"*The Prophet's Anthem* represents careful exegesis, thorough research, and theological insight at its best. Exploring one of the most exciting songs in Scripture and how it functions within the larger narrative of the book, Michelle Knight navigates the wealth of scholarship on Judges and also pushes it forward. Scholars and serious students alike will be 'most blessed' by this masterful contribution to scholarship on Judges."

— Elizabeth Backfish, Associate Professor of Hebrew Bible,
Jessup University

"*The Prophet's Anthem* is a judicious close reading of Judges that emphasizes the rhetorical and theological role of Judges 5 as an inset song. Michelle Knight successfully and winsomely argues that Judges 5 closes the second phase of YHWH's salvific work in Judges. This bold assertion challenges the scholarly consensus that each judge's cycle shows Israel's progressive decline and makes *The Prophet's Anthem* a must read for scholars and students of the book of Judges."

— Jillian L. Ross, Associate Professor of Biblical Studies,
Liberty University

"Judges 5 is often marginalized from studies of the narrative form of Judges. But with clarity and close attention to the text, Michelle Knight demonstrates how it fulfils key narrative functions within the book, and is thus more closely integrated to it than has been previously recognized. This meticulously argued volume will be essential reading for future studies of both Judges and integrated poems in Hebrew narrative."

— Rev. Dr. David G. Firth, Tutor in Old Testament,
Trinity College Bristol

"Like many students of Scripture, I have wondered about the nature and function of the Song of Deborah (and Barak) in the development of the overall message of the book of Judges. Michelle Knight has answered my questions. In the process, she has also demonstrated the wisdom of Jewish scribes in classifying Judges as a prophetic rather than a historical book. Grounded in rigorous analysis and composed in very readable—at times lyric—prose, Knight raises the blinds and helps us grasp the brilliant ray of light that shone into the dark world that was Israel at the end of the second millennium BCE. She shows that this Song celebrates the victories that YHWH had won on behalf of his people in chapters 3–4 and warns her people that if they ever forget God's righteous acts for their benefit, he will not intervene in their conflicts with enemies. Sadly, when their rebellion and the seductive power of alien gods eclipsed the visage of YHWH as their gracious Lord and Savior, he turned off their lights and left them to their own devices in a world that grew ever darker. Anyone who needs help making sense of the biblical book of Judges must read this book."

— Daniel I. Block, Gunther H. Knoedler Professor Emeritus of
Old Testament, Wheaton College

THE PROPHET'S ANTHEM

The Song of Deborah and Barak in the Narrative of Judges

Michelle Knight

BAYLOR UNIVERSITY PRESS

© 2024 by Baylor University Press
Waco, Texas 76798

All Rights Reserved. No part of this publication may be reproduced, stored in a retrieval system, or transmitted, in any form or by any means, electronic, mechanical, photocopying, recording, or otherwise, without the prior permission in writing of Baylor University Press.

Cover and Book Design by Elyxandra Encarnación
Cover image: Deborah. Illustration for Old Testament Portraits by Cunningham Geikie (Strahan, 1878). Portraits drawn by A. Rowan and engraved by G. Pearson. Digitally cleaned image. © Look and Learn / Bridgeman Images

Paperback ISBN: 978-1-4813-2160-0

The Library of Congress has cataloged the hardcover as follows:

Names: Knight, Michelle E., 1985- author.
Title: The Prophet's anthem : the Song of Deborah and Barak in the narrative of Judges / Michelle Knight, Baylor University Press.
Description: Waco, Texas : Baylor University Press, [2024] | Includes bibliographical references and index. | Summary: "A literary analysis of the prophetic "song" in the book of Judges, highlighting its significance for the development of the biblical book's themes"-- Provided by publisher.
Identifiers: LCCN 2024025211 (print) | LCCN 2024025212 (ebook) | ISBN 9781481321594 (hardcover) | ISBN 9781481321624 (adobe pdf) | ISBN 9781481321617 (epub)
Subjects: LCSH: Bible. Old Testament. Judges V--Criticism, interpretation, etc. | Deborah (Biblical judge) | Barak (Biblical judge)
Classification: LCC BS1303 .K57 2024 (print) | LCC BS1303 (ebook) | DDC 222/.3206--dc23/eng/20240701
LC record available at https://lccn.loc.gov/2024025211
LC ebook record available at https://lccn.loc.gov/2024025212

Contents

List of Figures and Tables　　vii
List of Abbreviations　　ix

Introduction　　1

    1   Judges 5 in Form and Content　　13

    2   Judges 5 in Its Narrative Cycle　　33

    3   Characterization in the Song and the Savior Stories　　77

    4   Plot and Themes in the Song and the Savior Stories　　121

    5   The Narrative Function of the Song of Deborah and Barak in the Book of Judges　　141

Appendix: Lexical and Text Critical Analysis　　145

Bibliography　　171

List of Figures

1	Stages of Divine Activity in Judges	125
2	Speeches of Divine Intermediaries	126
3	The Narrative Structure of the Core of Judges	128
4	Plot Development in the Core of Judges	129

List of Tables

1	Lexical Parallels in the Descriptions of Barak and Sisera	48
2	Lexical Parallels in the Descriptions of Ehud and Jael	90

List of Abbreviations

ÄAT	Ägypten und Altes Testament
AB	Anchor Bible
ABD	*Anchor Bible Dictionary.* Edited by D. N. Freedman. 6 vols. New York, 1992
ABRL	Anchor Bible Reference Library
ANET	Ancient Near Eastern Texts Relating to the Old Testament
AnOr	Analecta Orientalia
AUSS	*Andrews University Seminary Studies*
BAR	*Biblical Archaeology Review*
BASOR	*Bulletin of the American Schools of Oriental Research*
BBR	*Bulletin for Biblical Research*
BerOl	*Berit Olam*
BHK	*Biblia Hebraica.* Edited by R. Kittel. Stuttgart, 1905–1906, 1925, 1937, 1951, 1973
BHQ	*Biblia Hebraica Quinta*
BHRG	Merwe, Christo van der, Jackie Naudé, and Jan Kroeze. *A Biblical Hebrew Reference Grammar.* Sheffield, 1999
BHS	*Biblia Hebraica Stuttgartensia.* Edited by K. Elliger and W. Rudolph. Stuttgart, 1983
Bib	*Biblica*
BibInt	Biblical Interpretation Series
BibIntSup	Biblical Interpretation Supplement
BLS	Bible and Literature Series
BN	*Biblische Notizen*
BRev	*Bible Review*
BSac	*Bibliotheca Sacra*
BTAT	Barthélemy, Dominique. *Josué, Juges, Ruth, Samuel, Rois, Chroniques, Esdras, Néhémie, Esther.* Vol. 1 of *Critique textuelle de L'Ancien Testament.* Orbis biblicus et orientalis 50/1. Fribourg, 1982
BTB	*Biblical Theology Bulletin*

CBQ	*Catholic Biblical Quarterly*
CBR	*Currents in Biblical Research*
ConBOT	Coniectanea Biblica, Old Testament
DCH	*Dictionary of Classical Hebrew*. Edited by D. J. A. Clines. Sheffield, 1993–
DDD	*Dictionary of Deities and Demons in the Bible*. Edited by Karel van der Toorn, Bob Becking, and Pieter W. van der Horst. 2nd extensively rev. ed. Leiden, 1999
ErIsr	*Eretz-Israel*
ETL	*Ephemerides Theologicae Lovanienses*
FCB	Feminist Companion to the Bible
FOTL	Forms of the Old Testament Literature
FRLANT	Forschungen zur Religion und Literatur des Alten und Neuen Testaments
GKC	Gesenius, Friedrich Wilhelm. *Gesenius' Hebrew Grammar*. Edited by E. Kautzsch and Sir Arthur Ernest Cowley. 2nd English ed. Oxford, 1910
HALOT	Koehler, L., W. Baumgartner, and J. J. Stamm. *The Hebrew and Aramaic Lexicon of the Old Testament*. Translated and edited under the supervision of M. E. J. Richardson. Electronic ed. New York, 1999
HBM	Hebrew Bible Monographs
HBT	*Horizons in Biblical Theology*
HTKAT	Herders theologischer Kommentar zum Alten Testament
IBC	Interpretation: A Bible Commentary for Teaching and Preaching
IBHS	Waltke, B. K., and M. O'Connor. *An Introduction to Biblical Hebrew Syntax*. Winona Lake, 2004
ICC	International Critical Commentary
Int	*Interpretation*
ISBL	Indiana Studies in Biblical Literature
JBL	*Journal of Biblical Literature*
JETS	*Journal of the Evangelical Theological Society*
JHS	*Journal of Hebrew Scriptures*
JJS	*Journal of Jewish Studies*
JLCRS	Jordan Lectures in Comparative Religion Series
JNES	*Journal of Near Eastern Studies*
Joüon	Joüon, Paul S. J., and Takamitsu Muraoka. *A Grammar of Biblical Hebrew*. Subsidia Biblica 27. 2nd rev. ed. Rome, 2006
JQR	*Jewish Quarterly Review*
JSem	*Journal for Semitics*
JSNTSup	Journal for the Study of the New Testament Supplement Series
JSOT	*Journal for the Study of the Old Testament*
JSOTSup	Journal for the Study of the Old Testament Supplement Series

JTS	*Journal of Theological Studies*
LHBOTS	Library of Hebrew Bible/Old Testament Studies
LSAWS	*Linguistic Studies in Ancient West Semitic*
LXX	Septuagint
LXXA	Codex Alexandrinus
LXXB	Codex Vaticanus
MT	Masoretic Text
NAC	The New American Commentary
NETS	*A New English Translation of the Septuagint: And the Other Greek Translations Traditionally Included under That Title.* Edited by Albert Pietersma and Benjamin G. Wright. Oxford, 2007
NICOT	New International Commentary on the Old Testament
NIDOTTE	*New International Dictionary of Old Testament Theology and Exegesis.* Edited by W. A. Van Gemeren. 5 vols. Grand Rapids, 1997
NIVAC	The NIV Application Commentary
OBO	Orbis biblicus et orientalis
OTE	*Old Testament Essays*
OTL	Old Testament Library
OtSt	Oudtestamentische Studiën
PEQ	*Palestine Exploration Quarterly*
Proof	*Prooftexts: A Journal of Jewish Literary History*
SBLAIL	Society of Biblical Literature Ancient Israel and Its Literature
SBLSS	Society of Biblical Literature Semeia Studies
SJOT	*Scandinavian Journal of the Old Testament*
Syr.	Syriac Peshiṭta
TBN	Themes in Biblical Narrative
TDOT	*Theological Dictionary of the Old Testament.* Edited by G. J. Botterweck, H. Ringgren, and H.-J. Fabry. Translated by J. T. Willis, G. W. Bromiley, and D. E. Green. 15 vols. Grand Rapids, 1974–
TJon	Targum Pseudo-Jonathan
TRu	*Theologische Rundschau*
TynBul	*Tyndale Bulletin*
UT	Gordon, C. H. *Ugaritic Textbook.* AnOr 38. Rome, 1998
VT	*Vetus Testamentum*
VTSup	Supplements to Vetus Testamentum
Vulg.	Vulgate
WBC	Word Biblical Commentary
ZAW	*Zeitschrift für die alttestamentliche Wissenschaft*
ZECOT	Zondervan Exegetical Commentary on the Old Testament

Introduction

Few texts in the Hebrew Bible rival the fifth chapter of Judges in its academic impact and imposing ambiguity. The text itself is riveting; the final scene of the composition graphically describes a homicide and its aftermath with a level of rhetorical flourish that has captured the imagination of biblical interpreters, artists, historians, and archaeologists alike. In the field of biblical studies, the text's complexities—and potential insights—are renowned. The poem's unique style of parallelism, archaic language,[1] resemblance to Ugaritic literature, and pairing with a synoptic prose account have all garnered significant attention. From 1990 to 2009 alone, more than one hundred studies addressed Judges 4, Judges 5, or the two chapters together.[2] Such attention

---

[1] In this work, I will not adopt a theory of the song's age or priority in relation to the prose account. Due to the apparent compositional selectivity of the book of Judges, I assume that the song serves a literary function in the overarching narrative. This permits a variety of compositional theories, including (1) an ancient song being preserved, roughly as it was composed; (2) an ancient song being heavily adapted to fit the concerns of its new literary context; or (3) a song being written for the book of Judges at the time of its composition/compilation, using archaic language that was stylistically appropriate for its genre. While the first option strikes many as incompatible with the assertion that the song is firmly linked to its context, Gregory T. K. Wong ("Song of Deborah as Polemic," *Bib* 88 [2007]: 20–22), who emphasizes the polemical nature of the song and its "contribut[ion] to two ongoing motifs within the book," argues for the plausibility of the first option. I am inclined, at minimum, to designate the majority of the song as "old poetry," following Mark S. Smith, *Poetic Heroes: Literary Commemorations of Warriors and Warrior Culture in the Early Biblical World* (Grand Rapids: Eerdmans, 2014), 211–33.

[2] These studies (including commentaries) are outlined succinctly in Tyler Mayfield, "The Accounts of Deborah (Judges 4–5) in Recent Research," *CBR* 7 (2009): 306–35. Rudiger Bartelmus, "Forschung am Richterbuch seit Martin Noth," *TRu* 56 (1991): 221–59, demonstrates the disproportionate attention Judg 5 has received in a review of literature from Martin Noth to the end of the twentieth century. He observes that 120 (40 percent) of around three hundred studies pertaining to individual chapters or units in Judges are dedicated to all or part of the Song of Deborah.

devoted to the intricacies of the song itself is well-deserved but leaves comparatively underdeveloped an account of what made the poetic text ideal for its context. Scholars have helpfully considered the compositional relationship between the prose account and the poetic account,[3] and thereby the purposes of inserting the song in its narrow literary context, while others have begun to explore its role in the larger narrative complex of Judges. Whether the song is indeed ancient, as has long been assumed, or written and/or heavily adapted by a later hand, its inclusion in its narrative context affects the dynamic of the book of Judges.

The implications of the song's embeddedness in its present position in the Judges narrative is the central concern of this book. The question of its inclusion might be addressed diachronically and compositionally, to discern the process of, and motivations for, its insertion into a larger literary complex. Efforts have been made toward this end. James Watts addressed the inclusion of Judges 5 in *Psalm and Story: Inset Hymns in Hebrew Narrative*, in which he explored the role of poems embedded in narrative contexts. In analyzing the relationship of Judges 4 and 5, Watts observed that the song supplies "direct evaluative judgments" lacking in the intentionally constrained prose account with which it is paired.[4] In his view, few links exist between the Song of Deborah and the larger narrative of Judges. Watts thus limited his discussion to the function of Judges 5 within the account of the battle against Sisera: "Beyond [Judges 4–5], the psalm contains reminders of the tribal lists in Judges 1, and anticipates the tribal discord of the latter part of the book. Apart from such thematic allusions, however, the psalm's role is limited to the immediate narrative context."[5] Following academic consensus, Watts concluded the "poem and prose were already together before they were redacted as a unit into the

---

[3] The compositional relationship between Judg 4 and 5 is likely complex. Whether the prose account is dependent on (some form of) the poetic account (as has been long assumed), or whether the poetry has been updated to reflect the concerns of the prose is up for debate. Questioning the assumption of dependence entirely, Athalya Brenner opines that the two accounts might have circulated independently and concurrently, in "A Triangle and a Rhombus in Narrative Structure: A Proposed Integrative Reading of Judges IV and V," *VT* 40 (1990): 129–38. In a subsequent article, K. Lawson Younger affirms that such complementary battle reports are attested in the ancient Near East and that Judg 4–5 presents, indeed, "two sides of the same coin." See "Heads! Tails! Or the Whole Coin?! Contextual Method and Intertextual Analysis: Judges 4 and 5," in *The Biblical Canon in Comparative Perspective*, vol. 4 of *Scripture in Context*, ed. K. Lawson Younger, William W. Hallo, and Bernard F. Batto, ANET 11 (Lewiston: Edwin Mellen, 1991), 109–46.

[4] James W. Watts, *Psalm and Story: Inset Hymns in Hebrew Narrative*, JSOTSup 139 (Sheffield: JSOT, 1992), 96.

[5] Watts, *Psalm and Story*, 89.

larger framework."⁶ In his view, such a compositional history makes sense of the limited links between the song and the rest of the book, on one hand, and on the other, offers a probable explanation for this poem being inserted in the narrative at this point. For my purposes, I hold this compositional assumption loosely, so as to explore the possibility that literary considerations may have determined why "a psalm was added precisely here and nowhere else in the Judges narrative."⁷

Hans-Peter Mathys addressed Judges 5 as an example of the late poems and prayers added to earlier texts to offer much-needed theological direction. According to Mathys, these editorially inserted psalms ("Redaktionell eingesetzte Psalmen") drew out the significance of their surrounding narrative contexts for later generations.⁸ Judges 5 in particular urged the community to respond gratefully to God's salvific feats.⁹ While he argued the song is not compositionally uniform, he traced how its revision focuses especially on YHWH; moreover, he showed how the reworked song interpreted the events of the battle as examples of the deity's consistent action toward those faithful to him.¹⁰

Stephen Weitzman analyzed a host of biblical and extra-biblical examples of ancient Near Eastern poetry embedded in narrative to reconstruct the scribal practice of combining prose and poetry. Like Watts, he observed similarities between the convention of pairing prose and poetic accounts in the Hebrew Bible and other ancient Near Eastern literature. He proposed that Judges 5, like Exodus 15, was included with the prose episode in the manner of Egyptian battle accounts (e.g., the Piye Stela) "to promote God as invincible ruler and to render him the hero of battles in which his participation was difficult to represent."¹¹ Like Mathys, Weitzman concluded that, with a growth in canon consciousness, later redactors imposed songs on the biblical material in hopes of providing the same interpretive clarity as did these earlier songs.¹² Regarding the song, Weitzman states that "implicitly in Deborah's prophecy in 4:9 . . . is a rebuke of Barak *for not interpreting the battle properly.*"¹³ While reconstructing the process by which the song came to

---

[6] Watts, *Psalm and Story*, 92.
[7] Watts, *Psalm and Story*, 96.
[8] Hans-Peter Mathys, *Dichter und Beter: Theologen aus spätalttestamentlicher Zeit*, OBO 132 (Freiburg: Universitätsverlag Freiburg Schweiz Vandenhoeck, 1994), 318.
[9] Mathys, *Dichter und Beter*, 319.
[10] Mathys, *Dichter und Beter*, 175.
[11] Steven Phillip Weitzman, *Song and Story in Biblical Narrative: The History of a Literary Convention in Ancient Israel* (Bloomington: Indiana University, 1997), 35–36.
[12] Weitzman, *Song and Story in Biblical Narrative*, 129.
[13] Weitzman, *Song and Story in Biblical Narrative*, 35, emphasis original.

be attributed to Deborah and Barak, Weitzman observes the rhetorical effect of doing so: "Barak's participation in the song signals that his view of the battle has finally converged with that of Deborah, who has all along recognized God's central role in the battle."[14] Even though his concern is largely compositional—considering these inset songs as a standard convention in narrative structuring—Weitzman's observations about interpretation and Barak's witness are crucial and especially relevant.

In another volume on songs in biblical narrative—*Twice Used Songs: Performance Criticism of the Songs of Ancient Israel*—Terry Giles and William J. Doan build on the work of Watts through the lens of performance criticism, highlighting how the song functions as an "invitation for the reader to join in the celebration."[15] The song transforms those "spectating" into "participants in a shared enactment of identity."[16]

Each of these works begin to name the significance of this particular song within the scope of the book of Judges. The song invites response, recalls YHWH's past deeds, and offers an alternative interpretation. The incorporation of an extended prophetic response to YHWH's deliverance, in a book concerned with human responses to divine intervention, constitutes a strategic and theologically pregnant literary move. What is clear from the combined witness of such observations is that the song's effect has been often underappreciated in holistic accounts of the book of Judges. In what follows, then, I join the chorus of those considering the question of the song's function in its narrative context. My distinct approach is as follows: I do so literarily, according to the norms of biblical poetics, rather than exploring the compositional history of the song and the editorial process of its inclusion. Moreover, I focus especially on the song's effect on the entire narrative, rather than its relationship to, and integration with, the prose account of Judges 4. Even the most insightful of the studies that have explored the narrative function of Judges 5 have done so *primarily* (though not exclusively) in terms of its immediate context—Judges 4. Even if the so-called hero stories circulated independently before being combined, the book of Judges in its preserved form is often assumed to constitute a coherent narrative.[17] My goal, then, is to use

[14] Weitzman, *Song and Story in Biblical Narrative*, 35.
[15] Terry Giles and William J. Doan, *Twice Used Songs: Performance Criticism of the Songs of Ancient Israel* (Peabody, Mass.: Hendrickson, 2009), 75.
[16] Giles and Doan, *Twice Used Songs*, 84.
[17] The text I aim to describe (and where necessary, reconstruct) is the "final form"—the edition of the book recognized as authoritative by the compiling community at the beginning of its transmission process. Ellis R. Brotzman and Eric J. Tully (*Old Testament Textual Criticism: A Practical Introduction*, 2nd ed. [Grand Rapids: Baker, 2016], 222–25) articulate the goal of textual criticism in similar terms. In the case of Judges, that text—the

the methods of narrative criticism to explore the song's role synchronically. I approach this task at two levels: (1) to identify as precisely as possible what the song is and what it does in and of itself; and then more extensively, (2) to trace what interpretive difference the song in its location makes for reading and interpreting Judges. Given the growing "sub-field of biblical research ... on the topic of inset psalms in their literary contexts,"[18] a book-length study of one such poem—with special attention to how the song affects an interpretation of the whole of Judges—is warranted.

The remainder of the introduction will focus on defining two aspects of foundational importance for this inquiry, namely, (1) an account of "narrative function" and outlining a procedure for determining it; and (2) a description of the overarching narrative of the book of Judges, as defined by its prologue (Judg 1:1–3:6) and epilogue (17:1–21:25). Arguably, it is these chapters that provide the shaping and interpretive lens by which the book of Judges can be understood as a coherent narrative within which the song has a discernible function.

The Narrative Function of Embedded Poetry

The shift from prose to poetry in the Hebrew Bible is more easily intuited than it is defined.[19] James Kugel names this dynamic in his work on biblical poetry, in which he defines "what is called biblical 'poetry'" as a "complex of heightening effects used in combinations and intensities that vary widely from composition to composition."[20] These characteristic heightening effects, however, are recognizable, even if they are inconsistently and variously applied across the Hebrew Bible. Drawing on Russian formalism, Kugel observes a range of features that "strangeify" the language and "[mark] the

---

"received text"—seems to be singular (in contrast to, e.g., Jeremiah) and is often coterminous with the Masoretic Text. In my translation, I preserve the pointing of the Masoretic Text in all but one instance, that is, 5:5. "Is often assumed to": This generalization is not without exception. An especially poignant critique of this assumption is offered by Greger Andersson, *The Book and Its Narratives: A Critical Examination of Some Synchronic Studies of the Book of Judges*, Örebro Studies in Literary History and Criticism 1 (Örebro: Örebro University, 2001).

[18] James W. Watts, "Biblical Psalms outside the Psalter," in *The Book of Psalms: Composition and Reception*, ed. Peter W. Flint and Patrick D. Miller, VTSup 99 (Leiden: Brill, 2005), 289, drawing on observations by Lyle Eslinger.

[19] In fact, in his work on "inset psalms," Watts (*Psalm and Story*, 14) relies on "the intuitive recognition of a group of psalms in narrative contexts" to define the parameters of his analysis, though he does eventually restrict his study to *psalms*, rather than poems broadly, based on the presence of an appeal to praise God (15).

[20] James L. Kugel, *The Idea of Biblical Poetry: Parallelism and Its History* (Baltimore: Johns Hopkins University Press, 1998), 94.

language as *special*."²¹ Perhaps the most prevalent and pervasive elements of this elevated style are "terseness" and parallelism, which Adele Berlin has argued are definitive for identifying the presence of poetic language.²² To identify poetic discourse embedded in narrative contexts, then, is to observe a text dominated by denser clauses constructed in parallel.²³ Additional stylistic elements—inverted word order, ellipses, metaphor, etc.—accompany these features to varying degrees to facilitate categorization of poetic units. A departure from the surrounding prose narrative may also be signaled by introductory phrases that announce a shift to a genre considered poetic (e.g., Num 21:17: "Then Israel sang this song").

Prose narrative is rarely in need of being identified, given its prevalence in the Hebrew Bible. It is, indeed, "the predominant mode of expression," especially in the Former Prophets.²⁴ Narratives may incorporate a variety of subgenres—including various poetic types, alongside lists, letters, dialogue/discourse, genealogies, etc.—but may be generally identified by their attempt to recount and explain events in a (largely) linear fashion. The components of narrative literature are well established: narratives feature the point of view of a narrator, construe a sequence of events through plot, unfold in a particular setting, introduce and develop characters, and often organize themselves around central themes and motifs that contribute to conveying meaning. On the level of discourse, Hebrew prose narrative is most easily identified by a sequence of clauses featuring a clause-initial *wayyiqtol*, often in the third person. Various kinds of departures from the sequence of *wayyiqtol* clauses signal shifts at multiple levels (i.e., grammatical, pragmatic, stylistic, etc.) within the unfolding narrative.

The inclusion of a poem within a narrative framework is one such departure. At minimum, the shift to poetic discourse involves an interruption in the flow of the narrative. Studies of inset poetry published in the late twentieth century—most notably those described earlier in the chapter—suggest that these interruptions often have a similar purpose, that is, these songs "reshaped the surrounding literary structures in order to strengthen a theological focus on the acts of God, and/or provide models of proper worship through prayer

---

[21] Kugel, *Idea of Biblical Poetry*, 92, emphasis original.

[22] Adele Berlin, *Dynamics of Biblical Parallelism*, rev. and exp. ed., Biblical Resource Series (Grand Rapids: Eerdmans, 2008), 5.

[23] "Density" corresponds roughly to what Berlin terms "terseness" and is the word Jan Fokkelman chooses to describe the "compact and concentrated form" that poetry takes in the Hebrew Bible in *Reading Biblical Poetry: An Introductory Guide*, trans. Ineke Smit (Louisville: Westminster John Knox, 2001), 15.

[24] Adele Berlin, *Poetics and Interpretation of Biblical Narrative*, BLS 9 (Winona Lake, Ind.: Eisenbrauns, 1994), 13.

and hymnody for readers to imitate."²⁵ Understanding how exactly the song is introducing its theological agenda, what genre it adopts in doing so, and what difference it makes in its context requires analyzing the poem and its context in terms of standard components of narrative. Those narrative elements prioritized by Watts in his own work are fitting: in terms of its position in and effect on the plot; the characterization of particular individuals in the prose and poetic texts; and the level of continuity of vocabulary and themes between the psalm and its surrounding narrative.

In what follows, I employ a version of Watts' methodological paradigm by analyzing the function of the song on the level of plot, character, and theme. Though Watts does not clearly define the concept of "plot relations" by which he assesses an inset hymn's effect on the plot, his conclusions suggest that the narrative must explicitly "anticipate" the imbedded song or include "repercussions" unambiguously attributed to it to serve a notable narrative purpose.²⁶ By Watts' reckoning, the Song of Moses is the only such hymn anticipated by the preceding plot. A more robust analysis of scenic development and plot advancement in the surrounding narrative is beneficial, with a special emphasis on the placement and significance of the song in that unfolding plot. In addition to the plot, Watts analyzes "the psalm's contribution to the characterization of its speakers and sometimes other characters in the narrative."²⁷ Judges 5 is only one example of a poem that is replete with character-focused reflection that extends beyond its speaker(s). As a result, each of the characters in the poem must be addressed, so as to measure and describe how the song contributes to characterization in the overarching narrative. The third element of Watts' analysis of hymnic narrative function is its "semantic and thematic links" to its context, which he terms "thematic emphases." Watts assesses to what degree the "psalm and its immediate and extended contexts share vocabulary and themes" and, based on those data, analyzes the "thematic relationships between prose and poetry."²⁸ While a prevalent lexeme should not be confused with a theme, repeated words or groups of semantically related terms in a certain proximity constitute a stylistic device that gestures toward

---

²⁵ Watts, "Biblical Psalms outside the Psalter," 289.
²⁶ Regarding the Song of Hannah, Watts (*Psalm and Story*, 21) argues, "The psalm does not affect the plot of the story in any way. The preceding narrative *does not anticipate* Hannah's Song, nor does the subsequent account contain any *references to or repercussions from it*" (emphasis mine). Compare his comments on the Song of Moses: "Thus the song is *explicitly anticipated in the narrative's plot*, the only psalm in a narrative context of the Hebrew Bible for which this is the case" (64–65, emphasis mine).
²⁷ Watts, *Psalm and Story*, 17.
²⁸ Watts, *Psalm and Story*, 17.

underlying themes.[29] These repeated and/or emphasized lexemes offer a rich field of inquiry for understanding just what the song is doing both in its narrow and broader literary context.

The Overarching Judges Narrative

In its contours, the structure of the book of Judges is nearly uncontested among interpreters. Few challenge the tripartite structure of a double introduction (or prologue[s]), a cyclically organized collection of shorter narratives (or "deliverer accounts," *Retterbuch*), and a conclusion (or appendix[es], dénouement).[30] Having observed these natural divisions, studies of Judges have long posited theories identifying the source document and ideological milieu to which each of the sections belong. Scholars of the last two centuries have generally assigned the opening and closing chapters to an editor and historical context different from that of the stories collected in the core chapters. Regardless of the text's historical provenance, synchronic studies have traced how the three sections of Judges cohere.[31] The content framing the book shares themes, organization, and "rhetorical structure" with the cyclical center.[32]

The first portion of Judges (1:1–3:6) consists of two subunits. The first (1:1–2:5) reports (and implicitly assesses) the degree to which individual tribes faithfully applied חרם in the lands allotted to them by Joshua. Set in the time of the elders who outlived Joshua (1:1; cf. 2:7),[33] this section contrasts

---

[29] When describing the process of reading the text theologically, Elmer Martens ("Accessing Theological Readings of a Biblical Book," *AUSS* 34 [1996]: 229) suggests that the "message [or, in our verbiage, theme] of a book will almost always congeal into key terms which, in good rhetorical fashion, will be repeated."

[30] Most place the divisions at 1:1–3:6, 3:7–16:31, and 17:1–21:25.

[31] Of course, this is not universally acknowledged (on which, see n. 17 above). Cynthia Edenburg (*Dismembering the Whole: Composition and Purpose of Judges 19–21*, SBLAIL 24 [Atlanta: SBL, 2016]) is representative (and right) when she cautions that literary structures just as readily indicate editorial semblance of unity as they do unity of composition. It is the volume of links—beyond the book's simple structure—and the extent of their rhetorical continuity that most convincingly point toward thematic and composition unity, as has been demonstrated in Gregory T. K. Wong, *The Compositional Strategy of the Book of Judges: An Inductive, Rhetorical Study*, VTSup 111 (New York: Brill, 2006), 188–90. Based on these data, Wong argues that "the two peripheral sections were composed specifically to introduce and conclude the present form of the central section" (190).

[32] This language belongs to Wong (*Compositional Strategy of the Book of Judges*, 186): "Not only does the rhetorical structure of the prologue mirror the overall arrangement of the central section, even its idiosyncratic peculiarity finds parallel in the latter."

[33] The duplicate notice of Joshua's death is an interpretive crux that complicates the chronology of the opening chapters. Yairah Amit (*The Book of Judges: The Art of Editing*, trans. Jonathan Chipman, BibInt 38 [Boston: Brill, 1999], 136–41) suggests the second

the relative faithfulness of Judah and Simeon with the tempered success of the Northern tribes and the utter failure of Dan. Judges 2:1–5 concludes the unit with YHWH's rebuke through his messenger, in which he details the hardship Israel will experience when he no longer drives out the land's inhabitants before them. After a second notice of Joshua's death—a reminder of the experiential (and, consequently, spiritual) divide between those who entered Canaan under Moses' successor and those growing up in the land—Judges 2:6–3:6 details the struggle of the next generation(s), namely, the generation(s) under the leadership of the judges. Judges 2:11–23 describes the characteristic actions of all parties in the period, including a summary of divine activity that reiterates and supplements YHWH's recent declaration: not only would he delay the fulfillment of the Israelite settlement (as he had already stated) but he would also test the faithfulness of his people in fulfilling his conquest-related directives (and thereby demonstrate their waywardness) when they were settled among the nations and subject to their religious influence.

Amit rightly characterizes the relationship of these introductory chapters to the book's cyclical center as expository; in her words, Judges 1:1–3:6 "plays a decisive role in constructing the cognitive system of the reader."[34] The twofold announcement of the divinely facilitated presence of Canaanites in the land (2:3, 21; 3:1–6) provides the narrative context for the influence of non-Yahwistic religion on the generations on whom the remainder of the book focuses. Moreover, the cycle of Israelite behavior and divine response in Judges 2:6–3:6 establishes a pattern for chapters that follow, which consist of a series of similarly patterned conflicts.[35] Amit shows how the central section is the specific, concrete "application of the general expository description."[36] Rather than a list of events (a chronicle of sorts), the happenings of the Judges period are introduced as a series of actions related by cause and effect, with

---

notice signals a generational perspectival shift from the elders who outlived Joshua to the Judges generation. I adopt her interpretation, given the presence of Caleb in the first chapter.

[34] Amit, *Book of Judges*, 121. To define 1:1–3:6 as "exposition," Amit relies on Meir Sternberg, *Expositional Modes and Temporal Ordering in Fiction* (Baltimore: Johns Hopkins University Press, 1978).

[35] Elie Assis, "The Function of Repetition and Contradiction in the Paradigm of the Judges (2:11–19)," *Scriptura* 119 (2020): 1–10, argues there are two contradictory patterns at play in these expository sections, one that is featured prominently in the book (the people are drawn to idol worship, they are motivated by the judge to [temporarily] abandon their idolatry, and then they return to it upon the judge's death) and another that highlights a slightly different pattern (the people "deliberately forsake God," God sends plunderers, and the people are not persuaded; 8). Assis' efforts to complicate the so-called cyclical pattern are warranted, even if the factors he identifies may not be as contradictory as he claims.

[36] Amit, *Book of Judges*, 123.

a clear inciting problem (2:10), purpose/vision (2:22, 3:1) and trajectory (i.e., increasing corruption; 2:19). The second unit of the introduction demonstrates minimally that the cycles of 3:7–16:31 constitute a coherent plot.[37] According to the introduction, that overarching macroplot may be summarized as YHWH's testing of the fidelity of the post-Joshua generations of Israelites, in the partially dispossessed land of Canaan. The major players are thus threefold: the Israelites—already identified as those who "did not know YHWH" (2:10)—their covenant partner YHWH, and the inhabitants of the land, whose leaders are portrayed as cruel, powerful, and mere pawns at the mercy of YHWH.[38]

It is worth noting that the nations with whom the Israelites interact in the stories that follow are only rarely indigenous to the land; more frequently they are invaders. Certainly some were left (2:21; עזב) by Joshua after his death, and according to the logic of Judges 1, these are the Canaanites who influenced the Israelites to abandon their fidelity to YHWH. The battles of the Judges period, though, are dominated by those the deity "caused to rest" (2:23, 3:1; נוח; often translated "left") as a *response* to Israelite failure to drive out the Canaanites. This lexical shift helps to explain the presence of the Philistines in the list of those posing a threat in Canaan in 3:1; this list consists not merely of those who were indigenous but also those whom God more recently granted settlement in the land, when he had previously promised to grant that rest to Israel (e.g., Deut 3:20; 12:10; 25:19; Josh 23:1).

Following the central chapters of the book of Judges is a section consisting of two subunits: chapters 17–18 and 19–21. The first concerns the establishment of the Danite shrine (by way of the unsanctioned service of Micah's opportunistic Levite);[39] the second addresses the threatened חרם of Benjamin by fellow Israelites in response to the rape, death, and postmortem mutilation

---

[37] Here I rely on the definition of plot provided in Jan P. Fokkelman, *Reading Biblical Narrative: An Introductory Guide*, trans. Ineke Smit (Louisville: Westminster John Knox, 1999), 76–78, especially in terms of the "course of action, that is the course of events in a story, as a *trajectory*."

[38] The description of Adoni-Bezek in 1:5–7 defines the readers' expectations regarding Canaanite kings in the stories that follow. As to the reader's expectations of the Israelites, I explore the contextual and canonical significance of their collective ignorance (2:10) in "The Prophet's Song of Victory: Judges 5 within a Trajectory of Theological Training in the Book of Judges," *BBR* 33 (2023): 287–303. That article touches briefly on several of the same arguments I make in the pages that follow, but does so primarily through the lens of revelation.

[39] Daniel I. Block (*Judges, Ruth*, NAC 6 [Nashville: Broadman & Holman, 2001], 491) argues that "the primary function of chap. 17 has been to provide necessary background for the establishment of the aberrant cult site at Dan." For the "opportunistic" nature of the Levite's ministry, see K. Lawson Younger, *Judges, Ruth*, rev. ed., NIVAC (Grand Rapids: Zondervan, 2020), 423.

of an anonymous Levite's nameless concubine. Both units exhibit a sense of escalation, in which the covenant transgressions of a single (but representative) individual have devastating national ramifications.

In their relationship to the foregoing cyclical core, most interpreters have highlighted the culminating function of these episodes. Synchronic studies of Judges have traced the deterioration of Israelite fidelity in the overarching narrative that reaches a thematic climax in the conclusion. In these final stories the generalized syncretism that characterizes Israel in the core of Judges comes into focus through a veritable catalogue of Israelite covenant transgressions.[40] Judges 17–21 portrays the Israelite people as bereft of traditional Yahwistic (i.e., Deuteronomic) morality through intertextual links to pentateuchal covenant stipulations and, even more straightforwardly, textual parallels with Judges 1:1–3:6. With the latter literary strategy, the narrative uses contrastive repetition to portray Israel's religious degradation. Perhaps the most striking of these parallels is the implementation of חרם warfare. That which the people of God were unfaithful in executing against those inhabiting the land in the introduction, they are willing to execute faithfully against their kinsmen in the conclusion. In fact, the external foes of Israel are absent from the book's final chapters; the conclusion is concerned to reveal the depths of Israelite corruption in the days when YHWH had given them over to their rejection of his sovereign protection.

Most recently, David Beldman has analyzed Judges 17–21 and its "strategies of ending." He characterizes the relationship of these chapters to the preceding in terms of three interconnected modes of narrative closure: (1) completion, meaning the standard mode of ending that ties up the narrative's loose ends; (2) circularity, or the echo of semantic, syntactic, and plot-level features from the narrative's beginning (mentioned above); and (3) entrapment, indicating the strategy by which the appearance of new narrative features "give rise to a reevaluation of how they might cohere with the general pattern of the book."[41] The first two strategies of ending reflect observations similar to those of recent synchronic studies. With reference to the third, Beldman reflects on

---

[40] Most importantly, the repeated statement that everyone "did what is right in his own eyes" is a Deuteronomic expression describing covenant infidelity, specifically in relation to cultic malpractice (Deut 12:8). Just as "doing the evil in the eyes of YHWH"—another Mosaic phrase—indicates the worship of foreign deities throughout the book's core, so too does its opposite at the book's end. Jillian Ross (*A People Heeds Not Scripture: Allusion in Judges* [Eugene, Ore.: Pickwick, 2023], 189–214) outlines these transgressions, especially in relation to Deut 12–13.

[41] David J. H. Beldman, *The Completion of Judges: Strategies of Ending in Judges 17–21*, Siphrut: Literature and Theology of the Hebrew Scriptures 21 (Winona Lake, Ind.: Eisenbrauns, 2017), 145.

the refrain "in those days, there was no king in Israel," which foregrounds monarchic concerns that are arguably less explicit earlier in the narrative. He rightly challenges the popular notion that the book (or at least these chapters) promotes a centralized government. He asserts instead that the main concern of the narrative culminating with this refrain is to argue that "[the Israelites] already had a king, Yahweh, and until they repaired their relationship with him by means of covenant renewal and fidelity they would continue to spiral out of control."[42] As Beldman has so aptly described, the conclusion to the book of Judges bemoans Israel's rejection of YHWH and the devastating consequences of their resultant theological deprivation. The final chapters of Judges, then, punctuate a claim anticipated in the introduction and narrated in the book's core: that the people of Israel repeatedly did evil in YHWH's eyes—which was good in their own eyes—and in so doing, failed miserably to remain faithful to their Sovereign when entrenched among Canaanites in the land of promise.

It is precisely into this spiritual decline that Israel's God sent a prophet to offer an extended reflection on a singular battle. But to what end?

---

[42] By arguing that YHWH (not a human monarch) is the king mentioned by the refrain, Beldman follows (and also critiques) the argument of Wong, *Compositional Strategy of the Book of Judges*, 212–23.

1
Judges 5 in Form and Content

Judges 5 is notoriously difficult and contentious on source critical, text critical, philological, and form critical grounds. The analysis in this chapter identifies the text assumed by this author,[1] the presumed poetic structure of the composition, an analysis of the text's formal structure, its proper generic classification, and an interpretive summary, the details of which inform the rest of the volume.

Translation and Division of Cola[2]

וַתָּשַׁר דְּבוֹרָה	1	Then Deborah sang
וּבָרָק בֶּן־אֲבִינֹעַם		—and Barak ben-Abinoam—
בַּיּוֹם הַהוּא לֵאמֹר:		on that day, saying,

Part 1
Stanza 1

בִּפְרֹעַ פְּרָעוֹת בְּיִשְׂרָאֵל	2	"At the unbinding of hair in Israel,
בְּהִתְנַדֵּב עָם		at the volunteering of the people,
בָּרֲכוּ יְהוָה:		bless YHWH!
שִׁמְעוּ מְלָכִים	3	Listen, oh Kings.
הַאֲזִינוּ רֹזְנִים		Give ear, oh Rulers.
אָנֹכִי לַיהוָה אָנֹכִי אָשִׁירָה		I, to YHWH, I will sing.
אֲזַמֵּר לַיהוָה אֱלֹהֵי יִשְׂרָאֵל:		I will give praise to YHWH, the God of Israel.
יְהוָה בְּצֵאתְךָ מִשֵּׂעִיר	4	Oh YHWH, at your going out from Seir,
בְּצַעְדְּךָ מִשְּׂדֵה אֱדוֹם		at your striding from the territory of Edom,

---

[1] See appendix for a lexical and text-critical analysis.
[2] Unless otherwise noted, all English translations are mine. Scripture references follow the versification of the MT unless alternate versification is indicated.

	אֶרֶץ רָעָשָׁה	the earth shook,
	גַּם־שָׁמַיִם נָטָפוּ	even the heavens poured,
	גַּם־עָבִים נָטְפוּ מָיִם׃	even the clouds poured water.
5	הָרִים נָזְלוּ מִפְּנֵי יְהוָה	The mountains quaked before YHWH,
	זֶה סִינַי מִפְּנֵי יְהוָה אֱלֹהֵי יִשְׂרָאֵל׃	this one, Sinai, before YHWH, the God of Israel.

Stanza 2

6	בִּימֵי שַׁמְגַּר בֶּן־עֲנָת בִּימֵי יָעֵל	In the days of Shamgar ben-Anath, in the days of Jael,
	חָדְלוּ אֳרָחוֹת	roads fell into disuse.
	וְהֹלְכֵי נְתִיבוֹת	Those who walked on paths
	יֵלְכוּ אֳרָחוֹת עֲקַלְקַלּוֹת	walked on crooked roads.
7	חָדְלוּ פְרָזוֹן בְּיִשְׂרָאֵל חָדֵלּוּ	Villagers held back in Israel—they held back,
	עַד שַׁקַּמְתִּי דְּבוֹרָה	until I arose, Deborah,
	שַׁקַּמְתִּי אֵם בְּיִשְׂרָאֵל׃	I arose, a mother in Israel.
8	יִבְחַר אֱלֹהִים חֲדָשִׁים	God chose new ones;
	אָז לָחֶם שְׁעָרִים	then fighting was at the gates.
	מָגֵן אִם־יֵרָאֶה וָרֹמַח	Certainly no shield was seen—nor spear
	בְּאַרְבָּעִים אֶלֶף בְּיִשְׂרָאֵל׃	among forty thousand in Israel.

Part 2

Stanza 3

9	לִבִּי לְחוֹקְקֵי יִשְׂרָאֵל	My mind is on the leaders of Israel,
	הַמִּתְנַדְּבִים בָּעָם	those who volunteered themselves among the people.
	בָּרֲכוּ יְהוָה׃	Bless YHWH!
10	רֹכְבֵי אֲתֹנוֹת צְחֹרוֹת	Those who ride on tawny donkeys,
	יֹשְׁבֵי עַל־מִדִּין	those who sit on blankets,
	וְהֹלְכֵי עַל־דֶּרֶךְ שִׂיחוּ׃	those who walk on the way, tell of it!
11	מִקּוֹל מְחַצְצִים בֵּין מַשְׁאַבִּים	At the sound of those who distribute water between the watering places,
	שָׁם יְתַנּוּ צִדְקוֹת יְהוָה	there they recount the righteous acts of YHWH,
	צִדְקֹת פִּרְזֹנוֹ בְּיִשְׂרָאֵל	the righteous acts of his villagers in Israel:
	אָז יָרְדוּ לַשְּׁעָרִים עַם־יְהוָה׃	Then the people of YHWH went down to the gates.
12	עוּרִי עוּרִי דְּבוֹרָה	'Awake, awake, Deborah!
	עוּרִי עוּרִי דַּבְּרִי־שִׁיר	Awake, awake—utter a song!

	קוּם בָּרָק	Rise up, Barak,
	וּשֲׁבֵה שֶׁבְיְךָ בֶּן־אֲבִינֹעַם:	and take captive your captives, ben-Abinoam!'
13	אָז יְרַד שָׂרִיד לְאַדִּירִים עָם	Then the remnant triumphed against the mightiest people;
	יְהוָה יְרַד־לִי בַּגִּבּוֹרִים:	YHWH triumphed for me over the warriors.

Stanza 4

14	מִנִּי אֶפְרַיִם שָׁרְשָׁם בַּעֲמָלֵק	From Ephraim, their root among Amalek,
	אַחֲרֶיךָ בִנְיָמִין בַּעֲמָמֶיךָ	after you, Benjamin, among your people,
	מִנִּי מָכִיר יָרְדוּ מְחֹקְקִים	from Machir the leaders went down,
	וּמִזְּבוּלֻן מֹשְׁכִים בְּשֵׁבֶט סֹפֵר	and from Zebulun musterers with the scribe's staff.
15	וְשָׂרַי בְּיִשָּׂשכָר עִם־דְּבֹרָה	The officials of Issachar with Deborah,
	וְיִשָּׂשכָר כֵּן בָּרָק	and Issachar likewise with Barak,
	בָּעֵמֶק שֻׁלַּח בְּרַגְלָיו	into the valley were sent at his feet.
	בִּפְלַגּוֹת רְאוּבֵן גְּדֹלִים חִקְקֵי־לֵב:	In the ranks of Reuben were great leaders of heart.
16	לָמָּה יָשַׁבְתָּ בֵּין הַמִּשְׁפְּתַיִם	Why do you stay between the sheepfolds
	לִשְׁמֹעַ שְׁרִקוֹת עֲדָרִים	to listen to the sounds of flocks?
	לִפְלַגּוֹת רְאוּבֵן גְּדוֹלִים חִקְרֵי־לֵב:	The ranks of Reuben had great searching of heart.
17	גִּלְעָד בְּעֵבֶר הַיַּרְדֵּן שָׁכֵן	Gilead across the Jordan stayed,
	וְדָן לָמָּה יָגוּר אֳנִיּוֹת	and Dan—why does he sojourn among the ships?
	אָשֵׁר יָשַׁב לְחוֹף יַמִּים	Asher remained at the shore of the sea,
	וְעַל מִפְרָצָיו יִשְׁכּוֹן:	and in his bays he stays.
18	זְבֻלוּן עַם חֵרֵף נַפְשׁוֹ לָמוּת וְנַפְתָּלִי	Zebulun [was] a people who risked their lives—and Naphtali—
	עַל מְרוֹמֵי שָׂדֶה:	on the heights of the field.

Stanza 5

19	בָּאוּ מְלָכִים נִלְחָמוּ	Kings came, they fought,
	אָז נִלְחֲמוּ מַלְכֵי כְנַעַן	then the kings of Canaan fought,
	בְּתַעְנַךְ עַל־מֵי מְגִדּוֹ	in Tanaach, near the waters of Megiddo.
	בֶּצַע כֶּסֶף לֹא לָקָחוּ:	Spoil of silver they did not take.
20	מִן־שָׁמַיִם נִלְחָמוּ	From the heavens they fought—
	הַכּוֹכָבִים מִמְּסִלּוֹתָם נִלְחֲמוּ עִם־סִיסְרָא:	the stars from their courses fought with Sisera.
21	נַחַל קִישׁוֹן גְּרָפָם	The Wadi Kishon washed them away—
	נַחַל קְדוּמִים נַחַל קִישׁוֹן	the ancient wadi, Wadi Kishon.
	תִּדְרְכִי נַפְשִׁי עֹז:	March on, my soul, with might!

	אָז הָלְמוּ עִקְּבֵי־סוּס	22 Then the hooves of the horses hammered
	מִדַּהֲרוֹת דַּהֲרוֹת אַבִּירָיו:	from the galloping, galloping of his steeds.
	אוֹרוּ מֵרוֹז אָמַר מַלְאַךְ יְהוָה	23 'Curse Meroz,' said the envoy of YHWH,
	אֹרוּ אָרוֹר יֹשְׁבֶיהָ	'Fervently curse her inhabitants,
	כִּי לֹא־בָאוּ לְעֶזְרַת יְהוָה	for they did not come to the help of YHWH,
	לְעֶזְרַת יְהוָה בַּגִּבּוֹרִים:	to the help of YHWH against the warriors.'

Part 3

Stanza 6

	תְּבֹרַךְ מִנָּשִׁים יָעֵל	24 Most blessed among women is Jael,
	אֵשֶׁת חֶבֶר הַקֵּינִי	wife of Heber the Kenite.
	מִנָּשִׁים בָּאֹהֶל תְּבֹרָךְ:	Of tent-dwelling women, she is most blessed.
	מַיִם שָׁאַל חָלָב נָתָנָה	25 Water he requested; milk she gave.
	בְּסֵפֶל אַדִּירִים הִקְרִיבָה חֶמְאָה:	In a bowl for nobles she presented cream.
	יָדָהּ לַיָּתֵד תִּשְׁלַחְנָה	26 Her [left] hand to the tent peg she reached,
	וִימִינָהּ לְהַלְמוּת עֲמֵלִים	and her right hand to the workers' mallet,
	וְהָלְמָה סִיסְרָא	and she hammered Sisera.
	מָחֲקָה רֹאשׁוֹ	She shattered his head,
	וּמָחֲצָה וְחָלְפָה רַקָּתוֹ:	and she smashed and pierced his temple.
	בֵּין רַגְלֶיהָ כָּרַע נָפַל שָׁכָב	27 Between her feet he knelt, he fell, he lay.
	בֵּין רַגְלֶיהָ כָּרַע נָפָל	Between her feet he knelt, he fell.
	בַּאֲשֶׁר כָּרַע שָׁם נָפַל שָׁדוּד:	Where he knelt, there he fell, destroyed.

Stanza 7

	בְּעַד הַחַלּוֹן נִשְׁקְפָה	28 Through the window she looked down.
	וַתְּיַבֵּב אֵם סִיסְרָא בְּעַד הָאֶשְׁנָב	The mother of Sisera lamented through the veil,
	מַדּוּעַ בֹּשֵׁשׁ רִכְבּוֹ לָבוֹא	'Why do his chariots tarry to come?
	מַדּוּעַ אֶחֱרוּ פַּעֲמֵי מַרְכְּבוֹתָיו:	Why do the steps of his chariots delay?'
	חַכְמוֹת שָׂרוֹתֶיהָ תַּעֲנֶינָּה	29 The wisest of her women were answering her;
	אַף־הִיא תָּשִׁיב אֲמָרֶיהָ לָהּ:	even she was replying to herself,
	הֲלֹא יִמְצְאוּ יְחַלְּקוּ שָׁלָל	30 'Surely they are finding and dividing the plunder:
	רַחַם רַחֲמָתַיִם לְרֹאשׁ גֶּבֶר	a womb or two for every single man,
	שְׁלַל צְבָעִים לְסִיסְרָא	plunder of colored cloth for Sisera,
	שְׁלַל צְבָעִים רִקְמָה	plunder of colored cloth, embroidered cloth,

צֶבַע רִקְמָתַיִם לְצַוְּארֵי שָׁלָל׃	two pieces of colored, embroidered cloth for [his] spoil's necks.'
כֵּן יֹאבְדוּ כָל־אוֹיְבֶיךָ יְהוָה 31	Thus may all your enemies perish, oh YHWH,
וְאֹהֲבָיו כְּצֵאת הַשֶּׁמֶשׁ בִּגְבֻרָתוֹ	but may those who love him be like the going out of the sun in its might."

Formal Analysis

The integrity of the song has been discussed at length. Its thematic unity, lexical delimitation, alliteration,[3] and interstanzaic repetition have struck many as the product of careful composition, rather than evidence of textual corruption or careless integration of sources. Still others, however, point to certain textual factors as evidence of editorial activity within the song itself. In his 2008 monograph, Charles Echols offers an argument for the song's "liturgical reworking," attending especially to the "isolation of Psalm-like verses" at the beginning and end of the song, as well as the absence of YHWH's name in the song's key moments of apparent divine intervention (5:20–21).[4]

Even in his largely diachronic analysis, Echols makes observations that point to the legitimacy (if not also the necessity) of an approach that assumes the intelligibility and integrity of Judges 5. In arguing for evidence of the reworking of the song, Echols observes that the song's redaction is "relatively seamless" and "attests to the artisanship of the reviser(s)."[5] Moreover, Echols' reconstruction is prefaced by the admission that "it is impossible to adjudicate incontrovertibly the question of [the song's] unity," because arguments for its (compositional) unity "cannot be unequivocally falsified."[6] Echols' statement is based on the works of scholars such as Alexander Globe, Michael David Coogan, Artur Weiser, and Jan Fokkelman,[7] who have argued that the song

---

[3] Elizabeth Backfish offers an analysis of alliteration in Judg 4–5 in "The Function of Alliteration in the Prosaic and Poetic Accounts of the Deborah Cycle," *JSOT* 44 (2020): 551–62. She observes that alliteration in the poem "both reinforces the structure of parallel lines and strophes and creates links beyond individual poetic units" (556).

[4] Charles L. Echols, *"Tell Me, O Muse": The Song of Deborah (Judges 5) in the Light of Heroic Poetry*, LHBOTS 487 (London: T&T Clark, 2008), 90–91.

[5] Echols, *"Tell Me, O Muse,"* 200.

[6] Echols, *"Tell Me, O Muse,"* 90.

[7] Alexander Globe, "The Literary Structure and Unity of the Song of Deborah," *JBL* 93 (1974): 493–512; Michael David Coogan, "A Structural and Literary Analysis of the Song of Deborah," *CBQ* 40 (1978): 143–65; Artur Weiser, "Das Deboralied: Eine gattungs- und traditionsgeschichtliche Studie," *ZAW* 71 (1959): 67–97; Jan P. Fokkelman, "The Song of Deborah and Barak: Its Prosodic Levels and Structure," in *Pomegranates and Golden*

evinces structural, stylistic, formal, and thematic unity. Whether this unity is *authorial*—as some of these studies suggest—or *editorial* is the question that divides interpreters who deem the song a unified entity. Echols' remarks resemble the earlier observations of Joseph Blenkinsopp, who has proposed that, whatever the text's prehistory, its preserved form is sensible and fitting in its present location. Blenkinsopp describes the posteditorial unity of the song as a "theological" one, which "corresponds closely to that which can be deduced from the hand which has edited the 'heroic' tales of the Judges."[8] The compositional argument Blenkinsopp (and similarly Echols) makes corresponds to my own literary observations, that is, a continuity of themes and concerns both (1) within the song and (2) within the rest of the book of Judges, regardless of the song's origins. Therefore, while oral and written sources may have been consulted in composing (or restructuring) the song in its present form, perhaps even to fit its present context, this analysis will be concerned with the preserved version of the piece.[9]

The song divides into three clear thematic units: part 1 (5:2–8) establishes the theological and anthropological situation prior to the battle (i.e., the superior might of YHWH and the emphatically weakened Israel); part 2 (vv. 9–23) focuses on the leaders of the tribes of Israel and their participation (or lack thereof) in YHWH's miraculous feats of military vindication; and part 3 (vv. 24–31) celebrates the death of Sisera and its aftermath—the climax of the battle between Israel, their God, and the Canaanites.[10]

References to ישראל in its first colon (5:2), central colon (5:3), and last colon (5:5) formally demarcate the first stanza. This short stanza also mentions יהוה six times.[11] The stanza consists of two strophes: 2–3 and 4–5. The phrase יהוה אלהי ישראל concludes the first and second strophes and formally

---

Bells: Studies in Biblical, Jewish, and Near Eastern Ritual, Law, and Literature in Honor of Jacob Milgrom, ed. David P. Wright, David Noel Freedman, and Avi Hurvitz (Winona Lake, Ind.: Eisenbrauns, 1995), 595–628.

[8] J. Blenkinsopp, "Ballad Style and Psalm Style in the Song of Deborah: A Discussion," *Bib* 42 (1961): 62. For the view that the poem evinces "multiple theological views," see Mark S. Smith and Elizabeth Bloch-Smith, *Judges 1: A Commentary on Judges 1:1–10:5*, Hermeneia (Minneapolis: Fortress, 2021), 302.

[9] For a slightly more nuanced definition of this "preserved version," see chap. 1, n. 17, and appendix.

[10] I have identified seven stanzas, though stanzas 1 and 3 could easily be divided to create nine slightly smaller units, just as stanzas 1 and 2, and similarly 6 and 7, could be combined for a structure of five stanzas. My divisions agree with those of Fokkelman, "Song of Deborah and Barak," 595–628, whose insights have facilitated the current study.

[11] Coogan, "Structural and Literary Analysis," 153; Fokkelman, "Song of Deborah and Barak," 602.

emphasizes the centrality of YHWH and his relationship with Israel in the poem that follows.

The second stanza begins in verse 6. The parallels with the opening of the first stanza—two temporal (or circumstantial) clauses introduced by the preposition בְּ—suggest that the two stanzas should be considered part of a larger unit. ישראל continues to be a focus, but its role is locative rather than relational—the stanza's central and final statements identify the state of affairs in the area inhabited by Israelites (5:7c, 8d; בישראל). Verse 8 includes the first instance of a particle that will prove to be an important structural element in the poem—namely, אז. Introducing five statements about the progression of the battle, this adverb signals significant advances in the victory over Sisera.[12]

Part 2 commences with a slightly longer stanza that divides into two strophes: 9–11c (demarcated by enveloping references to ישראל) and 11d–13 (in which an inclusio is formed by statements in 13a–b that are phonologically and lexically reminiscent of 11d). That this stanza introduces a new movement is evidenced by features reminiscent of the beginning of part 1: first, the repetition of three lexemes from the second verse, namely, עם, ישראל, and the root נדב; second, an identical invocation to bless YHWH (cf. 5:2); third, a second identification of the song's addressees (5:10; cf. 5:3); fourth, another plural imperative (שיחו in 5:10; cf. 5:3); and fifth, a second person address (5:12; cf. 5:4).[13] This structural unity highlights that the might of YHWH in part 1 is mirrored here by a stanza that emphasizes the willingness of his leaders. The hymn to YHWH in 4–5 finds its counterpart in 11d–13, which reflects Deborah's and Barak's leadership roles and recounts the beginning of the battle. Just as YHWH went out (יצא) at the song's beginning, so now the people join YHWH in going down to (ירד) battle. The cohesion of the stanza is reinforced by an inclusio: the unit begins and ends with a statement that includes the first-person pronominal suffix (לבי in 9a and לי in 13b).[14] Pierre Auffret notes another pattern of structural importance in the stanza: that the lexeme ישראל (the first of two parallel terms for the Israelites in v. 9), which

---

[12] The significance of אז is noted by Nadav Na'aman, "Literary and Topographical Notes on the Battle of Kishon (Judges IV–V)," *VT* 40 (1990): 424. Nadav's suggestion that the action of v. 13 must constitute an event in the battle distinct from that described in v. 11 misinterprets the structural significance of the adverb, since אז may appear in a line that is repeated for structural purposes (rather than to distinguish between two separate events). To say that אז is used as "a stylistic device to introduce a stressed phrase" in a string of subsequent events is likely closer to the mark (*HALOT*, 26).

[13] So also Coogan, "Structural and Literary Analysis," 152–53.

[14] Many unnecessarily emend the line to reflect a third person suffix.

envelopes the first strophe, is matched by the lexeme עם (the second term for the Israelites in v. 9), which envelops the second strophe.[15]

The fourth stanza makes up the center of part 2. Most clearly delineated by the tribal list it contains, the stanza describes more extensively the עם from 5:11 and the שריד in 5:13. The stanza mentions ten tribes of Israel.[16] The section divides neatly into three strophes, each consisting of three segments (vv. 14–15c, 15d–16, and 17–18). The most obvious self-contained unit concerns Reuben (vv. 15d–16) and is enveloped by two phrases with identical surface structure (though one puzzling lexical distinction persists). The two remaining strophes commence with four lines bound tightly by lexical repetition (מן in the first strophe and the root שכן in the last), followed by sets of lines with their own syntactical and thematic cohesiveness. Sasson has observed the tribal arrangement is influenced by matriarchy; Ephraim begins the list of tribes born of Rachel, Zebulun is the first of those born of Leah, and Gilead is the first of the concubines' descendants.[17]

The fifth stanza rounds out part 2 of the song, turning from a description of purely human activity to recounting the miraculous nature of the details of the battle. Four strophes make up the stanza: verses 19, 20–21b, 21c–22, and 23. The first two strophes invite comparison by the repetition of the root לחם at their respective starts, which creates poetic balance that highlights an offensive imbalance.[18] The recurrence of אז in the third strophe shifts attention from the heart of the battle to the next significant event: the retreat of Canaan's army. The final strophe (5:23) effectively concludes the stanza and part 2, invoking the root בוא to reflect the beginning of the stanza (5:19) and the record of YHWH's action "against the warriors" (בגבורים; cf. 5:13) to mimic the beginning of the larger poetic unit.[19] Structurally (and thematically), the battle has come full circle.

---

[15] Pierre Auffret, "En ce jour-la Debora et Baraq chanterent: Étude structurelle de Jg 5, 2–31," *SJOT* 16 (2002): 119–20, building upon Fokkelman, "Song of Deborah and Barak," 595–628.

[16] Strictly speaking only eight are mentioned by name, but most recognize that Macir represents Manasseh and Gilead represents Gad by way of "poetic substitution" (Alexander Globe, "The Muster of the Tribes in Judges 5, 11e–18," *ZAW* 87 [1975]: 173).

[17] Jack M. Sasson, *Judges 1–12: A New Translation with Introduction and Commentary*, AB 6D (New Haven: Yale University Press, 2014), 320–22.

[18] After all, the strophe says of the Canaanites: "spoil of silver they did not take" (5:19). See Fokkelman, "Song of Deborah and Barak," 616–17.

[19] That the verse both concludes the fifth stanza and so aptly introduces the next has led some to describe the formal function of the strophe to be "transitional" (e.g., K. Lawson Younger, *Judges, Ruth*, rev. ed., NIVAC [Grand Rapids: Zondervan, 2020], 191). "Invoking the root": Fokkelman, "Song of Deborah and Barak," 617.

Part 3 includes two dramatic vignettes describing the relationship of two women to Sisera, the mighty leader of the Canaanite army. Focus on a particular character distinguishes one stanza from the next—namely, Jael in verses 24–27 and Sisera's mother in verses 28–30. In reference to the role of Jael in Sisera's defeat, stanza 6 commences with a blessing (ברך), a feature shared by the other two cola that begin parts 1 (5:2: ברכו יהוה) and 2 (5:9: ברכו יהוה). The emphatic nature of this final blessing is accentuated not only by the shift in focus (from YHWH to Jael) and form (from invocation to pronouncement) but also by its juxtaposition with the curse (ארר) of Meroz at the end of the preceding stanza. The root ברך also defines the boundaries of a chiastically arranged tricola that, together with verse 25, makes up the first strophe, whose limits are determined mainly by agency and subject matter. The remainder of the stanza describes the death of Sisera in detail: the second strophe (5:26) consists of verbs describing Jael while the verbs of the third strophe (5:27) describe Sisera. The poetic style of the stanza matches the growing intensity of the scene; the chiastic repetition of the first strophe is duplicated and intensified by semantic, synonymous parallelism in the tricola of verse 26c–e, wherein the last colon features an extra verb for climactic effect. Likewise, the final strophe repeats verbs verbatim to slow the account and emphasize the final unrepeated verb: שָׁדוּד. With this weighty passive participle, a "chain of seven *Qal* perfects comes to its chilling climax."[20]

The poem's final stanza shifts attention from Jael to Sisera's mother. Lexical continuity accentuates the unity of part 3: attention given to the "head" (ראש, though the lexeme is used distributively to mean "every single"; 5:30)[21] and the "neck" (5:30; צואר) invites comparison to the previous stanza (cf. 5:26). The stylistic similarity of the stanzas heightens this effect; the highly repetitive parallelism of verse 30 is remarkably similar to that of verse 27 (note that שלל is mentioned four times, צבע three times, and רקמה twice). Three strophes make up the final stanza, each of the first two consisting of a set of partially semantically synonymous bicola followed by direct speech (5:28 and 5:29–30). A shift to second-person pronominal suffixes sets apart the final strophe (5:31), whose terminal position hints at its thematic prominence—not only for the stanza but also for the song.

---

[20] Fokkelman, "Song of Deborah and Barak," 622. This strophe is a fine example of climactic parallelism.

[21] *HALOT*, 1165. Daniel I. Block (*Judges, Ruth*, NAC 6 [Nashville: Broadman & Holman, 2001], 243, n. 455) points out that the expression occurs only here in the Hebrew Bible. See *GKC* §134q for a similar distributive construction with אחד rather than ראש or ראשון.

Genre

To this point, the poetic composition of Judges 5 has been called a "song" for two reasons: (1) the narrative introduction that indicates it was sung (שִׁיר) and (2) the long-standing tradition of referring to the chapter as the "Song of Deborah." A more precise label is warranted.

A study of genre necessarily begins with a delimitation of the piece being considered. The superscription of Judges 5:1 formally sets off the song from the surrounding narrative, while the formulaic editorial tag at the end of the chapter (5:31c) signals a return to narrative prose and the literary dénouement of the Deborah-Barak cycle. At minimum, the piece is embedded poetry. But what sort of inset poem is it?

As discussed in the previous section, the consensus of scholars is that the intervening text is a composite, that is, a composition that developed over time, incorporating additions and being adapted for a new setting (or settings). Echols argues that the original poem is an example of "heroic poetry" in praise of human characters. Like the book of Judges, the song underwent a "profane-to-sacred transformation" of at least one revision, with the result that the edited composition "praises both the heroes and Yahweh."[22] Given that Echols is assigning a genre to a hypothetical version of the piece, he is analyzing a very different text than I. Instead, I will ascertain genre according to the text's self-presentation as a meaningful entity (i.e., synchronically).

The criteria for genre identification, especially regarding the place of "function" within that discussion, are contested. At minimum, the "organization of [a text's] content, in other words, by its structure"—including syntax—is an essential (and relatively uncontested) aspect of generic categorization.[23] This assessment includes an account of rhetorical devices, stylistic phenomena, arrangement, and characteristic expressions. Such structural observations also involve relating the individual text to the "typical structure on which it rests," without imposing a predetermined, ideal form upon the text.[24] In addition to (1) structures, genres are generally associated with specific (2) settings; and (3) intentions/purposes/rhetorical functions. "Setting" in its contemporary usage is applied far beyond the classical German concept (*Sitz im Leben*) and is often eclipsed by more literary concerns, especially in instances where a text lacks explicit evidence of being circulated apart from its surrounding context.[25] The third category, related to "function," is difficult to pin down but is founded on the recognition that "no communication takes place without a

---

[22] Echols, *"Tell Me, O Muse,"* 199–200.
[23] Serge Frolov, *Judges*, FOTL 6b (Grand Rapids: Eerdmans, 2013), 7.
[24] Rolf Knierim, "Old Testament Form Criticism Reconsidered," *Int* (1973): 462.
[25] Knierim, "Old Testament Form Criticism Reconsidered," 448–49.

purpose."[26] The analysis of a piece's purpose or function is multifaceted and involves distinguishing between the purpose or function of a genre generally and a text specifically. In the words of Rolf Knierim:

> The function of a genuine genre can be completely different from the function of this genre in a text or from the function of a text. The function of a text can be explained diachronically (in terms of its traditional type) or synchronically (in terms of its context).[27]

In assessing the genre of Judges 5, then, I here speak briefly to all three of these criteria—structure, setting, and function—recognizing that any conclusions I offer at this point about the song's function are preliminary.

By studying Judges 5:2–31b as an embedded genre with an unclear compositional history, I elevate its narrative framing (i.e., *Sitz in der Literatur*) as a determinative element of genre classification. My concern is not to describe how the song functioned within Israelite life outside of its present literary context at a given historical moment but to discern its function as a genre distinct from its prose surroundings (i.e., form and structure) and embedded in this precise narrative context, including its implied authorship (5:1; "Deborah . . . with Barak") and setting ("on that day").

To begin, in terms of stylistic phenomena, the composition is clearly poetic, insofar as it features the characteristic brevity, imagery, and parallelism of the biblical Hebrew poetic corpus. Poetry, of course, is a medium shared by a range of genres, even within the Hebrew Bible. Observing the organization of its content is helpful in assigning a narrower characterization. As many have observed, the arrangement of the piece is largely historical, incorporating a discernible series of events, even punctuated by the sequential adverb אז, "then" (5:8, 11, 13, 19, 22). Its genre, then, is in some way related to historical recapitulation. The reported setting of the composition is also relevant. Based on the superscription ("on that day"), many have categorized the song as a "victory ode" of the sort sung by "dancing women who celebrated [the victors'] feats in song."[28] Evidence of women celebrating this way appears even later in the book of Judges (11:34). While Deborah's song is at least related to this tradition, it seems to defy the standard features of the genre, since it gives little attention to the events of the battle itself.[29] Others have observed that the

---

[26] Frolov, *Judges*, 9.
[27] Knierim, "Old Testament Form Criticism Reconsidered," 466.
[28] Globe, "Literary Structure and Unity," 495. Susan Niditch, *Judges: A Commentary*, OTL (Louisville: Westminster John Knox, 2008), 76, labels Judg 5 a "beautiful and moving example of the traditional type of the woman's victory song."
[29] Gregory T. K. Wong, "Song of Deborah as Polemic," *Bib* 88 (2007): 3.

song features phrases and invocations generally associated with hymns and have opted for the classification of "victory hymn."[30] The shortcoming of calling the song a "hymn" of any kind, though, lies in its peculiar focus on human participation. David Beldman emphasizes this discontinuity in his comparison of Judges 5 with Exodus 15, observing that "in the Song of Moses, Yahweh is not just the primary actor, he is the only actor, apart from the futile efforts of his enemies"; by contrast, "the exploits of the human actors . . . get sustained coverage in the poem [of Judges 5]."[31]

The disposition of the song toward the events recorded in Judges 5 is another facet of analysis that is helpful in assessing genre, especially in reference to the ambiguous category of the poem's purpose or function. The song at points glorifies both human and divine participants for what unfolds, and is generally celebratory. However, the song ultimately criticizes those who did not offer themselves willingly to the Israelite war effort (esp. in vv. 15–17, 23). For this reason, Wong categorizes it as a "polemic against Israelite non-participation in military campaigns against external enemies."[32] In terms of its disposition, then, the song is marginally focused on the specifics of the battle, is only partially commemorative, and is rhetorically polemic, if not also something more.

At this point, a return to the superscription of Judges 5:1 is necessary, as well as the preceding narrative to which the song is appended (marked as such by the closure of the cycle in 5:31, not 4:24). While the narrow setting of the song has been considered, its implied authorship has not generally been the focus of scholarship beyond the fact that Deborah is a woman, and thereby one expected to greet men upon their return from battle. Judges 5:1 does in fact associate the song with Deborah *and Barak*, though Deborah's voice is treated as primary through the first-person singular references throughout, which Fokkelman aptly designates the "lyrical I."[33] Deborah's role in the preceding narrative is therefore crucial. Based on her designation as a prophet in 4:4, Serge Frolov rightfully argues the song is "a prophet's poetic recapitulation of the past," designed to "reveal the theological import of recounted events." He labels the unit a "prophetic historical exemplum," which is uncharacteristically narrow in its historical focus.[34] The genre is

---

[30] See, e.g., Robert G. Boling, *Judges*, AB 6A (New York: Doubleday, 1975), 117.

[31] David J. H. Beldman, *Judges*, Two Horizons Old Testament Commentary (Grand Rapids: Eerdmans, 2020), 100, following Wong, "Song of Deborah as Polemic," 21.

[32] Beldman, *Judges*, 100.

[33] Fokkelman, "Song of Deborah and Barak," 611.

[34] Frolov, *Judges*, 134, 366. Regarding the irregularity of its historical scope, Frolov helpfully contrasts the song with Deut 32, which spans centuries in its recounting (and projecting) of Israelite history. By contrast, Judg 5 reflects on a single battle.

a "type of prophetic discourse that describes YHWH's involvement in the past so as to teach something about his involvement in the present," most often detected among the Latter Prophets.[35] The benefit of Frolov's label over Wong's otherwise helpful proposal (i.e., "historical exemplum" rather than "polemic") is that it better accounts for the historical structure of the piece, as well as the fact that its disposition toward events is both evaluative and explanatory. Moreover, it draws attention to the authoritative stance of its speaker within the narrative world. Surely the song celebrates victory and faults Israelites for not participating adequately, but as Frolov argues, it also reveals the "theological import" of what has transpired, and it does so with the authority of YHWH's spokesperson. Bob Becking's suggestion that the song is a "topical song," which reports on recent events and has the twofold function "to inform and to convince" is similar, though Frolov's classification according to the song's prophetic quality is more precise.[36] The study that follows will both substantiate this characterization of the song and reflect on its implications for understanding the song's function within its larger literary context. While I agree wholeheartedly with Frolov's classification, "prophetic historical exemplum" is a bit of a mouthful, so I will often refer to the poem in Judges 5 under the title "the Song of Deborah and Barak" (due to the narrative superscription), "the song" in shorthand, "the poem" more generally, and with supplemental descriptive phrases as I deem helpful.

Interpretive Summary

In 5:1, the narrator attributes the song to Deborah and Barak, despite the prevalence of 1cs pronouns and verbal forms that are explicitly attributed to Deborah in verse 7 ("until I, Deborah, arose"). These first-person references permit the reader to hear the song in Deborah's "voice," while celebrating the willingness of the general to join in the song of the prophet.

According to the divisions established in the previous section, part 1 (vv. 2–8) describes the theological and anthropological foundations for the conflict that transpires in the battle at the Kishon. The first stanza is primarily theological while the orientation of the second is anthropological, though not rigidly so. In fact, before launching into lines in praise of YHWH, the song identifies the occasion for Deborah's praise in terms of human action: the Israelites' wholehearted devotion and active participation in the battle (v. 2). The

---

[35] Frolov, *Judges*, 366.
[36] Bob Becking, "Deborah's Topical Song: Remarks on the Gattung of Judges 5," in *Biblical Narratives, Archaeology, and Historicity: Essays in Honour of Thomas L. Thompson*, ed. Łukasz Niesiołowski-Spanò and Emanuel Pfoh, LHBOTS 680 (London: T&T Clark, 2019), 191.

following cola suggest that Israel is not yet the song's primary audience; the kings and rulers of Canaan must heed the prophet's words. The emphatic repetition of the divine name in Deborah's address signals to the reader that the first stanza provides the theological convictions that will guide the remainder of the poem. These convictions are anchored historically with an allusion to YHWH's theophany at Sinai (vv. 4–5). By drawing upon this event, the stanza establishes both the awesome might of YHWH and his special relationship to Israel (cf. "the God of Israel" in vv. 3d, 5b). The vision of cosmic upheaval recounted for the song's Canaanite audience clearly establishes the proper response of the created world to an encounter with Israel's God. These kings themselves witnessed a similar storm-like cosmic upheaval when they experienced firsthand YHWH's might in battle (vv. 20–22).[37]

The focus on YHWH's might in the song's opening lines contrasts starkly with the weakened state of Israel in the second stanza. The turmoil in the days of Shamgar and Jael arrested commerce and rendered travel unsafe. The fragile agrarian communities of Israel were crippled by the repeated invasion of oppressors.[38] As a result, those who lived in these villages (i.e., פרזון) were reluctant to engage their oppressors, or even to engage in normal activity.[39] However, these Israelites' tendency to shrink back in the face of military occupation stops abruptly when Deborah arises as a prophet in Israel. One short line in the poem seems to summarize the cycle of oppression and deliverance that characterizes the book of Judges: "God chose new ones [leaders]" (v. 8). As he did repeatedly in the period, God rescued Israel from oppression by raising up new leaders. In this particular battle, that activity began with Deborah, whose prophetic voice emboldened the people and their general, Barak.[40] Despite the change the song implies in verses 7b–c and 8a, the stanza continues to emphasize the weakness of Israel. While the nation's leaders were willing, its military resources were limited. According to verse 8, Israel's stash of weaponry was meagre in the face of a well-armed invading host (whose impressive chariots were furnished with iron enhancements).[41]

---

[37] On the double function of the theophany as recollection and preparation, see Alexander Globe, "The Text and Literary Structure of Judges 5,4–5," *Bib* 55 (1974): 178.

[38] The appendix offers a brief explanation of how the use of פרזון implies a lack of security, because it denotes villages that lacked walls (cf. Ezek 38:11).

[39] Judg 6:2–4, 11 illustrates the impact of Midianite and Amalekite oppressors on the economic and social patterns of daily life for Israel. The "dens in the mountains" and Gideon's hidden winepress reflect the danger of standard trade routes and activity during wartime.

[40] This matches the chronology and emphasis of the prose account, in which Deborah's leadership is established before she mediates God's call to Barak.

[41] Cf. Judg 4:3, 13. Statements highlighting Israel's lack of weaponry are not limited to the song or to Judges; 1 Sam 13:19–23 (esp. v. 22) makes a similar theological claim.

The weakness of Israel provides the backdrop against which YHWH triumphed mightily with the help of his willing leaders. The detailed description of Israel's shortcomings highlights the extraordinary nature of YHWH's victory. Part 2 as a whole (vv. 9–23) reflects on the ways God and his people participated in the events of the battle. Just as part 1 was introduced by an invocation, so too is the song's second major section. While Deborah initially addressed Canaanite kings, those participating in travel and commerce seem to be the subject of her imperative in verse 10.[42] The cessation of travel and trade emphasized in verses 6–7 (in which the operative verb is חדל, "to cease") is matched in verses 10–11 by a scene that depicts the normal movement and interaction of people in Israel (רכב, "to ride"; הלך, "to walk"). To highlight the dramatic change in circumstances, the song addresses those who have benefited directly from YHWH's deliverance. The abrupt shift from the description of a war-torn people in the second stanza to a picture of buzzing commerce in the third envelops (and thereby highlights) the poem's second statement of its occasion (v. 9): the time when the leaders and the people of Israel responded appropriately and engaged in the battle. Just as this joyous event prompted Deborah to sing of YHWH's mighty acts in the first stanza, so it caused the people of Israel to celebrate both the righteous acts of YHWH and those of the villagers who acted in this battle in accordance with YHWH's initiatives (v. 11). While the appropriate response of the Canaanite listener is to tremble in the face of Israel's Almighty God, the responsibility of the listening Israelite is to reflect on the events and share the good news. Unhampered by foreign oppressors and cruel plunderers, the people of Israel freely recount events as they go about their work with "tranquility and joy."[43]

In verses 11d–13, the text begins to describe the movement of Israelite troops. The remainder consists of the "righteous acts of his villagers" upon which the third stanza's addressees must reflect. The "people of YHWH" went down (ירד; cf. Judg 4:14) to the gates, which were identified as the location of the military activity reported after God installed new leaders in verse 8b. Verse 12 focuses on two such leaders, whom those "recounting" (v. 11b)

---

[42] J. David Schloen, "Caravans, Kenites, and *Casus belli*: Enmity and Alliance in the Song of Deborah," *CBQ* 55 (1993): 24–25, argues convincingly that those traveling comfortably in v. 10 are the very individuals whose economic livelihood was threatened by the conditions of v. 6.

[43] Brian Tidiman (*Le Livre des Juges* [Vaux-sur-Seine: Édifac, 2004], 137) describes the scene in this way when he encourages interpreters to focus on the general thought of the passage instead of its difficult terms; according to v. 11, both rural and urban life returned to normal because of the intervention of YHWH and his villagers.

the mighty acts of YHWH and his army address directly.[44] What appears interruptive is actually crucial in the flow of the song; this "song within a song" demonstrates the response of those who encountered the prophet's testimony—the very task with which they had been entrusted in verse 10c.[45] Using the vocabulary of military mustering, the speakers rouse Deborah to sing (עוּר) and encourage Barak to rise up (קוּם; cf. 4:14) and achieve the victory that is already assured.[46] That Barak did indeed "take captive [his] captives" is evident in verse 13, which describes Israel's supernatural triumph.

The last lines of the third stanza state that the remnant—the surviving warriors of Israel—secured this victory alongside YHWH in the battle at the Kishon. Two stanzas detail how this transpired: the fourth in terms of human agency and the fifth in relation to divine agency. The fourth stanza consists of one of the Hebrew Bible's list of tribal pronouncements (*Stammessprüche*; cf. Gen 49:1–27; Deut 33:1–29). While formally distinct from the canonically prior texts, the descriptions of the tribes included here mimic the vocabulary of other tribal blessings.[47] Indeed, the list of tribes in Judges 5 is organized matriarchally, as is the case for most of the tribal lists in the Hebrew Bible.[48] Reuben, the last son of Rachel and Leah to be introduced, broke from the pattern of his brothers and is the first of four disobedient tribes who refused the call to arms (the remainder of whom are descendants of Zilpah and Bilhah). Along with the kinsmen of Jacob's eldest son, these tribes fail to heed the call

---

[44] For a similar reading, see Trent C. Butler, *Judges*, WBC 8 (Nashville: Thomas Nelson, 2009), 142, though the "people" of whom Butler speaks seem to be the battle's *participants*, rather than those recounting it after the events transpire.

[45] Contra Raymond de Hoop, "Judges 5 Reconsidered: Which Tribes? What Land? Whose Song?" in *Land of Israel in Bible, History, and Theology*, ed. Jacques van Ruiten and J. Cornelis de Vos, VTSup 124 (Boston: Brill, 2009), 157–58, who argues the lines "disturb the line of thought of the poem" and indicate the fictitious addition of Deborah and Barak to an already-circulating victory song.

[46] While the root עוּר may simply mean to rouse oneself from slumber or inactivity (e.g., Isa 51:17; Hab 2:19), a figurative use of the imperative appears frequently in the sense of "rouse yourself for battle" (e.g., Ps 35:23; 59:5; 80:3; Joel 4:9; Zech 13:7).

[47] E.g., the description of Reuben in 5:15d–16c resembles a statement made about Issachar in Gen 49:14–15. The song portrays Reuben sitting/staying between the "sheepfolds" (ישׁב בין המשׁפתים), just as Jacob describes Issachar as a donkey crouching between them (רבץ בין המשׁפתים). See p. 165 below. The repetition of Issachar and the juxtaposition of these two tribes accentuates how the apparently pejorative statement in Gen 49:15 (given the prediction of מס) about Issachar is now more fitting of Reuben.

[48] Jack M. Sasson, "'A Breeder or Two for Each Leader': On Mothers in Judges 4 and 5," in *A Critical Engagement: Essays on the Hebrew Bible in Honour of J. Cheryl Exum*, ed. David J. A. Clines and Ellen van Wolde, HBM 38 (Sheffield: Sheffield Phoenix, 2011), 347–50. That the list begins with the descendants of *Rachel* is unique to Judges 5.

to battle, out of economic distress,⁴⁹ cowardice, or apathy. Rather than providing the reason for their absence (indeed, the prophet herself wonders "why" in vv. 16a, 17b), the stanza highlights lexically their inactivity in contrast to the valiant volunteers celebrated by the song; while the tribes of verses 14–15c "went down" (cf. v. 11d), Reuben, Gad, Dan, and Asher "stay," "remain," and "sojourn."⁵⁰ Of course, the use of the root ישב in reference to Reuben invokes Numbers 32, in which Moses anticipates the reluctance of Gad and Reuben to participate in Cisjordanian battles; to "stay" is not simply a sin of *reluctance* but a direct transgression of Moses' instruction to the tribes of the Transjordan.⁵¹

According to the fifth stanza, YHWH, not Israel, encounters Canaanite forces face-to-face. The poet introduces the rulers of Canaan as kings (following the pattern of the song's opening lines) and describes their military failure in terms of the inability to pillage. This reference to the spoils of war not only anticipates the emphasis on plunder that ends the song (again lamenting the lack thereof) but also emphasizes the reversal of fortunes that Canaan experienced because of YHWH's intervention. Since plundering was the modus operandi of the Canaanite oppressors (e.g., 2:14), this ode focuses on the deliverance of Israel from a specific and familiar form of oppression. The battle was as miraculous as one would expect after hearing YHWH's hymnic introduction in verses 4–5; the entire created order was at his disposal. The cosmic upheaval wrought by his entrance in the first stanza is matched by a similar scene here in which the stars and the Wadi Kishon fought at the whim of Israel's God.⁵² While these miraculous events only imply divine agency, the image of the Kishon washing away the Canaanite army echoes the moment when the Red Sea came crashing down on Pharaoh's chariots—when the Egyptians testified that "YHWH fights for [Israel]" (Exod 14:25). The deity's cosmic forces set the army's horses

---

⁴⁹ Thus Lawrence E. Stager, "The Song of Deborah: Why Some Tribes Answered the Call and Others Did Not," *BAR* 15 (1989): 50–64.

⁵⁰ As observed by Auffret ("En ce jour-la Debora et Baraq chanterent," 123), the repetition of the root חקק (vv. 14c, 15d) underscores this lexical contrast.

⁵¹ Jacob Wright ("War Commemoration and the Interpretation of Judges 5:15b–17," *VT* 61 [2011]: 516–17) emphasizes that the "rich pasturelands of the Gilead" (Num 32:1–5) would have tempted Reuben and Gad to remain across the Jordan. The song's reference to "sheepfolds" (משפתים) and "flocks" (עדרים) strengthens the literary parallel.

⁵² Alan J. Hauser, "Two Songs of Victory: A Comparison of Exodus 15 and Judges 5," in *Directions in Biblical Hebrew Poetry*, ed. Elaine R. Follis, JSOTSup 40 (Sheffield: JSOT, 1987), 272, argues that the use of מַיִם and שָׁמַיִם in vv. 19–20 are intentional references to the theophany of vv. 4–5.

to flight, thereby neutralizing the terrifying archetypal weapons of Canaan (i.e., the "chariots of iron"; 4:13).[53]

In an unexpected return to an evaluation of the battle's participants, the envoy of YHWH appears in verse 23. This transitional statement serves two primary functions.

First, the statement of the envoy provides a fitting conclusion to part 2. The second portion of the poem reflects successively on the triumph of the Israelites and their God; the first line of this section, in which Deborah praises YHWH because of the willingness of the people of Israel, is complemented by a statement exposing those who did *not* come to the help of YHWH. While the location and identity of Meroz is debated, Heinz-Dieter Neef has argued persuasively that Meroz is an Israelite settlement—why else would the envoy denounce its lack of participation?—whose military allegiance was to Canaan.[54]

Second, the placement of the curse (ארר) of Meroz highlights the benediction (ברך) of Jael in the next stanza by juxtaposing (and thereby contrasting) the response of two parties whose military allegiance is to Canaan (cf. Judg 4:17). Chiastic, lexical repetition emphasizes that Jael was "most blessed" among women, despite being a non-Israelite.

Like parts 1 and 2 of the song, part 3 begins with a blessing (cf. vv. 2, 9), as noted above. Because to this point only YHWH was the recipient of blessing, the shift to praise the action of a specific individual is striking. Repetition of the verb "to hammer" (חלם) ties the events that transpired in Jael's tent to the flight of the enemy horses in verse 22; Jael's victory over Sisera was the climax of the Battle of Kishon.

The dramatic language of Sisera's fallen body "between [Jael's] feet" has led scholars to suggest that the scene is thoroughly sexual.[55] From my perspective, however, the scene is more concerned with Sisera's unexpected

---

[53] The "hammering" of the horses' hooves probably refers to their flight as they broke loose from chariots and reared wildly in the chaos of the flooded battlefield. For a similar conjecture see Block, *Judges, Ruth*, 238; Butler, *Judges*, 153.

[54] Heinz-Dieter Neef, "Meroz: Jdc 5,23a," *ZAW* 107 (1995): 118–22, highlights the association of the envoy of YHWH with contexts banning covenant-making with other nations (e.g., Exod 23:23–33). By his reckoning, such a covenant is the criterion by which Meroz is explicitly *cursed*, rather than simply confronted as are the inactive tribes at the end of the fourth stanza. Followed by Lee Roy Martin, "From Gilgal to Bochim: The Narrative Significance of the Angel of Yahweh in Judges 2:1," *JSem* 18 (2009): 339–40.

[55] E.g., Niditch, *Judges*, 81–82; Richard G. Bowman, "Narrative Criticism: Human Purpose in Conflict with Divine Presence," in *Judges and Method: New Approaches in Biblical Studies*, ed. Gale A. Yee (Minneapolis: Fortress, 2007), 72–73. While this interpretation is possible, one that accounts for the motherly imagery of the vignette would be closer to the mark.

subjugation. While Sisera may have intended sexual exploitation (cf. 5:30), Jael emerges in the narrative as a warrior who subdued the enemy at her feet in military victory.[56] In a poem that carefully focuses on who acts and who does not, it is noteworthy that Sisera's last action was not his at all—the verb שדד is passive. Just as YHWH incapacitated the vast forces of Sisera's army, so Jael, as an extension of YHWH's military program, incapacitated Sisera.

In the seventh stanza the song's composer introduces Sisera's mother, who waited anxiously for the return of her son. Nervously she lamented Sisera's absence, wondering what delayed his chariots (v. 28). These lines use imagery reminiscent of the second stanza, in which a war-torn Israel was incapable of traveling freely (or safely); now the mighty chariots of the Canaanite general "hesitated" (בשש; v. 28c). Sisera's mother and her household expected not only to greet the victorious son but also to meet the captured women who would bear children for him.[57] Their expectations were confounded by the reality of which they were not yet aware: Sisera would fail to return with plunder and the warrior responsible for *his* capture and murder was a simple, tent-dwelling woman. The stanza illustrates graphically the implications of the earlier statement that the kings of Canaan took no "spoil of silver" (v. 19d); moreover, it ironically casts the subjugator of women as being subjugated by a woman.

The action ends abruptly with this dramatic reversal. As the song's audience contemplates the gravity of Sisera's defeat and the profound impact of YHWH's most recent intervention, the poet also reflects on the preceding events. With a direct address to YHWH, the prophet wills that all of God's enemies would perish like Sisera. As if her attention shifts back to her audience, the prophet refers to YHWH in the third person, declaring that those who demonstrate covenant loyalty to YHWH (אהב) would go forth in battle with the might of a sunrise. The song ends not by expressing the superiority of Israel but by associating the preceding victory with fidelity to (and the fidelity of) YHWH. Considering the curse of the Israelite settlement Meroz, the benediction of the non-Israelite Jael, Deborah's taunt of the inactive tribes, and the praiseworthy actions of the willing leaders, the Song of Deborah and Barak consistently celebrates covenant fidelity expressed through obedience to settlement-related directives. With Deuteronomic vocabulary the prophet assured her audience that generous blessing comes to those who remain uncompromisingly loyal to YHWH, the God of Israel.

---

[56] Cf. Ps 18:38 and 2 Sam 22:29. Alexander Globe, "Judges V 27," *VT* 25 (1975): 364–65, nicely captures the martial overtone of the vocabulary.

[57] The use of the crude term "womb" (רחם) to describe the women, as well as their identification as part of the plunder, highlights their intended role as "breeders" for their new master. The suitable translation "breeder" comes from Sasson, *Judges 1–12*, 279.

Conclusion

The difficulties posed by Judges 5 notwithstanding, the Song of Deborah and Barak is as poetically sophisticated as it is intelligible as a portrait of a notable Canaanite-Israelite military skirmish. While the given translation (not to mention the accompanying appendix) leaves some questions unanswered, this rendering of Judges 5 suggests that a historically plausible and literarily unified interpretation is possible. The summary above provides the contours of one such interpretation. Using Deborah's voice and the supporting tenor of Barak, the composition recounts the Battle of Kishon with theologically robust and pedagogically motivated language. Given its association with Deborah, a prophet of YHWH, the song represents a prophetic interpretation of the battle and a divinely authorized assessment of Israelite faithfulness. This interpretation of the composition is most evident when read in its near literary context—the task of the next chapter.

2
Judges 5 in Its Narrative Cycle

The standard interpretations of the Kishon battle account in Judges 4–5 have one thing in common: a tendency to treat Judges 4 and Judges 5 as synoptic accounts, rather than a unified narrative about the battle. There are good reasons for doing so, including, but not limited to, the fact that the details vary between the two accounts and that, at least at face value, they seem to address differing concerns; however, one must not disregard the clear textual (perhaps editorial) cues that encourage the accounts to be read together as one narrative cycle.[1] Those cues include the deferral of the sign of cyclical closure until 5:31 and the note that the song was delivered "on that day" in 5:1. This analysis, then, addresses the song as a climactic moment in a unified narrative about the Battle of Kishon, which contributes to the plot, characterization, and themes of Judges 4–5.

Plot

The narrative of Judges 4 may be divided into the following scenes:[2]

---

[1] The vocabulary of "cycle" indicates the textual pericope traditionally identified by Judges scholars that (in this case) stretches from 4:1–5:31 and is demarcated by standard formal elements, historically identified as "cyclical" or "editorial."

[2] According to Shimon Bar-Efrat, *Narrative Art in the Bible* (New York: T&T Clark International, 2004), 96, a scene is demarcated by the characters participating in it; when characters change, a new scene begins. For this reason the outline above lists the major participants in every scene. Shifts in characterization often accompany clauses that depart from the verb-initial *wayyiqtol*, which are termed "episode-bounding" in D. F. Murray, "Narrative Structure and Technique in the Deborah-Barak Story, Judges 4:4–22," in *Studies in the Historical Books of the Old Testament*, ed. J. A. Emerton, VTSup 30 (Leiden: Brill, 1979), 162 et passim. By contrast, acts are delineated by location, time, and/or subject matter. Given the number of troop movements in the chapter, I use the term "location" loosely. In this case, the first act encompasses everything that takes place near the Kishon (in short, the "battlefield"), whereas the second act takes place in a completely different, nonmilitary locale (i.e., the tent of Jael). On the whole, my analysis resembles that of

A   Narrative Prologue: Introduction of the Conflict (4:1–5; Jabin, Israelites, YHWH)
B   Act 1: The Battle at Kishon (4:6–16)
    Scene 1: Mustering Israelites (4:6–10; Deborah, Barak)
    Scene 2: Mustering Canaanites (4:11–13; Kenites, Sisera)
    Scene 3: YHWH's Triumph (4:14–16; Deborah, Barak, Sisera, YHWH)
C   Act 2: The Tent of Jael (4:17–22)
    Scene 1: Jael Kills Sisera (4:17–21; Jael, Sisera)
    Scene 2: Barak Visits Jael's Tent (4:22; Jael, Barak)
D   Conclusion of the Conflict (4:23–24; Jabin, Israelites, YHWH)

The beginning of the Deborah-Barak narrative cycle is marked by its formulaic vocabulary. As is the pattern in the book of Judges, 4:1–2 begins the narrative with reference to elements of the macroplot established in Judges 2:6–3:6, that is, a standard sequence of events that frame each of the individual microplots that make up the book of Judges. These elements include the apostasy of Israel ("they again did the evil"), the response of YHWH ("sold them"), and the Canaanite king whom the deity used to test Israelite response under political pressure ("Jabin, king of Canaan, who reigned in Hazor"). Background information in verses 2 and 4 transitions toward the microplot by introducing the two agents of YHWH and Jabin who feature prominently in the ensuing conflict:[3] Deborah and Sisera, respectively. In verses 3 and 5, the narrator caps off his introduction to the conflict with the event that sets the battle in motion: the people seek YHWH's intervention through his prophet.

With Deborah's summons to Barak in verse 6 the plot actions surrounding the Battle of Kishon begin. As is standard in battle reports,[4] the primary means of plot progression throughout act 1 is dialogue punctuated by summary narration. In fact, exchanges between the prophet and the Israelite general provide the organizing scheme against which the plot develops. Not only does that dialogue constitute the bulk of narrative material but that which is *not* part of direct speech is also tied causally to it, often by means of explicit grammatical repetition (e.g., using identical syntax, verses 9f–10 provide

---

Alonso-Schökel ("Erzählkunst im Buche der Richter," *Bib* 42 [1961]: 158–66), but I depart from his construal by splitting the first act into three scenes rather than two.

[3]   Marked formally by verbless and participial clauses.

[4]   Admittedly, battle reports take a variety of forms. They often include, but are not limited to, the mustering of troops, enumeration of weaponry, a leader's instruction, summary of military movement, and reports of casualties. Joshua A. Berman, *Narrative Analogy in the Hebrew Bible: Battle Stories and Their Equivalent Non-Battle Narratives*, VTSup 103 (Leiden: Brill, 2004), 21.

the narrative fulfillment of Deborah's charge to Barak to muster the Israelite troops and her promise to follow him to battle).

With the onset of the second act, the pace of the narrative changes abruptly. Accompanying the shift in Sisera's location—from the chaos (המם; v. 15) of the battlefield to the peace (שלום; v. 17) of a Kenite homestead—is a shift in the pace of the narrative itself.[5] Whereas a single verbal form summarizes the entire battle between the Israelites and the Canaanites in verse 15, the narrator uses eight verbs in verse 21 to describe the death of Sisera. Such intricate description alongside more detailed dialogue contributes to the slowing of narrative time—a stylistic move that highlights the tent scene as the climax of plot development.[6] Geographical realities reinforce the scene's importance in plot progression; beginning with the introduction of characters in verses 1–5, events transpire at locales increasingly proximate to the tent of Jael.[7]

The two tent scenes that make up the second act mirror one another on the level of syntax, lexicography, and character dynamic. This kind of parallel scene structure occurs also in the first act. In both cases the narrative focuses on each of the generals in turn (though the order reverses chiastically in the second act). Given this double parallel arrangement, the narrative structure—along with important lexical cues—may be re-charted as follows:

    A   Introduction (יד יבין)
       B   Israelite Mustering (vv. 6–10; זעק)
          C   Canaanite Mustering (vv. 11–13 // vv. 6–10; זעק)
             D   Barak's Movements (v. 14; ירד)
                E   YHWH's Movements (v. 15a)
             D'   Sisera's Movements (vv. 15b–16 // v. 14; ירד)
          C'   Sisera (Canaanite) and Jael (vv. 17–21; קרא + יצא)
      B'   Barak (Israelite) and Jael (v. 22 // vv. 17–21; קרא + יצא)
    A'   Conclusion (vv. 23–24; יד בני־ישראל)

---

[5] Alonso-Schökel, "Erzählkunst im Buche der Richter," 163, observes this shift: "The scene reflects absolute contrast: previously, war and confusion (המם), here, peace (שָׁלוֹם); there, a warcamp (מַחֲנֶה), here a peaceful place (אֹהֶל)" (translation mine).

[6] Meir Sternberg, *The Poetics of Biblical Narrative*, ed. Robert M. Polzin, ISBL (Bloomington: Indiana University Press, 1985), 282.

[7] The odd intrusion of Heber pitching his tent in comparatively close proximity to the battle (a *wayyiqtol*, rather than an explicitly offline clause) contributes to this movement. John H. Stek, "The Bee and the Mountain Goat: A Literary Reading of Judges 4," in *A Tribute to Gleason Archer: Essays on the Old Testament*, ed. Walter C. Kaiser and Ronald F. Youngblood (Chicago: Moody, 1986), 56.

While the arrangement above may appear oversimplified, this analysis reveals two important narration techniques employed by the storyteller: first, the contrastive juxtaposition of Canaanite and Israelite experience, and second, a regression of focus away from Sisera at the beginning and end of the narrative. Certainly Sisera is in the background of both scenes (quite literally in the last scene), but the attention to the response of the Israelite protagonist before and after his experience with the enemy general suggests that the defeat of Sisera and the Canaanite army is not the primary concern of the narrative, though it is the central plot point.[8]

In verse 22 the focus particle הנה signals that the point of view in the final moments of the tent scene is Barak's. Thus, the story of the Battle of Kishon ends with the perception of an imperceptive Israelite general, who has just witnessed the defeat of his mighty enemy at the hands of a foreign civilian women—Jael.[9] How the general will respond to YHWH's most recent revelation remains to be seen, but the narrative's plot-level emphasis on the invitation issued to Barak and his response to YHWH's initiative (i.e., the plot components that precede and follow the central conflict with Sisera) introduces a perspectival trajectory that will continue in the song.

Diverting back to the narrator's perspective, verses 23–24 summarize the details of the Battle of Kishon in terms of the macroplot: the faithfulness of Israel to YHWH, measured by the tribes' performance in battle against the oppressors du jour. "On that day" YHWH claimed victory as the leader of the Israelite army, and yet, the narrator notes that the hand of Israel bore down oppressively upon Jabin until he was destroyed. By the empowerment of YHWH, Israel responds faithfully and its fortunes are reversed—the balance of power has shifted from the "hand of Jabin" (יד יבין) in v. 2 to the "hand of

---

[8] In "Chiasmus in Biblical Narrative: Rhetoric of Characterization," *Proof* 22 (2002): 273–304, Elie Assis summarizes the consensus among scholars that plot-level chiasmus "focuses the reader's attention on the center of the unit, where the central idea or turning point is situated. . . . The introduction is parallel to the resolution, the rising action to the falling action, and in the middle stands the climax" (273). In the narrative of Judges 4, the center of the chiasm (act 1, scene 3) is the turning point in the narrative, while the true resolution of the conflict (and what I have called the "climax") comes in the second act.

[9] I acknowledge that the term "civilian" is anachronistic. By describing Jael as such, I am highlighting one implication of being a woman in the military context of the ancient Near East, that is, one generally not responsible for (if not also actively excluded from) military service. According to this analysis, for the narrator to highlight that a "woman" killed an enemy combatant is to emphasize that she is completely removed from the paradigm of battle. For a discussion of Jael's explicitly nonmilitary characterization, see below p. 63. For the argument that the connotation of "woman" in the text is "civilian," see p. 72.

Israel" (יד בני ישראל) in v. 24.[10] The detail that Israel completely destroyed both Jabin and his army is necessary to communicate that this battle was won in a manner that pleased YHWH; incompletely executing settlement-related directives (i.e., חרם) had always been the people's downfall.[11]

This indication that Israel had responded appropriately to YHWH leads naturally to a second event that transpired "on that day" of victory: a celebratory song—more aptly, a prophetic rendering of the battle concerned with gauging Israel's devotion to YHWH, as measured through the people's responsiveness to the call to battle. The superscription "Deborah, with Barak son of Abinoam, sang on that day" (5:1; cf. "on that day" in 4:23) continues the narrative flow initiated in the previous chapter. Not only does the sequence of *wayyiqtols* continue uninterrupted—indeed, the standard indicator of cyclical closure does not appear until after the song (5:31)—but also the narrator shifts back to Barak's perspective as he joins the prophet in a song recounting events. As Watts notes, the narrative of Judges 4 does not "anticipate" the song itself in the way that Deuteronomy 31:19–22 anticipates the Song of Moses, but the summative statements in Judges 4:23–24 signal a shift toward the theological concerns of the song that follows, just as the perspective of the song follows naturally from the end of the tent scene in verse 22. As a culminating moment in the narrative of the Battle of Kishon—and not merely a poetic recitation of events included for an alternate perspective—the Song of Deborah and Barak redirects attention to the crisis of the macroplot introduced in Judges 2:6–3:6—namely, the testing of Israelite commitment to YHWH in the context of military engagements with the land's inhabitants.[12] Given the evaluative bent of the macroplot, it is therefore fitting that the song includes blessings, curses, and the language of אהב—an expression of covenant commitment. These Deuteronomic features evaluate Israelite faithfulness to the "commands of YHWH, which he commanded their fathers by the hand of Moses" (3:4), a narratorial move that is central to the macroplot.

Beyond adding extended evaluative content to the brief summary at the end of Judges 4, the song contributes plot developments of its own. Using temporal adverbs (אז) to mark the progression of the skirmish, this poem retells the story of battle again, introducing theological material and battle

---

[10] Ellen van Wolde, "Deborah and Ya'el in Judges 4," in *On Reading Prophetic Texts: Gender-Specific and Related Studies in Memory of Fokkelien van Dijk-Hemmes*, ed. Bob Becking and Meindert Dijkstra, BibInt 18 (New York: Brill, 1996), 288.

[11] See, e.g., Josh 7:1–9; 15:63; 16:10; Judg 1:27–36; 1 Sam 15:1–11. Cf. Josh 10:40, 11:20–23.

[12] Because the text expresses this "test" primarily in terms of characterization, this chapter will address the nature of this evaluative scheme in the next section.

scenes entirely lacking from the prose account. Related to plot development, the most significant new material is stanza 2—the dilapidated conditions of the people of Israel before God's intervention—and stanza 7, the humiliation of the defeated conqueror's household. The entirety of the second stanza is summarized with one simple statement in the initial verses of the previous chapter: "He strongly oppressed the Israelites for ten years" (4:3c). By contrast, the song's seventh stanza includes a vignette at which the preceding narrative does not even hint. Thus, the cycle of Judges 4–5 ends with entirely new information about the household of Sisera. The last scene of the previous chapter concluded with Barak's having witnessed the remarkable triumph over Sisera; now, having benefited from the prophet's theological reorientation, Barak joins Deborah in summoning the people of Israel to reflect on the scene in Jael's tent and its wide-ranging implications. The supplemental perspective afforded by the end of the song thus facilitates a transition from individual-centered reflection at the end of Judges 4 (that of Barak on the defeated Canaanite general) to community-oriented and prophetically amplified reflection in Judges 5 (that of the people of Israel on the defeated Canaanites).

The chapter's final verse (v. 31) concludes the prophetic utterance and resumes the sequence of *wayyiqtols* from the previous chapter, only here giving the formulaic signal of cyclical closure (v. 31c). The first word of 5:31a (כן) signals the nature of the relationship between the Song of Deborah and Barak and the remaining battles of the period: the prophet wills that "in this way" all of YHWH's enemies would perish. In short, the battle is exemplary. The poetic, prophetic rendition of the Battle of Kishon—especially part 3—has a paradigmatic quality that explicitly qualifies it for reflection at the level of the macroplot. The observation of Mathys is insightful: while the song recounts an event, it does so with fewer ties to the details of what occurred than it does to Israelite motivation. In this way it is somewhat deprived of its contingency ("Ihrer Kontingenz ein Stück weit beraubt") and becomes an example of how God treats those who love him.[13]

Based on these observations, I summarize the contribution of Judges 5 to the cycle's plot development as follows: Deborah's creative, theologically laden retelling of the events at Kishon does not simply replay the events of the battle, nor provide a secondary, more imaginative account of the scene. Instead, the voices of Deborah and Barak provide public, evaluative commentary that is entirely at home in the narrator's summative comments at the

---

[13] Hans-Peter Mathys, *Dichter und Beter: Theologen aus spätalttestamentlicher Zeit*, OBO 132 (Freiburg: Universitätsverlag Freiburg Schweiz Vandenhoeck, 1994), 176.

end of the previous chapter; the formulaic language of 4:23–24 contextualizes the song as a performative event associated with the Kishon battle. Given the song's paradigmatic quality, it provides direct interpretation of the events in Judges 4 in light of the macroplot. It is instructive that the song's additional plot-level content (i.e., stanzas 2 and 7; scenic details that add temporal and spatial dimension, not simply characterization) is not immediately relevant to the battle per se but rather to its effectiveness in reversing the balance of power in Canaan. The function of the Song of Deborah and Barak in the plot development of Judges 4–5 is thus *expositional*; insofar as the macroplot is the "real story" in the book, the song's function is to supplement and interpret plot elements so as to reveal their enduring theological and covenantal implications.

Character

A reader expecting to identify with the cycle's major players might be disappointed; none of the cast's personalities is developed very fully.[14] Instead, the narrative develops the characters only insofar as they contribute to the forward movement of the microplot (Israel's deliverance) and ultimately the macroplot. I have suggested that the macroplot consistently construes the events in terms of three major players—namely, YHWH, Israel, and its oppressors. The judges—in tandem with the other salvific agents God calls to action (e.g., Jael)—function as the means by which the deity accomplishes his purposes and thus act as major players in individual accounts of his salvific exploits, that is, the microplots. In each of the cycles, the introductory and concluding verses typically address the three major characters while the intervening verses focus on YHWH's salvific agent(s). Judges 4 adheres to this pattern, as we shall see below.

Israelites

The first character (or in this case, a collective group of characters) mentioned in the narrative of Judges 4 is the בני ישראל—the Israelites. The verbs related grammatically to this noun phrase frame chapter 4 and are restricted to the cyclical unit's introduction and conclusion.[15] In verses 1–5, the Israelites (1) again did

---

[14] P. J. Nel, "Character in the Book of Judges," *OTE* 8 (1995): 198, observes that "presentation of character [in the book of Judges], whether direct or indirect, appears to serve the overall plot or secondary motifs of the different stories. It does *not* serve to create characters, complex and unpredictable, through an understanding of their psychological dispositions and forces of personality."

[15] In addition to the overarching chiasm(s) mentioned in the previous section, Stek ("Bee and the Mountain Goat," 55) argues that the actions of the Israelites in the narrative

"the evil" in the sight of YHWH, (2) had been sold into the hand of Jabin, king of Canaan, (3) cried out to YHWH, (4) experienced twenty years of cruel oppression under Sisera, and (5) went to Deborah for assistance, or "the judgment." By noting the severity of Israel's oppression, the opening verses certainly acknowledge Israel's culpability in their circumstances but front the agency of the aggressor. The cycle depicts the Israelites not simply as sinful and militarily occupied but also suffering. Such an introduction sets the stage for a reversal of Israel's fortunes on the one hand and contributes to the portrait of Sisera on the other.

The chapter's closing verses (4:23–24) offer the only other references to corporate Israel. Here, (1) God leads them to battle (the Israelites are the *object* of the verb), (2) their hand "pressed harder and harder" against Jabin, and (3) they—not YHWH—destroyed him. Even more than the rest of the cyclical conclusions in Judges, the last clauses of the chapter attribute victory to the Israelites. Unique to Judges 4 is the statement that "the hand of the Israelites pressed (הלך) harder and harder against Jabin, king of Canaan, until they destroyed (כרת) Jabin, king of Canaan" (4:24).[16] According to this statement, the victory was decisive and the destruction of the enemy was total.

The focus on Israel's military participation at the end of chapter 4 reflects a move toward the emphases of the next chapter. Far more than in chapter 4, the account of the battle on the lips of Deborah and Barak emphasizes the agency of the entire people of Israel. The composition in chapter 5 refers to Israel corporately—using the terms ישראל and עם־יהוה—and according to tribes. Scholars studying the portrayal of Israel in the song tend to be interested most in the (seemingly) incomplete tribal list occupying verses 14–18, which chastises several tribes, labels two obscurely (Machir [Manasseh]; Gilead [Gad]), and completely omits two southern tribes (Simeon and Judah).[17] For this

---

cycle are arranged in a "thematically concentric [pattern] with reinforcing verbal links." He provides the following diagram:

  A The Israelites again did evil in the eyes of YHWH (4:1)
      B YHWH sold them into the *hands* of *Jabin king of Canaan* (4:2)
          C and the Israelites cried to YHWH (4:3)
          C' and God subdued . . . Jabin king of Canaan before the Israelites (4:23)
      B' The *hand* of the Israelites bore down ever harder on *Jabin king of Canaan* (4:24)
  A' And the land enjoyed peace forty years (5:31).

[16] Moreover, the noun יָד is the subject of the verbal root הלך only here in the Hebrew Bible. This singular construction serves the unique thematic purposes of the chapter. The Ehud narrative uses a similar statement with a passive verb: "Moab was subdued on that day under the hand of Israel" (3:30).

[17] On the tribal/geographical referent of Machir and Gilead in Judg 5, see Magnus Ottoson, *Gilead: Tradition and History*, trans. Jean Gray, ConBOT 3 (Lund: CWK Gleerup, 1969), 136–43.

reason, some have questioned the legitimacy of the traditional conception of a tightly bound "people of Israel" at the time of the judges.[18] In addition, most of the tribes listed in Judges 5 are missing from the battle report of Judges 4, in which only two tribes earn mention (i.e., Zebulun and Naphtali; cf. 4:6, 10). Others attribute the discrepancy to competing traditions. At the very least, one may make the literary observation that the song expands the presentation of Israel in Judges 4 and thereby includes a more holistic (i.e., supratribal) presentation and assessment of Israelite involvement in the conquest.

From the opening of the song, the centrality of Israel's role is apparent. The opening lines introduce the prepositional phrase בישראל ("in/among Israel") that occurs four more times in the poem. These five references to the collective character "Israel" demonstrate an optimistic reality: a certain willingness to participate in battle (vv. 2, 11) despite Israel's weakened state (vv. 7, 8).[19] Put simply, the song initially portrays Israel as a victorious underdog. While the prose narrative states briefly that the people of Israel were cruelly oppressed, the song spends almost an entire stanza reflecting on the war-torn condition of Israelite civilian life. Only after the singers explore thoroughly the depths of Israel's desperation do they consider the reemergence of Israelite prosperity after the victory. They emphasize equally that the unexpected victory at Kishon is a result of Israel's relation to its deity; the repeated appellation "YHWH, God of Israel" (vv. 3, 5) grounds the character of Israel in its collective election by and covenant with YHWH. That covenantal relationship is the backdrop against which the people's actions are pronounced "righteous" in verse 11—by responding to the muster, the people of God faithfully fulfilled their designated role in battle. As in the enveloping verses of the previous chapter, the Israelites are characterized in terms of their (un)faithfulness to YHWH.

References to the collective noun ישראל (or the parallel noun עם) occur only in the first three of seven stanzas; however, the fourth stanza is pivotal for the characterization of the tribal league. While the text lists individual tribes in lieu of the collective noun ישראל, the presence of a (partial) tribal list contributes to the literary portrait of the collective. Only at this point in the battle account does the text reveal that the response of Israel was not monolithic.

[18] By contrast, K. Lawson Younger ("Judges 1 in Its Near Eastern Literary Context," in *Faith, Tradition, and History: Old Testament Historiography in Its Near Eastern Context*, ed. A. R. Millard, James K. Hoffmeier, and David W. Baker [Winona Lake, Ind.: Eisenbrauns, 1994], 226–27) argues of Judg 5, "Regardless of the tribal delineation within it, the song emphasizes the national entity, Israel, a supratribal subject of historical action that existed *before* the war with the Canaanites."

[19] The reading of חדל proposed by Chaney (see p. 151, n. 24 below) would change the characterization of Israel in the song significantly.

This characterization marks a turning point in the cycle, in which the complexities of Israel's response come to the fore. With prophetic insight, Deborah problematizes the response of Reuben, Gilead [Gad], Dan, and Asher when summoned to battle. With this troubling portrait the song's depiction of Israel ends; the remaining three stanzas speak only of Canaanite entities, the deity, or other localized entities whose particular roles in the battle were noteworthy (i.e., Meroz, Jael).

Given this censure, the unique contribution of the song to the cycle's characterization of Israel may be summarized as follows: on the surface, the song mimics the prose account's portrayal of Israel (an oppressed people delivered by YHWH and victorious over Sisera) and emphasizes the reversal of fortunes Israel experienced after the battle (especially stanza 3). In the fourth stanza, the song more precisely describes the contribution of tribally delineated participants and thereby complicates the portrayal of Israel in the narrative cycle. The initially positive characterization of them takes a decisively negative turn; by the time the conflict on the battlefield is described in detail (vv. 19–22), the collective people of Israel is completely absent. In the crescendo of praiseworthy characters, it is Jael, the non-Israelite, upon whom the song focuses as the agent of salvation at the Kishon battle.

The Deity

The narrative account of the Kishon battle opens from YHWH's perspective. Even before the deity appears as the subject of any verb, the narrator notes YHWH's displeasure with the actions of Israel. The point of departure for the narrative is Israelite failure in the eyes of God. As is characteristic of the macroplot, Israel's God sold his people into the hands of an oppressor, so as to provide an opportunity to test their allegiance to him through another military crisis. After the transition to the microplot in 4:6, YHWH acted and spoke almost entirely by proxy. Through Deborah he assured Barak that he would deliver Sisera to him posthaste (v. 14).[20] Thus, Deborah's speech about YHWH characterizes him as communicative, active, and a faithful defender of his people. The chapter's battle report highlights this by including YHWH as an active agent in the heat of the battle. One verb in the chapter encompasses the entire battle—ויהם, "confused"—and YHWH is its subject.[21] In the scene that follows, YHWH is absent; however, Deborah describes the interaction between Jael and Sisera as YHWH's handiwork: "into the hand of a woman

---

[20] That YHWH does not deliver Sisera into the hands of Barak directly is crucial to the plot; however, by describing the opposing peoples in terms of their representatives, YHWH speaks truthfully and acts faithfully.

[21] Alonso-Schökel, "Erzählkunst im Buche der Richter," 162.

YHWH will sell Sisera" (v. 9).[22] The deity, then, is the definitive champion for Israel, just as 4:23 claims.

The prominence of YHWH in the accompanying song matches and exceeds his role in Judges 4. Without question the "hero" of the song of Deborah and Barak is YHWH. The first stanza is dedicated entirely to him and serves as the theological ground upon which the song stands. This theophany recalls YHWH's storm-like emergence from Sinai toward the land of promise and "represents the spiritual origins of the people as the covenantal partner of God."[23] From the outset, YHWH's covenant relationship with his people is the cause for celebration and the initiative for Israelite devotion. It is in accordance with this covenant that the actions of YHWH are deemed "righteous" (5:11); as the patron deity of Israel, YHWH faithfully fought for his people, as he has throughout their history.[24] The appellation "YHWH, God of Israel" (vv. 3d, 5b) is thus apropos.

Even the turn of events precipitated by Deborah's emergence as a prophet ("until I arose") is attributed to אלהים in v. 8;[25] not even the song in her name permits Deborah to take credit for the events that transpire. A line ascribing triumph to YHWH tempers every recognition of Israelite initiative: the volunteering of the people is occasion to bless YHWH (vv. 2, 9); the righteous acts of the villagers are preceded by the righteous acts of YHWH (v. 11b–c); and the triumphant remnant is accompanied by YHWH, who went to battle on their behalf (v. 13).[26] Only in verse 11d does an action of corporate Israel lack a parallel action by their God, but even here the army is called "the people of YHWH" to highlight his agency.

By contrast, the fourth stanza is completely anthropocentric. Despite the prominence of YHWH in the song, these lines centered on the response of Israel confirm that the composition is not primarily concerned with depicting the power of YHWH to the enemies of his people; instead, the characterization of YHWH as a mighty hero for Israel is undoubtedly subordinate

---

[22] Observed by Robert H. O'Connell, *The Rhetoric of the Book of Judges*, VTSup 63 (Leiden: Brill, 1996), 112–13.

[23] Jan P. Fokkelman, "The Song of Deborah and Barak: Its Prosodic Levels and Structure," in *Pomegranates and Golden Bells: Studies in Biblical, Jewish, and Near Eastern Ritual, Law, and Literature in Honor of Jacob Milgrom*, ed. David P. Wright, David Noel Freedman, and Avi Hurvitz (Winona Lake, Ind.: Eisenbrauns, 1995), 598.

[24] Mathys, *Dichter und Beter*, 175, who argues the term has the effect of joining this victory to all those YHWH has fought previously.

[25] This interpretation requires translating v. 8a as "God chose new ones [leaders]," which is a debatable reading. For a defense of this translation, see appendix, p. 154.

[26] According to Fokkelman ("Song of Deborah and Barak," 599), "in stanzas I and III the chosen people are consistently presented vis-à-vis YHWH."

to the challenge to those who doubt the saving work of YHWH (Israelite or otherwise).

Much like the battle report of Judges 4, elsewhere the poem describes the mustering of Israelite troops (4:10, 14 // 5:11d, 14–15c, 18) and their pursuit of captives (4:15–16 // 5:12c–d, 22) but here restricts the description of the conflict itself to YHWH's activity. The fifth stanza is devoted to depicting the mighty deeds of YHWH in mythic proportions. These lines commemorate the participation of the forces of nature in the battle: the stars fighting from their courses and the Wadi Kishon overwhelming the army. Despite scholarly arguments to the contrary, the first of the two images is most likely one of divine intervention;[27] it thus contributes to the prophet's characterization of YHWH. The same YHWH who wrought cosmic upheaval in the song's theophany manipulated the natural order again, drawing the very stars from their courses as agents of destruction. The second image certainly connotes divine intervention, if by no other means than allusion to the imagery of Exodus. Not only is YHWH stronger than any Israelite foe but he also has the ability to bring the resources of the cosmos into his service, whether it be a heavenly body, a wadi, or—as we shall see—a woman perceived by society to be exceptionally vulnerable.

As in the narrative, YHWH recedes from view in the stanzas that portray the tent scene. Sisera's death at the hands of Jael and the contrasting expectations of his household take precedence in the song's final moments. However, when in verse 31 Deborah reflects on the devastation of Israel's enemies (vv. 26–30), she defines how these vignettes relate to the overarching theological theme of the poem: the fortune of Sisera and his household contrasts with that of "those who love [YHWH]," or, those who demonstrate covenant commitment to YHWH—in this context, through military initiative.[28] Wong opines that these lines raise "the nagging possibility" that the nonparticipating Israelites "would in the end suffer the same fate as those who are regarded as enemies of YHWH."[29] The final strophe reinforces the polemic undertones

---

[27] The motif of the heavens constituting the army of God in the biblical text (Isa 40:26; Dan 8:10) suggests the stars were acting as agents of YHWH. So argues Moshe Weinfeld, "Divine Intervention in War in Ancient Israel and in the Ancient Near East," in *History, Historiography and Interpretation: Studies in Biblical and Cuneiform Literatures*, ed. H. Tadmor and Moshe Weinfeld (Jerusalem: Magnes Press, 1984), 124–30.

[28] For a covenantal definition of אהב, see Daniel I. Block, *Deuteronomy*, NIVAC (Grand Rapids: Zondervan, 2012), 144, especially n. 9; Richard S. Hess, *Israelite Religions: An Archaeological and Biblical Survey* (Grand Rapids: Baker Academic, 2007), 168. Following William L. Moran, "Ancient Near Eastern Background of the Love of God in Deuteronomy," *CBQ* 25 (1965): 77–87, which documents the lexeme's use in common treaty parlance to describe the faithfulness and dedication owed by a vassal to a suzerain.

[29] Gregory T. K. Wong, "Song of Deborah as Polemic," *Bib* 88 (2007):18.

of the composition but also depicts YHWH as the righteous covenant partner of Israel who requires nothing short of (and no more than) wholehearted devotion to his purposes. Thus the characterization of YHWH that completes the Song of Deborah and Barak mirrors exactly that of the cycle's beginning (4:1): the God who evaluates the response of Israel in terms of his covenant relationship with them, that is, the God who is testing them (2:22–3:4). Thus, the theological portrait in Judges 4–5 is entirely consistent. The song contributes to the deity's character development by making explicit the theological assumptions that undergird the narrative of the battle at the Kishon; in their song the prophet and the general reorient readerly attention from the relative armament of Israelite and Canaanite forces to the overwhelming military might of Israel's God.

Jabin

As in Judges 3:8 and 3:12 (as well as 8:5 and 11:12), the narrator introduces the oppressor of Israel as the king of a people group settled in or militarily occupying Canaan. In this case, that oppressor is Jabin, king of Canaan. As Sasson has aptly stated, "There cannot be a more paradigmatic confrontation than between Israel and Canaan, more or less reprising the conflict in Joshua's days."[30] A debate persists regarding the relationship of Jabin, king of Canaan (or Hazor; 4:17) to Jabin, the king of Hazor mentioned in Joshua 11, which records the latter's death and the destruction of his city. While scholars have proposed a number of interpretive solutions to this apparent problem, the most popular—and the most persuasive—distinguishes the two figures and identifies the name Jabin as a sort of "dynastic" designation (like those of, e.g., Egyptian pharaohs) and imagines a partial resettlement of Hazor by his descendants.[31] On a literary level, Joshua 11 provides the cognitive backdrop for references to Jabin by emphasizing the prominence of Hazor in the region before its destruction and its king as head of a coalition of northern rulers. Whatever the historical reality, the text introduces the battle at the Kishon using vocabulary reminiscent of a generation past—once more Jabin reigned in Hazor, once more iron chariots terrorized

---

[30] Jack M. Sasson, "'A Breeder or Two for Each Leader': On Mothers in Judges 4 and 5," in *A Critical Engagement: Essays on the Hebrew Bible in Honour of J. Cheryl Exum*, ed. David J. A. Clines and Ellen van Wolde, HBM 38 (Sheffield: Sheffield Phoenix, 2011), 341.

[31] This now popular explanation of the similarly named figures and the presence of Hazor after its destruction is offered by Abraham Malamat, *Mari and the Early Israelite Experience*, Schweich Lectures 1984 (Oxford: Oxford University Press, 1989), 58. Malamat muses that the name Jabin may have been a "dynastic one at Hazor going back to Old Babylonian times," considering that a figure named Ibni-Adad appears in conjunction with Hazor in Mari texts.

the region, and once more the people of God experienced cruel oppression.³² To introduce Jabin, king of Canaan as the opponent of Israel is to emphasize not only the cyclical nature of Judges but also the regression of Israelite dominance in the generations after Joshua.

Mention of Jabin is limited to the opening remarks of the narrative (v. 2), Sisera's title (v. 7), the notice of Heber's political alliance (v. 17), and a closing summary of the prose account (vv. 23–24). The song in the next chapter never mentions Jabin by name, though it does recount an offensive by the "kings of Canaan," a broader designation that applies to Jabin (especially because Jabin is the only dignitary in the book who is designated expressly as "Canaanite"). He therefore "represents ancient Israel's more formidable enemy."³³ Jabin's participation in the battle at the Kishon is only by proxy; Sisera, the commander of Jabin's armies, is the active oppressor and the individual characterized as the opponent of Israel throughout both chapters. Still, despite Sisera's pervasive presence in the narrative, Jabin's function in the summative portions of Judges 4 identifies him as one of the battle's main characters.³⁴ By portraying Jabin as the initiator of Canaanite aggression—and the one who sent Sisera to battle—the narrator has on some level identified Jabin as parallel in narrative function to YHWH and his messenger Deborah, who sent Barak to battle.³⁵ The chapter's introduction and conclusion reinforce this; Ellen van Wolde observes how the three characters that appear in the early verses of Judges 4—namely, YHWH, Jabin, and the Israelites—also conclude the chapter.³⁶ As the account transitions from prose to poetry, Jabin's absence suggests his destruction was final and enduring; only insofar as he is one of the faceless "kings of Canaan" in 5:19–20 does the song find him worthy of mention. In the ongoing struggle

---

32   Observed by Robert B. Chisholm Jr., *A Commentary on Judges and Ruth*, Kregel Exegetical Library (Grand Rapids: Kregel Academic, 2013), 221.

33   Mark S. Smith and Elizabeth Bloch-Smith, *Judges 1: A Commentary on Judges 1:1–10:5*, Hermeneia (Minneapolis: Fortress, 2021), 251.

34   Daniel I. Block (*Judges, Ruth*, NAC 6 [Nashville: Broadman & Holman, 2001], 189) notes Jabin's prominence in other canonical references to the battle (e.g., 1 Sam 12:9; Ps 83:9).

35   Athalya Brenner, "A Triangle and a Rhombus in Narrative Structure: A Proposed Integrative Reading of Judges IV and V," *VT* 40 (1990): 130–31, describes Deborah and Jabin as "social, political, or religious initiator[s] of the action," opposed to Sisera and Barak, who are "clearly inferior in stature to the other, yet carr[y] the burden of execution." I depart from her argument by emphasizing that YHWH (with Deborah, his representative) is the most fitting counterpart to Jabin, given the summative frame in 4:1–5, 23–24.

36   According to van Wolde ("Deborah and Ya'el in Judges 4," 288), this intentional enveloping structure is especially clear given the narrator's choice to refer to Jabin differently in vv. 7 and 17.

of YHWH, the true King of Israel, against the "kings of Canaan," Jabin challenged YHWH and lost. The song's abstracted reference to "kings of Canaan" effectively identifies Jabin's significance in the book—he is merely one of the rulers YHWH has set out to dethrone as he dispossessed the inhabitants of Israel's inheritance.

Sisera

The narrator first introduces Sisera in relation to Jabin; Sisera was the general of the Canaanite king's army. As mentioned above, Sisera becomes the mode by which the narrative documents Jabin's aggression. Yet Sisera's unique and very personal encounter with one individual at a crucial point in the story (i.e., Jael) requires that he, rather than Jabin, is the primary microplot antagonist (and, consequently, the most consistently appearing character in the cycle). The narrator uses similar syntax, lexical overlap, and parallel plot structures to draw comparisons between Sisera—the primary antagonist—and each of the protagonists in turn.

The first of these is Deborah. Identical syntax draws the two characters into juxtaposition and raises the expectation that their roles in the narrative will be similar:

4:4 וּדְבוֹרָה אִשָּׁה נְבִיאָה אֵשֶׁת לַפִּידוֹת הִיא שֹׁפְטָה אֶת־יִשְׂרָאֵל בָּעֵת הַהִיא	4:2 וְשַׂר־צְבָאוֹ סִיסְרָא וְהוּא יוֹשֵׁב בַּחֲרֹשֶׁת הַגּוֹיִם׃
4:5 וְהִיא יוֹשֶׁבֶת תַּחַת־תֹּמֶר דְּבוֹרָה	

Sisera was the captain of Jabin's army just as Deborah was the prophet in Israel (and thus the representative of YHWH). The syntactical surface structure of verse 2b (*waw* + independent personal pronoun + participle [יֹשֵׁב] + prepositional locative phrase) parallels exactly that of verse 5a: Deborah carried out her judicial responsibilities under the Palm of Deborah just as Sisera led from חֲרֹשֶׁת הַגּוֹיִם. The structural equivalence of these introductions accentuates that both characters function as servants of their respective (and opposing) suzerains—namely, Jabin and YHWH.[37] When this plot-level expectation is complicated by Barak's emergence as Israel's general in verses 6–7, narrative details juxtapose the two military leaders. A pattern of meticulous lexical overlap in descriptions of Barak and Sisera replaces the syntactical parallels

---

[37] For a similar observation, see Daniel I. Block, "Deborah among the Judges: The Perspective of the Hebrew Historian," in *Faith, Tradition, and History: Old Testament Historiography in Its Near Eastern Context*, ed. A. R. Millard, James K. Hoffmeier, and David W. Baker (Winona Lake, Ind.: Eisenbrauns, 1994), 234.

relating to the prophet and the Canaanite general.³⁸ This word play is charted in table 1.

Table 1: Lexical Parallels in the Descriptions of Barak and Sisera

	Barak	Sisera
Instigation to Battle by YHWH	v. 6 (משך; vocative)	v. 7 (משך; object)
Troop Summons	v. 10 (זעק)	v. 13 (זעק)
Descent in Battle	v. 14 (ירד)	v. 15 (ירד)
Foot Movement	v. 10 (ברגליו)	v. 17 (ברגליו)
Jael Approaches	v. 22 (קרא + יצא)	v. 18 (קרא + יצא)

The first of the lexical pairs programmatically orients the reader to the relationship between the two characters. Deborah relayed YHWH's command to Barak to muster for battle in the same breath that she reported YHWH's intention to rouse Sisera to do the same (משך). In short, YHWH had appointed both Sisera and Barak to be major players in the Battle of Kishon. The repeated verbs in verses 10–15 reveal Sisera to be Barak's foil on the battlefield—where Barak was weak (commander of foot soldiers; v. 10), Sisera was strong (boasting an army led by nine hundred chariots of iron; v. 13). Given this initial assessment of their offensive capabilities, another set of parallels stresses a reversal of their fortunes: where readers expect Sisera's superior armament to ensure victory, they instead witness his flight "on foot" (v. 17)—the very lexical detail that originally indicated Barak's vulnerability.

Even though the prose account carefully traces the shift in Sisera's situation, it is concerned with more than the humiliation of Canaanite forces and their situational reversal. The triangulation of characters in the tent scenes (vv. 17–22) portrays Jael as Sisera's third and final opponent but does so without Barak's fading from view. As he was the last and most significant survivor of the Canaanite army, Sisera's death represents not only the utter destruction of the Canaanite army through an unexpected agent but also the means by which Deborah's prophecy was fulfilled and Barak witnessed the saving power of YHWH. Thus, Sisera's final role in the portrayal of Judges 4 is evidential; he is relegated to the backdrop in front of which YHWH displayed his might—a mere piece of staging in the theater of God's redemption.

The development of the depiction of Sisera from the prose to the song of Judges 5 is the most interesting and the most crucial for properly interpreting

---

[38] These parallels are compiled from Murray, "Narrative Structure and Technique," 169–71; Elie Assis, "The Choice to Serve God and Assist His People: Rahab and Yael," *Bib* 85 (2004): 85; and Stek, "Bee and the Mountain Goat," 66–67.

the narrative cycle. Given the shift toward the macroplot in 4:23–24, Sisera recedes from view in favor of his king, Jabin. His absence continues through the first five stanzas of the song (5:1–23). Until that point, the text identifies the enemy of Israel as a group of faceless "kings," whose flat characterization coheres with the standard stereotypical portrayal of foreign rulers in conquest narratives;[39] however, the last two stanzas are completely dedicated to Sisera and his household. In fact, the last four verses of the song introduce a small cast of characters for the sake of the characterization of Sisera—namely, his mother and her attendants.[40] While the scenic details initially allow the interpreter to pity his anxious mother, her conversation with the rest of Sisera's household "convinces the reader to reread, in a less generous frame of mind, the earlier lines that described a mother's worry."[41] By anticipating the swift return of Sisera (on his thematically relevant chariot, no less) and his conquest over vulnerable women, the perspective of the general's household reveals the irony and theological significance of his dying at the hands of a someone who is characterized as vulnerable. Thus, in both Judges 4 and 5, Sisera's strength is contrasted with the weakness of his opponents; in the prose account, these opponents are Barak and Jael in turn, while in the poem, the composer focuses on Jael. The cycle thus consistently emphasizes the (seemingly) unprecedented devastation of Sisera, once in the context of military prowess (especially in chapter 4), and later in a far more intimate and personal manner (in the last stanzas of chapter 5). By reflecting on his familial ties, socioeconomic status,[42] and sexual intentions toward captives of war (as articulated by his mother's attendants), the song's more socially and perhaps ethically accented characterization suits its macroplot concerns. In fact, in verse 31, Deborah implies that Sisera

---

[39] Eglon in Judg 3:12–30 is a significant exception.

[40] That the mother has no other designation aside from her relation to the Canaanite general reinforces the notion that any degree of personal detail serves Sisera's characterization.

[41] Jo Ann Hackett, "Violence and Women's Lives in the Book of Judges," *Int* 58 (2004): 359. Amy Cottrill ("Moral Injury and Humanizing the Enemy in Judges 5," in *Moral Injury: A Guidebook for Understanding and Engagement*, ed. Brad E. Kelle [Lanham, Md.: Rowman & Littlefield, 2020], 154) builds on this observation through the lens of moral injury.

[42] The shift in imagery from the itinerant family's tent to the secure, latticed home of the city-dweller seems to continue the song's contrast of vulnerable, unwalled Israelite settlements to the fortified, well-guarded, and, consequently, economically superior dwellings of the Canaanites. See Lawrence E. Stager, "The Song of Deborah: Why Some Tribes Answered the Call and Others Did Not," *BAR* 15 (1989): 55. On the association of fortified cities with the land's inhabitants (of which Sisera is representative), see Deut 6:10; 9:1; Josh 10:20.

represents all the "enemies" of YHWH—any who do not demonstrate covenant commitment to him, regardless of their political affiliations. What is strictly political in the prose expression of the battle is rendered personal, ethical, and, arguably, covenantal in the song.

Deborah

Few women feature as prominent leaders of any kind during the settlement period, at least according to the biblical material. Deborah is an exception to that generalization, so her presence in a series of male leaders invites consideration. Interpreters have often struggled to see past her gender; indeed, one key interpretive question is whether they ought to do so. In the following analysis, I argue that too narrowly focusing on her gender leaves other important dynamics underdeveloped. Underemphasizing her gender, however, distorts key themes the narrator develops in conversation with social perceptions and gendered expectations.

Deborah's narrative introduction in 4:4–5a consists of three circumstantial clauses. In two discrete semantic units, the first verbless clause addresses details of profession and socioeconomic status: Deborah was a woman prophet (אשה נביאה) and the wife of Lappidot (אשת לפידות).[43] In regard to the first description (אשה נביאה), many scholars appropriately identify the phrase as crucial for understanding her character development, though a tendency to highlight the noun אשה as separate from (and more important than) נביאה prevails. Elie Assis, for example, observes that the "unique protagonist" Deborah is characterized first as a woman, then a prophetess, and finally a judge. Regarding the first descriptor (that is, אשה), he argues that "the emphasis on Deborah's womanhood is conspicuous in the exposition."[44] Trent Butler concludes that Deborah's role as prophet is more important than her role as judge, but second to her role as a woman, which is "first and foremost in the narrative."[45] Masoretic accentuation and the absence of a conjunction, however, reduce the probability that "a woman" functions independently, rather than as a part of a larger syntactical

---

[43] The argument that the title "wife of Lappidot" is symbolic is popular (see, e.g., Susan Niditch, *Judges: A Commentary*, OTL [Louisville: Westminster John Knox, 2008], 65; Jack M. Sasson, *Judges 1–12: A New Translation with Introduction and Commentary*, AB 6D [New Haven: Yale University Press, 2014], 255–56), though descriptions elsewhere of prophets with similar familial descriptions suggest otherwise. Just as Huldah was the "prophetess (נביאה), wife of (אשת) Shallum the son of Tikvah, son of Harhas," so Deborah's description seems straightforward: she was Lappidot's wife. See 2 Kgs 19:2 (Isaiah); 22:14 (Huldah); cf. Jer 28:1; Zech 1:1, 7, in which the order is reversed and the patronymic precedes the designation נביא.

[44] Elie Assis, "Man, Woman and God in Judg 4," *SJOT* 20 (2006): 111, 114.

[45] Trent C. Butler, *Judges*, Women's Bible Commentary 8 (Nashville: Thomas Nelson, 2009), 90, 94.

unit (literally, "woman prophet").⁴⁶ This type of apposition is common to the Hebrew Bible; similar grammatically feminine constructions include אשה מינקת ("nurse"; Exod 2:7) and אשה אלמנה ("widow"; 1 Kgs 11:26, 17:9–10).⁴⁷ The Hebrew construction per se does not emphasize gender; indeed, such constructions occur in contexts not interested in gender roles. That being said, the grammatically feminine noun נביאה appears more frequently without the modification of אשה, which would suggest that the twice gendered phrase serves the purposes of the chapter at the level of pragmatics. Deborah's later prophecy mentioning an אשה will bring to the fore the importance of gender in thematic promise fulfillment; however, her initial introduction only hints at the theme by choosing a gendered (and thus, thematically appropriate) professional title.

The appearance of a female prophet, then, at this point in the narrative, is not unprecedented. Her title certainly mentions her gender, though primarily as a modifier of the vocational title "prophet." Moreover, women were known to prophesy both in Israel (e.g., 2 Kgs 22:14) and the ancient Near East broadly.⁴⁸ While it brims with thematic potential that will be later realized, 4:4a consists of a remarkably straightforward classification: Deborah was a prophet.

Just as the first clause addresses details related to Deborah's person, the following two participial clauses describe her activities. By invoking the root שפט—"she was judging (שפטה) Israel at that time"—the narrator notes that Deborah was participating in a kind of activity related to the normal office of "judge." Eight other individuals in the book of Judges are explicitly said to have "judged"—namely, Othniel, Tola, Jair, Jephthah, Ibzan, Elon, Abdon, and Samson. Of the various reconstructions proposed, my sense is that the title "judge" throughout the book of Judges is in continuity with the "judges" of Deuteronomy; they assist in decision-making (see Deut 17:8–9) in conjunction with other elements of tribal and national leadership, which range from resolving local disputes to dispensing wisdom or fulfilling the duties of a prophet (e.g., Samuel).⁴⁹ There is no textual indication (here or elsewhere)

---

⁴⁶ The conjunctive *mûnaḥ* serving the disjunctive *zaqef qaṭōn* sets off the descriptive phrase אִשָּׁה נְבִיאָה as a single meaningful unit.

⁴⁷ Consider also the following masculine examples: איש שר (Exod 2:14); איש ראש (Num 1:4).

⁴⁸ Due to the alleged rarity of female prophets in the Hebrew Bible or the supposed absence of official "prophets" during the time of the tribal league, some scholars (e.g., James Ackermann, "Prophecy and Warfare in Early Israel: A Study of the Debora-Barak Story," *BASOR* 220 [1975]: 12) have argued that the title "prophet" in this text is anachronistic. Sasson (*Judges 1–12*, 255) counters such claims.

⁴⁹ For a similar construal, see Mark J. Boda, "Judges," in *Numbers–Ruth*, vol. 5 of *The Expositor's Bible Commentary*, ed. Tremper Longman III and David E. Garland, rev. ed. (Grand Rapids: Zondervan, 2017), 1054.

that one should distinguish between so-called forensic judges and those who function as "saviors"—an argument which often relies on viewing Deborah as a more Deuteronomic (i.e., "forensic") judge, while her contemporaries served a different function. On the level of vocational designation, Deborah's title is identical, with the minor difference that hers is grammatically offset from the narrative mainline.[50] In line with her unique prophetic characterization, the narrative highlights Deborah's role as decision-maker over any other governing responsibilities.

The literary function of the note in verse 4b is to explain the next narrative event (v. 5b) in which the people sought from her "judgment" (משפט). As I have observed elsewhere: "While the nature of the question posed by the Israelites is unknown, the background for their inquiry is not. Deuteronomy 17:8 instructs Israel to 'go up' (עלה; cf. Judg 4:5b) to the Levitical priests and the judge (שפט; cf. Judg 4:4b) to receive the 'judgment' (משפט; cf. Judg 4:5b)."[51] Despite the way English translations tend to construe the syntax of verses 4–5, the ascent of the people for "judgment" is not narrative background but the first mainline action after that exposition.[52] As a prophet of YHWH, Deborah

---

[50] Canonically, authors remember Barak (often in lieu of Deborah) as the pertinent leader during the Battle of Kishon, perhaps because of his role as general (which was often shouldered by judges). Heb 11:32 lists Barak with the other judges separately from the prophets, as do the LXX and Syr. versions of 1 Sam 12:11 (cf. MT, בדן; for a discussion of the textual issues, see Block, "Deborah among the Judges," 229–53). Klaas Spronk ("Deborah, a Prophetess: The Meaning and Background of Judges 4:4–5," in *The Elusive Prophet: The Prophet as a Historical Person, Literary Character and Anonymous Artist*, ed. Johannes de Moor, OtSt 45 [Leiden: Brill, 2001], 241), uses 1 Sam 12:11 to support the opinion that a late redactor added Judg 4:4b; he hypothesizes that the historical Deborah never judged Israel at all. By contrast, my point is simply that later authors gravitate toward the general in recounting battles. This may suggest that Deborah is primarily remembered as a prophet.

[51] See Michelle Knight, "The Prophet's Song of Victory: Judges 5 within a Trajectory of Theological Training in the Book of Judges," *BBR* 33 (2023): 296. There I also observe that this mimics the pattern of Moses as spokesperson for God in Exod 18:13–23. The uniqueness of this authoritative vocabulary is highlighted by Yaakov S. Kupitz and Katell Berthelot, "Deborah and the Delphic Pythia: A New Interpretation of Judges 4:4–5," in *Images and Prophecy in the Ancient Eastern Mediterranean*, ed. Martti Nissinen and Charles E. Carter, FRLANT 233 (Göttingen: Vanderhoeck & Ruprecht, 2009), 109.

[52] Noted also by van Wolde, "Deborah and Ya'el in Judges 4," 287; Mark J. Boda and Mary L. Conway, *Judges*, ZECOT (Grand Rapids: Zondervan Academic, 2022), 255; and Smith and Bloch-Smith, *Judges 1*, 261. *Wayyiqtols* may on occasion function as continuation of a backgrounded sequence, but the shift in subject to the Israelites, who had been the subject of the previous *wayyiqtol* in v. 3, suggests a resumption of the narrative mainline here rather than a continuation of an offline narrative sequence.

interceded on behalf of the people for YHWH's intervention and subsequently indicated which campaigns had been approved by him.[53]

Thus from the outset of Judges 4, the narrator casts Deborah primarily as a spokesperson and representative for YHWH. In terms of the cyclical expectations earlier narratives suggest to the reader, Deborah represents the abiding word of YHWH to Israel's general; her summons to Barak to muster the troops is parallel to YHWH's action to "raise" a deliverer in the other cycles.[54] In fact, Judges 4 frames Deborah primarily as the deity's representative, thereby allowing YHWH's agency to be highlighted.[55] Wong observes that Deborah "functions more like an agent than a full-fledged character, and her role seems to be restricted mainly to the conveying of YHWH's will and not much else."[56]

Three times in Judges 4 Deborah addresses Barak, each time with the purpose of instructing (command) and reassuring (promise).[57] YHWH's instructions through Deborah about Barak's battlefield responsibilities are followed by the assurance that YHWH would deliver to him Israel's foe. Even before the battle began or Barak spoke, Deborah repeated a promise that YHWH had made numerous times before (cf. Deut 1:30–31; 3:18, 22; 7:21–24): he would fight before Israel and deliver to them the king of their enemies.

After Barak responded conditionally, Deborah's address uses the adverbial infinitive absolute to convey assertive agreement, while hinting at a forthcoming concession (הלך אלך; v. 9).[58] The concessive element in Deborah's discourse is more explicitly introduced with the rare limitative construction אפס כי

---

[53] On the authorizing voice of the prophet, see Hackett, "Violence and Women's Lives in the Book of Judges," 357. Robert G. Boling, *Judges*, AB 6A (New York: Doubleday, 1975), 81, 95, suggests that the Israelites' cry to God (צעק) is the same as the משפט they requested; they approached the prophet as the deity's representative. Followed and expanded by Spronk, "Deborah, a Prophetess," 236; Ackermann, "Prophecy and Warfare," 11; and Block, "Deborah among the Judges," 239. Block highlights Ackermann's observation that צעק and משפט are used to designate the appeal to (צעק) and decision (משפט) rendered by the king.

[54] Barry G. Webb, *The Book of Judges*, NICOT (Grand Rapids: Eerdmans, 2012), 183.

[55] Assis, "Choice to Serve God," 89. Given his persuasive argument that Deborah's characterization is flat, Assis may be overstating his case when he argues in a later essay that the tent scene functions to "reemphasize [Deborah's] prophetic *personality*" (emphasis mine). See "The Hand of a Woman: Deborah and Yael (Judges 4)," *JHS* 5 (2005): 12. To say that the final scene emphasizes Deborah's *prophecy* is more accurate.

[56] Gregory T. K. Wong, *The Compositional Strategy of the Book of Judges: An Inductive, Rhetorical Study*, VTSup 111 (New York: Brill, 2006), 243.

[57] The vocabulary of command/law and promise is indebted to Alonso-Schökel, "Erzählkunst im Buche der Richter," 161.

[58] On the use of the infinitive absolute in oppositional phrases in general and Judg 4:9 in particular, see Joüon, §123i.

("notwithstanding").⁵⁹ Verse 9 thus introduces a clarification to God's earlier promise in a way that shows how the initial promise remained unchanged (cf. 4:14, "Today is the day God has given Sisera into your hand"). Rather than punishing Barak, by this reading Deborah clarified the unexpected nature of YHWH's deliverance. After signaling the corrective orientation of her response, Deborah introduced a key narrative detail in the form of prophetic promise: into the hands of a woman—not the Israelite military officer or his army—God would deliver Sisera. Despite Barak's preoccupation with Deborah's command, both in speech and action the prophet emphasized the assurance she gave from YHWH. The verbs of movement in verses 9e–10 reiterate that Deborah was "with" (עִם; vv. 9f, 10c) Barak just as she assured him she would be. At a crucial moment in the battle she repeated her promise that God would hand over Sisera (v. 14c; cf. 7b).

After her final conversation with Barak, the prophet withdraws from the narrator's attention; however, that her promise would be fulfilled—and the interesting way in which this occurred—is the focus of the plot that follows. Every time Deborah had spoken in the previous act she used the key word "hand" and provided a lexical anchor for the theme of faithful promise-fulfillment that would reemerge in the second act. The literary portrait of Sisera's death at the "hand" of Jael (v. 21) at a climactic plot point highlights the fulfillment of these prophetic words at the tail end of the story, even though Deborah had not been present since verse 14. Just as Deborah's words in the previous act emphasize God's faithfulness to save, so do Jael's actions emphasize the fulfillment of YHWH's promise through Deborah.⁶⁰ Deborah's absence in this scene is consistent with her characterization elsewhere: a prophet's significance is associated with her message. Her words remain central to the narrative long after she recedes from view.

In its entirety, Judges 4 characterizes Deborah as the mouthpiece of God and a tangible representation of his promise to fight for Israel. As his representative, Deborah consistently reinforces the terms of God's special relationship (i.e., covenant) with Israel: YHWH promised to deliver Israel from bondage into the promised land, and the appropriate response to such a gift was wholehearted obedience. Like that of Moses, the prophet par excellence, Deborah's intermediary function demonstrates God's grace to a generation crying out for

---

⁵⁹ *HALOT*, 79; Joüon, §173a.

⁶⁰ Assis ("Hand of a Woman," 4) suggests that Jael is "Deborah's 'hand'—an extension of Deborah who carries out her prophecy." While Assis rightly emphasizes the continuing impact of the prophet in the last portion of the narrative, it is more precise to say that Jael represents the hand of YHWH.

YHWH's intervention.⁶¹ Like Moses, Deborah would not allow the people to overlook the extraordinary quality of the victory she experienced at Kishon. Consequently, immediately following the narrative summary of God's intervention (vv. 23–24), Deborah sang a song interpreting their experience, in much the same way her prophetic forefather did following the Exodus. Since the song is attributed to Deborah (and Barak), the entire composition contributes to the depiction of the prophet. Moreover, assuming the first-person statements may be attributed to her, the passage offers six elements of direct character development:

First, she would sing to YHWH. Coupled with the imperatives of perception (אזן, שמע) and response (ברך שיח) issued to the song's hearers, her role as songstress seems to exemplify an appropriate response to the events that had just transpired. Deborah's choice to highlight the people's own recounting of the battle in 5:11 (i.e., following the example she set forth in vv. 2–3) contributes to this sense.

Second, Deborah arose at the time of Israel's need and initiated the socioeconomic reversal celebrated by the song (v. 7). She reinforces her historical assessment with the self-description "mother in Israel," an honorific title most likely associated with authority in general and prophecy in particular.⁶² This title also suggests that the alignment of Deborah's ministry with YHWH's intervention in Judges 4 carries over to the song, in which the "mother in Israel" is a representative of the "God of Israel"—both set above Israel and intimately connected to it.⁶³ Similarly, Rannfrid Irene Thelle observes that "in a narrative-sequential or intertextual reading," like the one undertaken here, "by the time she is designated as אם בישראל, all of these behaviors [i.e., the "composite of her roles in Judges 4"] will come

---

⁶¹ Deborah is the first prophet (explicitly identified as such) since the time of Moses, who promised the emergence of prophetic figures in Deut 18; no נביא or נביאה is mentioned between Deut 34:10 and Judg 4:4. While Block ("A Prophet like Moses: Another Look at Deut 18:9–22," in *The Triumph of Grace: Literary and Theological Studies in Deuteronomy and Deuteronomic Themes* [Eugene, Ore.: Cascade, 2017], 365) asserts rightly that prophets may be designated by various terms, including "messenger" (cf. Judg 2:1), the term נביא lexically anchors Deborah's appearance in the Deuteronomic promise.

⁶² The phrase "mother in Israel" occurs only here and in 2 Sam 20:19, in which a city associated with prophetic authority is given the same title. Since Elijah and Elisha are also called "father" (cf. 2 Kgs 2:12, 13:14), the vocabulary of parentage seems apt to describe the prophet.

⁶³ Susan Ackerman (*Warrior, Dancer, Seductress, Queen: Women in Judges and Biblical Israel*, ABRL [New York: Doubleday, 1998], 37) presents a convincing analysis of the poetic parallels that reinforce this semantic relationship.

together to inform the designation of 'mother,' giving the label meaning on the basis of the previous information."[64]

Third, Deborah proclaims in the third stanza that her "mind is on" the leaders of Israel (v. 9). As in verse 2, the prophet identifies the willing participation of the militia as the occasion for her song of praise, though she personalizes her reflection both here and in verse 13 with first-person pronouns. As a leader of Israel and a representative of YHWH, she has an immediate relationship with both parties, as well as divine insight into the tribes' motivations.

Fourth, she recounts the people's call to her to rouse herself and sing a song (v. 12). One should not underestimate the martial overtones of the root עור. Deborah is (arguably) not depicted as a traditional "warrior" within the song, but, at minimum, such vocabulary depicts her as an active agent, present at the battle against Canaan, and the representative to whom the people called when they sought God's intervention (as in 4:5d). That God responded and intervened in accordance with the people's call permits her to claim that YHWH went down "for me" in verse 13. While all of Israel, including Deborah, is clearly in service to their Sovereign (and thus they fight for *him*), the language of 5:13 emphasizes God's responsiveness to the pain and needs of his people, presumably through his prophet.

The people call to Deborah not simply to rouse herself and facilitate YHWH's intervention but also to utter a song. As in the previous chapter, communication seems to be what the people expected and sought from Deborah—a request quite different from the thoroughly soldierly overture made to Barak. At the very least, the people expected Deborah to sing because she is an Israelite woman; however, the evaluative nature of the preserved song—along with the authoritative title she ascribes to herself in the previous stanza—prompts the hearer to expect something more than a simple victory song.

Fifth, in verse 15 the song mentions Deborah's presence in battle once more. Issachar was sent (שׁלח) to follow Barak into the valley, just as the narrator described in 4:14e (without mention of the specific tribe). Although the verse notes Issachar's response to Barak's muster, it first acknowledges the presence of the tribe's captains with Deborah. Thus the song corroborates the prose account's assurance that Deborah is present on Mount Tabor (cf. 4:10) and reiterates her role in relaying YHWH's plan of attack (cf. 4:6–7) and the commissioning of the troops to battle on the plains.

Sixth, referring to herself with a 1cs pronominal suffix, Deborah again interrupts her account in 5:21 with an encouraging cry. While the rest of her directives had been aimed at others, Deborah here speaks introspectively, in

---

[64] Rannfrid Irene Thelle, "Matrices of Motherhood in Judges 5," *JSOT* 43 (2019): 439.

the manner of the psalmist.[65] Having witnessed the wondrous acts of YHWH, she again modeled for the people an appropriate response: to draw strength and assurance from his demonstration of power, in the spirit of Deuteronomy 20:3–4: "Hear, O Israel, today you are drawing near for battle against your enemies: let not your heart faint. Do not fear or panic or be in dread of them, for YHWH your God goes with you to fight for you against your enemies, to give you the victory."

Given the narrow, vocationally oriented portrait of Deborah in the previous chapter, the song both echoes and expands the characterization of the prophet in the narrative cycle. Its mere literary inclusion strengthens the association of Deborah with authoritative, community-oriented utterances (as does the song's portrait of Deborah in vv. 7, 12). In form, the song demonstrates how Deborah acted as an intermediary between the deity and the people by addressing both audiences in turn (the deity: vv. 4–5, 31; the people: vv. 2–3, 9–10). In content, the song recounts (in far more detail than the narrative) the skirmish between the people of Israel and the Canaanite forces under Sisera from the personal perspective of Deborah, whose viewpoint is entirely absent heretofore. In keeping with her prophetic function, her perspective extends beyond the events of the day and grounds the events at Kishon in the theological context of Israel's relationship with YHWH through (1) the theophany of the first stanza, associated with Sinai; (2) the imagery of divine intervention in verses 20–21, reminiscent of Exodus; and (3) evaluative commentary included throughout. Deborah renders blessings and curses four times in the song based on covenant fidelity (specifically related to military involvement: vv. 2, 9, 23–24). Especially given the prominence of blessings and curses, the statements of the prophet may be interpreted as Deuteronomic—in verse 31 she speaks of "those who love" YHWH, a participle rife with covenantal overtones (cf. Exod 20:6; Deut 5:10; 7:9), and the desired result of testing YHWH imposes on Israel through prophets (Deut 13:3). The prophet's authoritative vantage point renders her moments of introspection worthy of emulation. Thus, her reaction to YHWH's intervention in verse 21 is not merely an emotional aside; on the lips of a prophet in a pedagogically motivated text, her statement exemplifies the very change of heart Deborah's ministry was oriented to inspire.[66]

---

[65] Consider Ps 103:1: "Bless YHWH, oh my soul" (ברכי נפשי את יהוה; with imperative instead of jussive).

[66] Mark S. Smith, "What Is Prologue Is Past: Composing Israelite Identity in Judges 5," in *Thus Says the Lord: Essays on the Former and Latter Prophets in Honor of Robert R. Wilson*, ed. Stephen L. Cook and John J. Ahn, LHBOTS (T&T Clark, 2009), 46–47, observes that the rhetorical effect of the first-person references in the poem, even aside

Barak

Barak's introduction is modest compared to that of Sisera and Deborah; two modifiers identify his family and provenance—he is the son of Abinoam from Naphtali. Naphtali's inability to drive out the Canaanites in 1:33 may be pertinent to the characterization of Barak as it relates to his extended family. Any military hesitancy he shows in the episode that follows is characteristic of his tribe. From his limited vantage point, he has precedent to expect trouble in battle.[67] Along with the first mention of Barak by name, these details come as the object of the collocation שלח + קרא + ל in 4:6, of which Deborah is the subject. Thus, Barak is first and foremost a recipient of a message from God through the prophet. Like Gideon and Manoah after him, Barak encountered a divine envoy—in this case, one who is clearly human. Like Moses once did for Israel, Deborah directly relays the commands to Barak with divine authority. In fact, in a book concerned to demonstrate Israel's disobedience to Moses' commands (cf. 3:4), Barak's response to Deborah's command (from YHWH) provides a measure of spiritual insight into the life of an Israelite leader after the death of Moses' successor.

The message Barak received is straightforward. God commanded Barak to (1) go, (2) muster (משך) troops to Mount Tabor, and (3) call up warriors (לקח) from Naphtali and Zebulun. This summons to and strategy for battle are followed swiftly by a guarantee of victory; Barak's responsibility is limited to pulling together a militia, while YHWH would deliver his foe. Having received a straightforward command (צוה) and the reassurance of God's victory (which has been promised for generations before this battle), on this occasion, Barak responded conditionally.

Interpretations of Barak's response fall into the following broad categories: (1) positive/faithful; (2) shameful/cowardly; and (3) disobedient/morally objectionable. While the first opinion is uncommon, the second is quite widespread. The consensus among Judges scholars that the narrator emphasizes Deborah's gender leads naturally to an emphasis on the characterization of Barak vis-à-vis his female counterpart(s), and more specifically, in terms of a shameful reversal of gender roles. Sternberg is representative when he suggests that "of the two leaders, it is [Barak] who plays the woman; and having been summoned to do a man's job, he refused to act unless the woman who delegated it to him comes along to give him moral courage."[68]

---

from any prophetic considerations, "express the imaginative participation of the composer in the battle, and, by implication, to invite the audience to do likewise."

67 The relevance of Barak's familial ties is noted by Sasson, *Judges 1–12*, 257.

68 Sternberg, *Poetics of Biblical Narrative*, 274. So also David J. Zucker and Moshe Reiss, "Subverting Sexuality: Manly Women; Womanly Men in Judges 4–5," *BTB* 45

Arie van der Kooij explains how the role reversal motif is associated with the motif of honor/shame when he summarizes van Dijk-Hemmes' conclusions as follows:

> Typical of the story [i.e., Judg 4] is the opposition of, first, Deborah and Barak, and secondly, of Jael and Sisera: in both cases the women turn out to be the stronger party, to the effect that the men are experiencing a most shameful fate: Barak, the general of the Israelite army, is not able to slay his opponent, Sisera, and Sisera, the general of a most powerful army (see v. 13), is slain by a woman.[69]

Later in his discussion, van der Kooij draws attention to the biblical catchword that has given prominence to the honor/shame reading of gender dynamics in Judges 4: תפארת (v. 9; "honor, splendor, fame"). Deborah's restriction on the divine promise to Barak stipulates that Barak's military involvement would not lead to his honor; instead, God would deliver Sisera into a woman's hands. However, to suggest that Barak would not experience honor does not consequently imply that he would experience shame, nor does it require that a woman's involvement would be the source of that shame. תפארת is not even an antonym of the standard Hebrew word for shame (בשת); in the context, it connotes something like "fame" or "glory," as in credit for victory.[70] In this light, Deborah's restriction is certainly corrective—he would not receive the credit for victory—but perhaps less condemnatory. Alternate interpretations have assumed that "the way that [Barak is] going" (on which no honor is to be found) is a gloss for his apparent cowardice; however, in Judges 4, "the way that you are going" seems to have a very concrete referent—literally, the direction in which Barak is about to set out. The most significant moment in the battle would transpire in Jael's tent, which is likely pitched near Kedesh-Naphtali in lower Galilee (to the east), whereas the military action would transpire at least ten miles west in the Jezreel Valley.[71] In this context, דרך denotes a geographic course rather than a

---

(2015): 34, in which Barak (with Sisera) is accused of "traditionally womanly characteristics (fear, subservience, need of protection, frailty)."

[69] Arie van der Kooij, "On Male and Female Views in Judges 4 and 5," in *On Reading Prophetic Texts: Gender-Specific and Related Studies in Memory of Fokkelien van Dijk-Hemmes*, ed. Bob Becking and Meindert Dijkstra, BibInt 18 (New York: Brill, 1996), 138. He is correct to assume that biblical characters would view wartime death by a woman as shameful; Abimelek says as much in 9:53–54.

[70] *HALOT*, 1773.

[71] The exact location of חרשת הגוים is debated, but the area is best understood as "the farmland of the Gentiles"—a spacious (and cultivable) plain ideal for assembling troops of charioteers. The song locates the battle at just such an area, namely, "Tanaach, by the waters of Megiddo" (5:19). Anson F. Rainey and R. Steven Notley, *The Sacred Bridge: Carta's Atlas of the Biblical World* (Jerusalem: Carta, 2006), 151.

moral, ethical, or behavioral one.[72] Given the vocabulary Deborah used and the geographical shifts accentuated by the plot structure, the prophet's words seem straightforwardly corrective: while Barak assumed he and his forces were central to YHWH's plans and thus requested that the prophet accompany them to the battlefield, Deborah explained that God would bring victory in a completely different setting through an agent not associated with the militia.[73] This appears to be the central connotation of the prophecy's reference to a "woman"; a noncombatant, whose social situation would normally render her inconsequential to military victory. Thus, the "shameful" interpretation of Barak's response not only misconstrues the chapter's gendered vocabulary but arguably inserts the otherwise absent concept of shame into the narrative.

The conditional response of Barak to Deborah's imperative suggests at least a level of disobedience in response to a divine command—a fact highlighted by those in the third category above. The Deuteronomic portrait of future prophets emphasizes that heeding the authorized voice of YHWH's messenger presents an opportunity for Israel to demonstrate their Yahwistic devotion (Deut 18:17–19); indeed, the narrative of Judges is framed in terms of assessing Israelite adherence to the directives of YHWH through a process of testing (see 3:4). While these canonical controls identify Barak's response as unfaithful, the final step in evaluating this construal is assessing the degree to which the present narrative highlights YHWH's command and Barak's response. In so doing, one observes that while Barak's response in verse 8 uses lexical repetition of הלך to highlight the directive elements of Deborah's words, and, consequently, his response to them, the prophet's initial statement (and indeed, her resumptive assurance in v. 14) emphasizes the divine promise. In fact, the narrative details surrounding Deborah's movements from that point on expressly emphasize divine faithfulness (i.e., YHWH's messenger was "with" Barak consistently, as she said she would be). Furthermore, the final scenes in Jael's tent accentuate the humiliation of Sisera through a degree of graphic narrative detail (v. 21) unmatched by the portrait of Barak. In short, the narrator gives little attention to issues of humiliation, shame, or disobedience in his portrayal of Barak; instead, the text presents Barak as a witness to the fulfillment of the prophet's words. Thus, the narrative of Judges 4 consistently characterizes Barak as one in need of assurance of YHWH's faithfulness. Barak's theological shortsightedness provides the desperate

---

[72] Or perhaps less directionally, but just as concretely: "the military campaign upon which Barak was about to embark," as Chisholm commends in *Judges and Ruth*, 228–29. So also Smith and Bloch-Smith, *Judges 1*, 270.

[73] Richard D. Nelson, *Judges: A Critical and Rhetorical Commentary* (New York: Bloomsbury T&T Clark, 2017), 79; Assis, "Man, Woman and God," 123.

context out of which his threatened disobedience develops. It is this basic misconception, rather than the resultant disobedience, that Deborah addresses most prominently when she confronts Barak.

In verses 23–24, the narrator invites the reader to witness the events of the battle from Barak's perspective, just as Jael invited him into her tent to find Sisera slain in the previous verse. In fact, with the reintroduction of Barak in 5:1, the narrator confirms that YHWH succeeded in correcting Barak's theological misconceptions by allowing him to witness Jael's unexpected participation in the battle at the Kishon. While Barak's conversation with the prophet earlier in the cycle demonstrated his need for a more Yahwistically oriented perspective, the narratorial note that Barak joined the prophet in her musical assessment of the battle signals to the reader that he has adopted the prophet's point of view and has consequently become a more responsible witness to the mighty acts of God.

All this suggests that in the cycle of Judges 4–5, Barak underwent an exemplary change of theological orientation. The song's ascription is its most important contribution to his character development; Barak's duet with the prophet emphasizes that the relationship between the general and the prophet of YHWH at the moment of victory was not antagonistic. Having witnessed the death of Sisera and now sharing in the prophet's extended recapitulation of it (stanzas 6–7), Barak echoed the prophet's conviction that Israel's Divine Warrior was poised to ensure victory even when an under-armed militia was not. Additionally, though restricted to two verses (vv. 12, 15), Barak's representation in the song is wholly optimistic. The final word on the Israelite general by the book of Judges is positive: he did command a successful militia, and, though initially hesitant, he did fight for YHWH. In the heat of battle, Israel turned to him (not the prophet) to "take captive" the enemies of YHWH (v. 12); on the battlefield, Issachar valiantly followed him into the fray (v. 15). Though Jael was the instrument by which YHWH solidified his victory over Canaan, Barak's leadership did not go unnoticed. This characterization of Barak helpfully demonstrates the asymmetrical nature of Judges 4–5. The viewpoint of the song is certainly *post*battle; it recounts what transpired from the perspective of those who knew its outcome. Thus, Barak is barely visible in the song (a fact that reflects his insignificance in the outcome of the battle), but when he appears, he is not censured because in the end he participated as directed. Ultimately, Barak "under[went] the perspectival transformation the audience is meant to undergo as it follows the story."[74]

---

[74] Steven Phillip Weitzman, *Song and Story in Biblical Narrative: The History of a Literary Convention in Ancient Israel* (Bloomington: Indiana University Press, 1997), 35.

Jael

The centrality of Jael in the narrative of the Kishon conflict is evident from the significant role she has already played in this analysis. Though Jael does not emerge until the beginning of act 2, the narrative twice anticipates her pivotal importance (as discussed above): first, in Deborah's assurance that YHWH would deliver Sisera into the hand of a "woman" (4:9); and second, in the narrator's scenic and political positioning of Heber the Kenite in relation to the ensuing battle (vv. 11, 17b).

The prophetic assurance of the delivery of Sisera into a woman's hands creates narrative suspense that only finds its resolution in Jael's emergence in verse 17. Her brief familial introduction is imbedded in the motive clause explaining Sisera's destination. The narrator identifies her as "wife of Heber the Kenite" to associate her with the character verse 11 describes. While Jael may not herself be a Kenite, she is married to one, and her marriage identifies her as a "borderland figure," whose political allegiance is not entirely clear.[75] Yet both verses 11 and 17b clarify that Heber's family had broken ties with Israel and extended some kind of allegiance to Canaan.

To some degree, then, Sisera's approach toward the Kenite camp forces a choice upon the anticipated woman. Assis observes that the introduction of Jael (v. 17) begins a pattern of obscuring her motives that continues throughout the narrative.[76] Many have accentuated how the ambivalence of Jael's political affiliation and her ambiguous motives introduce a level of suspense that highlights her choice to act on behalf of Israel. Ryan Bonfiglio observes,

> Judges 4 underscores the fact that Jael faces a choice between siding with the Israelites or with the Canaanites. By virtue of choosing the former, Jael becomes a heroine for Israel in a manner not unlike the various Israelite deliverers found throughout the book of Judges.[77]

Bonfiglio is partially correct—the portrait of Jael in the next chapter suggests that something about her response is praiseworthy. However, while Judges 4 carefully highlights Barak's response to YHWH's summons so

---

[75] This terminology is borrowed from Katharine Doob Sakenfeld, "Whose Text Is It?" *JBL* 127 (2008): 16. Lillian R. Klein, in *The Triumph of Irony in the Book of Judges*, JSOTSup 68 (Sheffield: Almond, 1988), 43, too hastily labels Jael an Israelite because of her actions in support of Israel.

[76] Assis, "Choice to Serve God," 88, following Yairah Amit, *The Book of Judges: The Art of Editing*, trans. Jonathan Chipman, BibInt 38 (Boston: Brill, 1999), 211.

[77] See Ryan P. Bonfiglio, "Choosing Sides in Judges 4–5: Rethinking Representations of Jael," in *Joshua and Judges*, ed. Athalya Brenner and Gale A. Yee, Texts at Contexts (Minneapolis: Fortress, 2013), 165, following Sakenfeld, "Whose Text Is It?" 16.

as to invite its evaluation, the material involving Jael provides no comparable explicit summons to the Kenite woman or a consequent reaction to assess. Moreover, the "peace between" Heber and the king of Hazor signals a diplomatic agreement of some kind, rendering Jael's allegiance much less ambiguous than often acknowledged;[78] her family was on some level allied with Canaan. These elements of characterization, alongside the narrative's inattention to her inner life (through direct or indirect characterization), suggest that Jael's motivations and intentions are not critical for understanding her part in what unfolds.

These details of Heber's location and political affiliation have a far more important function, that is, to quite literally distance Jael from the army of Israel. Not only is her family affiliated with Canaanite power structures but her tent is pitched at least ten miles away from the Kishon skirmish. Jael's political affiliation and geographical distance from the battle buttress the narrative feature that most distances her from the army: she is a female noncombatant who would never participate in battle.[79] Just as Deborah said he would, YHWH delivered Sisera into the hands of a woman (the connotation of which is now clearer), and he did so in a direction ("way") that Barak was *not* headed—that is, eastward (v. 9b–c)! By no standard metric might Jael be associated with Israel, Barak, or the Israelite forces. Perhaps the fact that Jael is so carefully "othered" by the text (according to gender and ethnicity, especially) explains Sisera's underestimation of the woman.[80] In either case, Jael's emergence in the plot sets the stage for YHWH to fulfill the unexpected promise of the prophet.

---

[78] Deut 20:10, for example, instructs the people to "offer peace" (קרא + אל + שלום) to those outside of Israel's inheritance, in contrast to those who fall under the חרם ordinance (Deut 20:16–18); they are to seek diplomatic solutions rather than hostile ones. It remains unclear whether an official treaty was in place. See D. J. Wiseman, "'Is It Peace?' Covenant and Diplomacy," *VT* 32 (1982): 311–26, who argues that שלום simply denotes a relationship of "nonhostility" between parties.

[79] Gale A. Yee summarizes: "As in most cultures, warriorhood in Israel is commonly regarded as a male activity, theologically reified in Yahweh as the warrior God. Women traditionally are noncombatants, the victims of rape or the spoils of war." From "By the Hand of a Woman: The Metaphor of the Woman Warrior in Judges 4," in *Women, War, and Metaphor: Language and Society in the Study of the Hebrew Bible*, ed. Claudia V. Camp and Carole R. Fontaine, Semeia 61 (Atlanta: Scholars Press, 1993), 110. Num 1:2–3 suggests the only Israelite individuals free of military obligation were women, children, and Levites.

[80] This is the suggestion of Isabelle Hamley, *God of Justice and Mercy: A Theological Commentary on Judges* (London: SCM Press, 2021), 47. Hamley describes Jael as "doubly other" and, like Ehud, underestimated by an overconfident leader (here, Sisera) expecting "fealty."

Like Deborah, Jael the Kenite begins to act immediately after the narrator introduces her. Just as Deborah calls for Barak and addresses him with a string of imperatives, in 4:18 Jael issues an imperative and a prohibition to Sisera. Many scholars have observed this pattern of action and initiative during Jael's encounter with the Canaanite general and contrasted her self-assertion and Barak's initial hesitation on the one hand and the failed actions of Sisera on the other.[81] Indeed, in verses 17–22 (esp. v. 21) the text uses a string of verbs that outnumber those used to describe any other character in the chapter. This plot-focusing technique slows the narrative time considerably and directs attention to Jael and the effortless quality of her interaction with a brutal, powerful military man. While Barak required theological correction and prophetic reassurance to act appropriately and the actions of Sisera were thwarted at every step, the actions of Jael were never frustrated. According to the narrative, Jael's encounter with Sisera involved no struggle or self-defense; instead, with every action Jael's subtle insurgency escalated unnoticed: he requested water, she provided milk (v. 19); without prompting (or resistance), she covered him (vv. 18, 19); when asked to stand guard, she collected instruments of tent-pitching (vv. 20–21); once Sisera had fallen asleep, she killed him (v. 21).[82] The narrator presents Jael as resolute and unwavering in executing her task. The simple *wayyiqtol* sequence in verse 21 especially contrasts the uncomplicated accomplishments of the woman with the hurried retreat and unexpected vulnerability of the Canaanite general, whose last action is to die at her hand.

Neither Jael nor the narrator comments on Sisera's death. Instead, Jael meets Barak's approach with a summons akin to Deborah's in the first act: לך (in this case, "come"). If by no other means than the lexical parallel, the narrative reveals that Deborah and Jael share a similar relationship to Barak—in both cases they issue an invitation to the Israelite general to witness and trust in the power of YHWH—the former as messenger of the divine word, and the latter as its "executor."[83]

The victory over Sisera in which Jael participates is not mentioned in the summary of verses 23–24. The corporate conquest of northern Canaan, including Israel's victory over Jabin, king of Canaan, here replaces the one-on-one

---

[81] See, e.g., van Wolde, "Deborah and Ya'el in Judges 4," 291–92.

[82] Adele Berlin, *Poetics and Interpretation of Biblical Narrative*, BLS 9 (Winona Lake, Ind.: Eisenbrauns, 1994), 70–71, likewise speaks of the "subtle dissonance" of Jael's actions.

[83] According to Assis ("Choice to Serve God," 89) the "concealment" of Jael's motives intentionally redirects attention from the Kenite woman to the prophecy that predicted her role. The label "executor" is Brenner's ("Triangle and a Rhombus," 129–38).

encounter of the tent scene in a manner consistent with the transition from microplot to macroplot. The Song of Deborah and Barak continues the shift from individual to corporate perspectives and yet revisits the role of Jael extensively. The prophet's song addresses Jael twice: once in a short temporal clause in 5:6 and again in a pair of vignettes recalling the details and repercussions of the tent scene (vv. 24–30).

First, the song contextualizes the events that transpired before Deborah's intervention in the second stanza with the phrase, "In the days of Shamgar ben-Anath, in the days of Jael." Referring to her only as יעל at this point in the song, the composer leaves the affiliation and significance of this heroine indeterminate, assuming her brief mention is enough for the audience to discern her import properly. Minimally, to associate her with Shamgar is to suggest that she too saved Israel (cf. 3:31). Second, immediately following the double cursing (ארר) of Meroz in 5:23, Deborah doubly blessed (ברך) Jael. Here, Meroz is a foil to Jael.[84] While the song provides only a summary of Meroz's transgression, it describes meticulously every detail of Jael's actions. By contrast, the song reflects theologically on Meroz's actions, while Jael's are only narrated. Thus the reader is left to assume that what Jael has done must be considered "coming to the help of YHWH," the very thing Meroz failed to do. Further, the only other character to be blessed in the song is YHWH (5:2, 9). For Jael to be blessed is for Jael to be aligned with YHWH, the God of Israel. In short, Jael was a faithful agent of YHWH in a way that Meroz was not.

In verse 24, poetic lines portray Jael as "most blessed among women" (תברך מנשים; v. 24a) and then "among tent-dwelling women most blessed" (מנשים באהל תברך; v. 24c). While in the intervening line (v. 24b) the song mimics the previous chapter's introduction of Jael as "wife of Heber the Kenite," the third colon identifies the Kenite as most blessed "among tent-dwelling women." The preceding narrative left the significance of a woman's participation to the imagination; by contrast, the song explicitly highlights one aspect of her characterization that is of particular interest to the composer: the defenselessness of the tent-dwelling existence. Given the song's interest in the relative insecurity of certain people groups in contrast to the fortified and weaponized city-states of northern Canaan, the portrait of Jael as a tent-dweller wielding a domestic instrument contributes to the thematic contrast between small unfortified communities and secure Canaanite cities. Similar to the portrait of oppressed, battered Israel in the second stanza, Jael's living situation makes her extremely vulnerable. In the song's final stanza, the weakness of her position as a civilian in an unfortified settlement is exacerbated by her sex; here

---

[84] Webb, *Book of Judges*, 204.

her vulnerability is a function of sexual conquest. The brutality of Sisera finds its match in the callous daydreams of his household, which expects a report of his sexual dominance over his female foes.

Given the depiction of Jael in the second and last stanzas, we may summarize the contribution of the Song of Deborah and Barak to the narrative's characterization of her as follows: First, the song confirms what was implicit in the pattern of prophecy fulfillment in Judges 4—Jael is YHWH's salvific agent. The juxtaposition of Jael's blessing and the cursing of Meroz in 5:23–24 insinuates that her actions may be interpreted as coming to the help of YHWH, that is, serving as one of his agents of salvation. Moreover, by pairing Jael with Shamgar in 5:6, the song suggests that the two characters played a similar role in the battles of the period. Thus, the song coordinates the heroine of the tent scene with at least one other prominent figure/event outside of the narrative cycle—the salvation of Israel through Shamgar (3:31; ישע). This element of contextual awareness is noteworthy; by extending Jael's portrait beyond the battle at the Kishon to the broader narrative of various saviors, the prophetic rendition situates Jael within the macroplot's overarching historical and theological construal.

Second, the song reflects on the theological significance of Jael's role as a *female* savior. Considering the song's disinterest with the motives of Jael on the one hand, and silence regarding the shame her victory may have been to Barak on the other, her initiative to participate in the purposes of YHWH is not of primary importance to the song (and arguably, the cycle). Instead, the song proclaims that she saved Israel (as described above) and, through the portrayal of Jael in the final stanzas, demonstrates that her vulnerability and perceived weakness are key to understanding her character's role in the microplot. Thus, the song more explicitly says what Judges 4 implied: for YHWH to deliver Sisera into the hand of a woman is to deliver the powerful enemy of Israel to someone unarmed, (perceived to be) weak, and vulnerable. In almost every detail, the characterization of Jael mirrors that of the Israelites. The next section will address the thematic significance of these parallels.

Thematic Emphases

In an effort to distinguish carefully between elements relating to plot, characterization, and themes, this section will be restricted to an analysis of "key words" and prominent semantic fields. I address major semantic emphases in the narrative and the song, while attending especially to any thematic development that occurs during the cycle. Because semantic and thematic emphases are not coterminous, the criterion by which I will determine a thematic emphasis is its explanatory power: "The best statement of the theme of a work is the statement that most adequately accounts for the content, structure, and development of the work."[85] Thus, each section will address the relationship between the identified lexical/semantic emphases and the theme to which they contribute.

Shimon Bar-Efrat provides three criteria for identifying a "key word" that may aptly apply to this discussion: (1) the frequency with which a lexeme occurs, relative to its frequency in the Hebrew Bible, especially in texts of a similar genre; (2) the frequency with which the word appears in the text under observation; and (3) the proximity of the repeated words in the text. Bar-Efrat reasons that lexemes more common to the Hebrew Bible must appear more densely and with greater proximity in a given text to qualify as "key words," while rarer words may appear more sparsely and at a greater distance to be worthy of the same classification.[86] The same three criteria apply to the selection of important semantic fields.

The Verbal Root הלך and Thematic Movement

As familiar as it is unexceptional, the root הלך is at home in most Hebrew narratives; yet its concentrated distribution in the account of Judges 4 is striking. In terms of narrative emphases, the beginning of the Deborah-Barak narrative contains little movement, so the absence of the root is appropriate; the first five verses are dominated by offline clauses. Not until the dialogue between Barak and Deborah begins in verse 6 does the root הלך appear; in fact, of its twelve appearances in the narrative, nine occur in dialogue between protagonists.[87] The first is an imperative addressed to Barak. Deborah simply instructs him to begin his movements toward Tabor. A common imperative, the verb does not find its narrative significance until verse 8, when Deborah's command to Barak (לך) is met with the following conditional statement, in which the root appears four times:

אם־תלכי עמי והלכתי   If you go with me, I will go
ואם־לא תלכי עמי לא אלך   But if you do not go with me, I will not go

---

[85] David J. A. Clines, *The Theme of the Pentateuch*, 2nd ed., JSOTSup 10 (Sheffield: Sheffield Academic, 1997), 23. Cf. Shimon Bar-Efrat, "Some Observations on the Analysis of Structure in Biblical Narrative," *VT* 30 (1980): 168: "Themes define the central issues of the narrative. They are embodied in the various narrative elements discussed before and serve as their focal point and as a unifying and integrating principle."

[86] Bar-Efrat, *Narrative Art in the Bible*, 212.

[87] Nelson (*Judges*, 79) rightly observes that the repetition of the root הלך "hold[s] together" the conversation and subsequent actions of Deborah and Barak, with special emphasis on Deborah instigating the action.

To emphasize her agreement, Deborah responded to this ultimatum by assuring Barak she certainly would *go* (הלך אלך עמך) with him, despite the fact that the glory of victory would be accomplished by another means. In fact, Deborah phrased her restriction using הלך as well: on the way that he is *going* (הולך) no credit awaits. The very concrete meaning of הלך in verses 6–8 suggests that the same might be said in verse 9; Barak wanted Deborah with him in battle, but she explained that God would conquer Sisera in a completely unexpected direction.

After all of this talk of "going," only once did someone in the story actually "go": in verse 9f, Deborah followed through on her emphatic assurance that she would "go with" (הלך + עם) Barak. As the scene unfolds, the narrator favors military vocabulary to describe standard troop positioning (ירד; עלה) and postbattle flight (נוס). Not until the abrupt change of scene in verse 17 does the vocabulary of battle fade and the lexical landscape become mundane again. After Jael had slain Sisera and Barak approached Jael's tent in pursuit of the enemy's general, Jael reissued the imperative to Barak from verse 6: לך (rather than סור, the word chosen to address Sisera). Though unspectacular in this context and dialogue pattern, the repeated directive draws an explicit connection between the death of Sisera at Jael's hands and the dialogue between Deborah and Barak in verses 6–9, in which the event is foretold.

A collocation involving the root הלך appears in verse 24: "The hand of the Israelites weighed consistently upon (ותלך יד . . . הלוך וקשה) Jabin king of Canaan." For the second time in the narrative, finite and infinitive forms of הלך are paired for a maximum lexical impact. While the English rendering here does little to represent the repetition of the root הלך,[88] it does reflect the distinction of the language of the report from the book's other summary statements, both in syntax and connotation. In this text the emphasis on Israelite agency and success is conspicuous, especially since the narrator's description uses a root associated with faithful response earlier in the chapter. Just as the narrator emphasized that Deborah followed through on her promise to stay with Barak (vv. 9b, 9g), so too does the narrator emphasize that God enabled the people of Israel (under the leadership of Barak) to fulfill Deborah's charge to their general: to go (הלך). While the microplot highlights Barak's initial hesitancy through prophetic command (לך), in the same breath the account accentuates lexically the trustworthiness of God's messenger on individual (to Barak, v. 22; הלך) and corporate (of Israel, v. 24; הלך) levels.

---

[88] The noun יד is the subject of the verb הלך only here in the Hebrew Bible; however, the idiom הלך (*wayyiqtol*) + הלוך (inf. abs.) + וְ + adj. occurs in Gen 26:15; 1 Sam 14:19; 2 Sam 18:25, and indicates increasing intensity or duration. See *HALOT*, 246; *GKC* §113u. Much like אשה נביאה, which is a normal—but thematically ideal—Hebrew construction, the syntax of v. 24 is normal, but apropos for thematic development.

The song of the prophet and the general in chapter 5 is unquestionably concerned with that same mustering call to Israel's militia. Nevertheless, after a theocentric introduction, verses 6–7 turn readerly attention to thoroughly civilian affairs for the first time in the cycle. The prophet uses the vocabulary of motion to assess the welfare of Israelite daily life: the political and economic turmoil characteristic of the days before YHWH's intervention caused normal trading and travel to cease, and those who journeyed (הלך) had to use obscure roadways. By contrast, in the next stanza those who traveled (הלך) freely could only attribute their freedom to the righteous exploits of YHWH and the Israelite troops (v. 11), on whom most of the song focuses.

As in the previous chapter, Judges 5 describes the events at Kishon in terms of fidelity to YHWH. Just as 4:24 had expanded its focus to speak of corporate Israelite faithfulness, so the song looks past the general to the militia he represents. This change in characterization precipitates a change in thematic expression; the mundane vocabulary of הלך (whose thematic significance was tied to the response of a single individual) is replaced by a martial semantic domain. In its most evaluative statements (5:14–18, 23), the song measures the faithfulness of tribal response with verbs of military movement: the faithful tribes descend (ירד) and are sent into (שלח + ב) the valley, while the unfaithful stay (ישב), remain (שכן), sojourn (גור), and "do not come" (לא + בוא). The juxtaposition of conquest (movement) and settlement (nonmovement) vocabulary reinforces poetically the ambivalent appraisal of Israelite success in the period.[89] The theological foundation upon which this correlation between faithfulness and military movement stands is clear from the song's bookends: the first stanza depicts the Divine Warrior valiantly going forth (יצא) to conquer the land of promise, marching (צעד) from the south. The last bicolon (v. 31a–b) associates covenant faithfulness with going forth (יצא) with the fervency of the sunrise. Those who are faithful to YHWH will rouse themselves to emulate the Divine Warrior, who is definitively on the move.

Therefore, in its literary context the Song of Deborah and Barak contributes to two significant thematic developments using this particular semantic domain. First, by exploiting a vocabulary of movement to assess the welfare of the Israelites in both mundane and military spheres, the song draws a correlation between the initiative of the Israelite militia specifically and the welfare of the people generally. The mustering of Israelite soldiers and their faithful execution of divine directives is an essential step in their own thriving. Thus, the vocabularic emphasis on mobility throughout Judges 4–5

---

[89] See, e.g., Josh 15:63; 16:10; 17:12; Judg 1:21, 27–36. Cf. Josh 11:23; 18:1.

shows that Israel's success in the land (measured by their ability to move freely) is fundamentally tied to their obedience to YHWH's muster. The third stanza correlates effectually the freely moving Israelite society with previous military movements of YHWH and his forces. Correspondingly, the enemy's *inability* to move freely—exemplified in the "hesitation" of Sisera's chariots (5:28)—is a testament to YHWH's triumph for Israel. Second, the song expands upon the previous chapter's thematic emphases in terms of motivation, internalization, and theological perspective. In Judges 4, both the prophet and the judge are presented as comparatively flat characters; their emotional state and theological convictions are untouched by the narrator. The song thus interprets the relatively straightforward account of the battle's events by describing the miraculous action of YHWH, discerning the motivations of key players (including the tribes as well as Sisera's family), and making accessible for emulation Deborah's internal convictions. Thus, the song ties the external phenomenon of movement to an internal disposition: willing participation in the work of God. For this reason the song reflects upon both the faithful triumphs of God and his army (5:11) and those leaders who "offered themselves willingly" (vv. 2, 9).

אשה and Gendered Vocabulary

Gender dynamics constitute a crucial feature of the Kishon battle accounts in Judges 4–5. Female characters uncharacteristically take center stage; they occupy significant roles in conjunction with their male counterparts, but they also "cooperate" and "compete" among themselves.[90] As I have already addressed how gendered labels contributed to characterization in Judges 4–5 above, the discussion here will summarize the contribution of the lexical emphasis on gender to thematic development in the cycle and the particular function of the Song of Deborah and Barak in that process. In Judges 4, the noun אשה is especially significant given its role in a crucial plot twist: the introduction of Jael as one of YHWH's delivering agents. Fronting the adverbial phrase "into the hand of a woman" in verse 9e reinforces syntactically the prioritization of this otherwise innocuous noun as a crucial element of narrative development.

Since the narrative uses אשה so intentionally in verse 9e, the earlier gendered introduction of Deborah has rightfully drawn attention. However, much like the first occurrences of the root הלך, in and of themselves the gendered

---

[90] Fokkelien van Dijk-Hemmes, "Mothers and a Mediator in the Song of Deborah," in *A Feminist Companion to Judges*, ed. Athalya Brenner, FCB 4 (Sheffield: Sheffield Academic, 1993), 111–12, highlights the dynamic of cooperation and competition that draws together the mothers in the text.

nouns associated with the introduction of Deborah are not significant (i.e., that Deborah is a woman is not as shocking as some scholars suggest). Granted that assumption, the double אשה in verse 4a gains its significance retrospectively as a potential antecedent to the prophetic word in verse 9. Despite this tantalizing lexical possibility, the prophet immediately excludes herself as the referent—the climax of the battle will unfold in a location different from the one in which she and Barak will find themselves.

How one measures the lexical impact of the noun אשה (and איש) here,[91] and throughout the narrative, depends on the sense the interpreter assigns to the introduction of Deborah in verse 4 and her response in verse 9. On the one hand, if the primary identifier for Deborah in verse 4 is "woman," and Deborah's rise in lieu of a male deliverer is the context through which the gender vocabulary in the narrative is to be read, then the promise that "the hand of a woman" will slay Sisera contributes to a theme of YHWH using strong women to shame weak men. From this perspective Murray argues that the narrative's theme is "the subjugation, at once self-imposed but divinely-ordered, of presumed authority-bearing men to presumed subservient women."[92] Similarly, Gale Yee invokes the vocabulary of the "shame syndrome" to describe a literary convention in which an empowered female protagonist ("warrior queen") is useful to the narrative as a foil to its male protagonist.[93] On the other hand, if the gendered introduction of Deborah is merely incidental (or better, largely anticipatory), and the central feature of her initial characterization is her prophetic ministry (as has been argued above), then establishing a pattern of female dominance is difficult until Deborah's response to Barak in verse 9, in which the "hand of a woman" becomes central. If Deborah's statement primarily provides theological clarification and correction, as I have argued, then the prominence of a woman in the prophecy connotes something other than shame to the male protagonist. Yee provides a helpful summary of the possible connotations of male/female contrasts in literature using insight from the anthropological study of

---

[91] The noun איש appears inconspicuously throughout the account as is required by standard battle report (and standard biblical Hebrew) syntax. Three of six times the noun occurs in the description of Barak's army: עשרת אלפי/אלפים איש ("ten thousand men"). Here the emphasis is not on the gender of the individuals so much as their number and comparatively scant armament. In the exchange between Jael and Sisera (4:20), the noun איש in the context likely translates "one" (i.e., "is there anyone . . . ?"), though there is a *possibility* that the question is ironic (i.e., suggesting that Sisera does not count as a man). The plausibility of such a reading, however, rests on a scene designed to demasculinize Sisera, against which I have argued.

[92] Murray, "Narrative Structure and Technique," 177.

[93] Yee, "By the Hand of a Woman," 115.

metaphor. She notes the following examples of commonly connoted binary oppositions:[94]

> man:woman :: warrior:noncombatant
> protector:protected
> conqueror:defeated
> destroyer:nurturer
> violent:nonviolent
> independent:dependent
> aggressive:meek
> dominant:submissive, etc.

Given the contrastive plot structure of Judges 4, thematic emphasis on the comparative strength of the two armies, and the unexpected appearance of a tent-dwelling woman at the climax of military victory, the connotation of a "woman" in the text seems to resemble the first binary opposition listed by Yee. By clarifying that a "woman" would kill Sisera, Deborah effectively assured Barak that a nonmilitant (an especially vulnerable one) would be responsible for the capture of the Canaanite general. Retrospectively, the narrative emphasizes that a character especially far removed from the Israelite army—politically, socially, and scenically—was the agent of YHWH's salvation.

By this reading, the gendered vocabulary of the chapter contributes less to a construal of shamefully reversed gender roles and more to an overriding theme of YHWH's faithfulness to his word despite the (perceived) weakness of his agents. Brenner is right to suggest that in the tent scene of Judges 4 (the climax of the microplot) the "emphasis is on the consequences, on Jael's fulfilling God's words, rather than on Barak's humiliation. The sociosexual element, then, features in chapter 4 inasmuch as it contributes to the advancement of the plot."[95] Identifying the enduring word of God (evidenced through the fulfillment of prophetic assurance) as thematically significant makes better sense of the relatively flat characterization of both Jael and Deborah, the latter's tendency to speak only the words of YHWH, the uncharacteristic emphasis on YHWH's direct intervention in the narrative, and Deborah's accompanying Barak to battle. Rather than shaming Barak for being less than a man, the chapter uses gendered vocabulary to highlight YHWH's ability to empower the (stereotypically) weak to fulfill his purposes and thereby to expose the theological blind spot

---

[94] Yee, "By the Hand of a Woman," 104.
[95] Brenner, "Triangle and a Rhombus," 131.

that underlies Israelite hesitancy in battle.⁹⁶ In the microplot's final moments, the Israelite general witnesses YHWH's ability to triumph over Israel's enemy using no more than a Kenite woman; Jael is to Sisera what Israel's militia had been to the sophisticated army of Jabin under Sisera.

Judges 5 develops gender-related themes differently.⁹⁷ On the level of lexicography, the nouns איש and אשה do not occur abstractly to draw gender concerns to the fore; any gender-related thematic development occurs on the level of characterization. The interest of interpreters in the gender dynamics of the song is due in part to its comparatively significant attention to women: the song's first-person voice is female, as are the focal characters of the last two stanzas. Given the accent on Jael's gender in Judges 4, her representation in stanzas 6 and 7 is particularly instructive. The vignette that depicts Jael subduing Sisera is formally parallel to a second vignette in which Sisera's family expects him to subdue women similar to Jael. The song thus exposes a compositional/editorial tendency in the cycle to highlight the perceived weakness and vulnerability of particular entities in contrast to their empowerment as agents of YHWH. Given this reading of Judges 4–5, the gender dynamics of the cycle are related to a third theme: military might.

Military Might

The relative insignificance of Israel is a major theme in the Pentateuch and Joshua,⁹⁸ one that is fundamental to the biblical portrait of Israelite election. In the book of Judges, this portrayal of Israel takes on a military tone. Judges 4–5 is no exception; using consistent semantic patterns, the Kishon unit emphasizes the weakness of Israel's militia in contrast to the strength of the Canaanite army. Because the serial occupation of God's people during the period is crucial to the macroplot, the crisis of the Kishon microplot involves military deficiency from the beginning. The narrator identifies the severe (lit. "strong"; בחזקה) oppression of Sisera's army with the quintessential symbol of Canaanite technological might—the chariot of iron (4:3; cf. 1:19).

---

⁹⁶ In "Deborah's War Memorial: The Composition of Judges 4–5 and the Politics of War Commemoration," *ZAW* 123 (2011): 527, Jacob Wright notes also that the prophetic and Jael-related material in Judges 4 contributes to an elevation of the deity; however, he emphasizes that the "diminution of the male warrior" is one of the narrative's central themes.

⁹⁷ Brenner ("Triangle and a Rhombus," 131) suggests that the gender-related elements in Judg 4 foreshadow the "pronounced space given to [them] in the second text (ch. v)." For my full assessment of Brenner's argument, see Michelle Knight, "Geometry and Psalmody: Characterization and the Role of Deborah's Song (Judges 5)," in *"Now These Records Are Ancient": Studies in Ancient Near Eastern and Biblical History, Language and Culture in Honor of K. Lawson Younger, Jr*, ed. James K. Hoffmeier et al., ÄAT 114 (Münster: Zaphon, 2022), 287–98.

⁹⁸ See esp. Deut 7:7, but also Num 13:31–33; Deut 4:38; 9:4–6; 10:14–19; 32:9–14.

Supplemented by the notice that the oppression dragged on for ten years, the emphasis on Canaan's advanced weaponry in the introduction is the backdrop against which the battle unfolds.

Throughout Judges 4, the narrative focuses much more on the strength of Canaan than the weakness of Israel. The observation that ten thousand men followed Barak on foot (ברגליו) in verse 10 only reflects Israelite weakness in contrast to the weaponry available to his foe. To demonstrate the discrepancy more poignantly, the narrative includes the iron chariots of Canaan with every mention of Sisera in battle; in verse 13, conspicuous syntax establishes the pattern and recalls the numeric verbiage of the introduction: "Then Sisera summoned all his chariots—nine hundred iron chariots—and all those accompanying him."[99] The consistent portrayal of Sisera as well-armed and militarily superior brings into sharp relief his incremental humiliation: he was robbed of his troops, his weapon (his chariot), reduced to the level of Barak's foot soldiers, and killed by an otherwise-vulnerable noncombatant politically allied with his own nation. As a result, the narrative also highlights the event that so emphatically weakened Sisera—the intervention of YHWH in verse 15. This pattern of attributing the weakening of Canaan to the intervention of Israel's patron deity continues in verses 23–24, in which summarizing statements show that Sisera's experience was representative of his army's: YHWH, the God of Israel, humbled Canaan (כנע . . . כנען).

Beginning in 5:1, Deborah offers an exposition of this theme. Her voice replaces that of the storyteller as the one drawing attention to the might of Israel's God. Even though Deborah praises Israel's warriors for their acts of heroism, it is YHWH—not the people—whom Deborah depicts as mighty. In this characterization the song continues the thematic trajectory of the narrative. Nevertheless, the song makes its own contribution when it dedicates an entire stanza to Israel's socioeconomic fragility. Israel's dereliction was only implied in the previous chapter by the severity of Canaanite oppression. In Judges 5 Deborah (with Barak) attends to the people of God, who are hopelessly occupied, geographically vulnerable, economically crippled, and woefully unarmed (5:6–7). In contrast to this tattered "remnant" (שׂרים; v. 13) of a militia, the song refers to the standing army of Canaan as mighty men (אדירים; v. 13) and trained warriors (גבורים; vv. 13, 23). Given the situation, the song's disturbing final stanza emphasizes that Israelite victory was surprising in the

---

[99] Sue Groom (*Linguistic Analysis of Biblical Hebrew* [Waynesboro, Ga: Paternoster, 2003], 155) notes this "anaphoric reference" with several more: the root זעק (v. 13, cf. v. 10); Barak, "son of Abinoam" (v. 12, cf. v. 6); Haroshet Hagoyyim (v. 13, cf. v. 2); and the Kishon (v. 13, cf. v. 7). Saturated with familiar vocabulary, these verses draw together details scattered throughout the narrative to prepare the reader for this central skirmish.

face of such might. In contrast to the vulnerable travelers described in 5:6–7 and the tent-dwelling woman in 5:24–26, Sisera's mother waits securely at the window in her well-fortified home (v. 28). Much like the Israelites in the previous chapter, she expects her son's triumph in correlation with the impressive charioteers under his command. The irony that her son has been subdued at the hand of a civilian, just as his mighty chariots have been destroyed by the divinely appointed forces of nature, underscores the unexpected turn of events that could only result from miraculous intervention—intervention like that of the strong warrior striding forth to battle in the opening stanza.

Thus the Song of Deborah and Barak employs the vocabulary of strength and weakness to highlight the unexpected outcome of the battle. By supplementing the assertion of the narrative that Canaan was militarily superior with the choral description of an impoverished and vulnerable Israel, the song capitalizes on the perception that Israel stood no chance of victory. After acknowledging the veracity of this assessment in stanzas 2–3, the prophet reorients the attention of her hearers with a theologically robust account of YHWH's mighty intervention. Only with the inclusion of the theophany of the first stanza does Israel's triumph start to make sense. While Judges 4 also emphasizes YHWH's agency in the battle, Judges 5 rhetorically invites Israel to assess its own strength from a more theologically informed perspective. To illustrate, in 4:9 the prophet had to reassure Barak that being insufficiently armed and lacking in numbers was irrelevant, because God would defeat Sisera using completely nonmilitary means (i.e., Jael). In the song, the prophet extends this theological realignment to the Israelite people en masse, who consistently underestimate the ability and determination of YHWH to deliver his people. When addressing a revitalized Israelite citizenry in verses 10–11, Deborah instructs those reveling in the change of their circumstances to convey properly (יְשִׂיחוּ; v. 10c) the specifics of the battle: the mixed responses of the tribes (stanza 4), the miraculous intervention of YHWH at Kishon (stanza 5), the decisive action of his underestimated salvific agent (stanza 6), and the devastation of Israel's foe at her hand (stanza 7). Therefore, the semantic emphasis on strength and weakness that contributes to characterization in both chapters consistently demonstrates the irrelevancy of Israel's weakness in appropriate self-perception. The might of YHWH is the only accurate measure of the people's fitness for battle.

Conclusion

The interpretive authority conferred on Judges 5 by its ascription to a prophet has a significant impact on the narrative in which it is embedded. Not only does it contribute additional content and perspectives to the prose account but it also offers something deeply theological: a paradigmatic, prophetic interpretation of the Kishon battle. Assuming this narrative framing, the song provides a level of hermeneutical control to the audience seeking revelatory clarity from the God of Israel. That clarity is offered not only by the prophet but also by the general she admonished. Despite the initial hesitation Barak had conveyed in the face of Canaan's superior armament at the beginning of chapter 4, the divine assurance Deborah offered roused Barak to battle and put him in a position to witness firsthand the miraculous quality of YHWH's saving work in battle and in the privacy of a Kenite woman's tent. Appropriately then, the ensuing song offers an opportunity for the entire community to witness the same. Deborah's unique prophetic insight lends authority to the song's theological claims as well as supernatural access to details of motivation, divine action, and benedictory (and condemnatory) pronouncements, all of which are normally reserved for the narrator in prose. Thus, the prophetic song provides a unique opportunity for a character in the microplot to reflect on issues related to the macroplot: the ongoing struggle between YHWH, Israel, and Canaan, in which Israel's suzerain YHWH seeks covenant faithfulness from his people Israel and serially tests the strengths of their bond through military conflicts with other kings.

Just as the narrative highlighted YHWH's role in the moment of battlefield victory (4:15), so the song demonstrates that the Divine Warrior presided over the Canaanite defeat (5:19–22). The song draws on mythic imagery and Israelite memory to address more forthrightly the people's central theological blind spot: YHWH's role as Divine Warrior and guarantor of victory. By transitioning from the battle to the scene in Jael's tent, the song mimics the prose in identifying the exchange between the Kenite woman and the Canaanite general as the climax of the Canaanite-Israelite conflict. Using the final stanza of the song to accentuate the vulnerability of a civilian woman near a combat zone, the song once more highlights the perceived weakness and defenselessness of particular entities in contrast to their empowerment as agents of YHWH. Given the unmistakable parallel between Jael and Israel's militia, the song's final stanzas confront the people of YHWH with the prophetic assurance that to hesitate in battle is to doubt his divine empowerment. Just as Barak's misconceptions about YHWH's role in battle had triggered a conditional and disobedient response to his messenger, so too is Israel's wariness in completing conquest directives ultimately a measure of (and an impediment to) their religious fidelity. As the next chapter will suggest, at this moment in the Judges macroplot, the poetic rendition of the Kishon battle draws a causal correlation between Israelite hesitancy and the thoroughgoing apostasy that characterizes the period.

3
Characterization in the Song and the Savior Stories

The focus of the next two chapters is the book's core (3:7–16:31; the "Book of Deliverers"), in which the song plays a vital role in developing the narrative characterization of four significant parties: Israel, its saviors, the nation's sundry oppressors, and YHWH. Just as 2:10–19 described these characters according to their roles in the conflicts of the period, so too must the reader consider them not simply as individuals but as representatives of these groups.

The Israelites

The cycle describing the exploits of Othniel against King Cushan-Rishathaim most closely resembles the second introduction of Judges and is thus prone to the same abstraction. The cycle is less concerned with individual details and historical flavor than with the aforementioned four entities of the macroplot. Therefore, the corporate entity בני־ישראל is as central to the narrative as the deliverer himself (i.e., the subject of as many verbal clauses as Othniel). The key characteristic of Israel in the initial cycle is its sinfulness. Whereas more frequently the book of Judges notes only "the evil" committed by Israel and its consequent suffering (e.g., 3:12, 4:1, 6:1), here the text clarifies that the people's transgression is that which was explicated in the previous chapter: they forgot YHWH and served the Baals and the Asherahs/Astarte(s) (3:7; cf. 2:11–13).[1] In fact, the narrative says nothing of the nature or degree of Israel's suffering or participation in battle; sin is the hallmark of its literary portrayal.

With the transition to the tale of Israel's conflict with Moab under the leadership of Ehud, the narrative similarly highlights the infidelity of Israel

---

[1] The goddess mentioned alongside Baal in Judg 2:13 (and 10:6) is not אשרות (pl. of Asherah) but עשתרות (pl. or rare sg. of Astarte; see N. Wyatt, "Astarte," *DDD*, 109–14). Only in 3:7 does the noun אשרות appear in the book of Judges; for that reason, Vulg. and Syr. opt for עשתרות, while LXX and TJon retain אשרות. The two goddesses are distinct in Canaanite religion, but here they serve the same literary function: to highlight the apostasy of Israel in terms of its service to foreign gods and goddesses.

after the death of Othniel (3:12). While it does not elaborate on specifics, the narrative does highlight the trespass by stating twice that Israel did the aforementioned "evil": once as the instigating event in the conflict (3:12a) and again in a purpose clause describing the reason for YHWH's action against his own people (3:12c). Here the textual accent is on the causal relationship between Israel's apostasy and subjugation. In keeping with an emphasis on Israel's culpability, the narrative mentions only the servitude imposed upon Israel (v. 14; עבד), not its consequent suffering under occupation.

The בני-ישראל appear in the initiating verses of the battle account when sending Ehud as their tribute-bearing representative (v. 15). By highlighting a common element of political occupation (i.e., offering tribute), the narrative reiterates the Israelites' subjugation to a foreign king, as well as their hand in supporting the initial efforts of the deliverer. After the private assassination of Eglon, Ehud musters Ephraim to fight against the Moabites; however, verse 27 clarifies the representative function of Ephraim in regard to the characterization of the people of Israel—the group mustered from the hill country of Ephraim is consequently called the בני-ישראל. Israel's militia is obedient, swift, and effective; twice the text emphasizes their complete annihilation of the enemy (vv. 28–29). Moreover, the Israelites strike (נכה; v. 29) Moab in the manner that they had been struck by Moab's king (נכה; v. 13). The narrative's final statement emphasizes the reversal of Israel's fortune: under its hand Moab was subdued (v. 30). This passive statement avoids accentuating the agency of the Israelites in the battle and focuses on the change in their *circumstances* already highlighted by the word play in verse 29; they literally gained the upper hand. In this way, Judges 3:12–30 not only portrays the Israelites as sinful before their punishment (as was the pattern of 3:7–11) but also emphasizes the change in their circumstances afforded by a decisive victory.

When the narrative turns to the events after Ehud's death (4:1), the text again mentions the sinfulness of the Israelites but does not dwell on their transgression; instead, it portrays the Israelites as objects of cruel oppression under a formidable foe. In the story of the Kishon battle, twice the text mentions the crying out of Israel: once in a formulaic statement (v. 3, tied causally to the oppression of their enemy) and again when a corporate envoy approached Deborah for direction in the present conflict (v. 5). Thus, the distress of the בני-ישראל, caused by the "hand" (v. 2) of a formidable opponent, dominates the narrative's introduction. By contrast, the complete annihilation of the enemy—by the "hand" of the people of Israel, no less (v. 24)—is the highlight of the cycle's end. Despite YHWH's empowerment of their victory, the text clearly acknowledges the agency of the people of Israel in the annihilation of Jabin's forces and, once again, the unlikely reversal of their circumstances.

This shift reveals a trend: the portrayal of Israel in the first three prose accounts shifts gradually from highlighting the Israelites' apostasy to emphasizing the degree to which their fortunes were reversed because of the salvation brought through YHWH's deliverers. This pattern comes to a climax with the Song of Deborah and Barak. Even more than the prose rendition of the Battle of Kishon, the song of Judges 5 focuses on the people of Israel, and more specifically the initial dilapidated condition of Israelite villages and the coalition's underwhelming militia. Interestingly, the song never mentions past Israelite transgression nor identifies it as the reason for the battle. Perhaps because the song is not primarily a retelling but instead a pedagogically motivated reflection, the song's focus on Israel is limited to assessing its people's response: retrospectively, their response to the muster, and prospectively, to the dramatic restoration of Israelite prosperity against all odds. At this point, the overarching narrative has focused on the salvation the people have received at YHWH's hand and the way they have reacted to that salvation. Israel's developing characterization in the first three narrative cycles prepares the reader to join Deborah and Barak in considering how effectively Israel responded to the decisive, gracious interventions of Israel's God. Especially given the song's contextual awareness and covenantal focus, Judges 5 helps to define the first three cycles as, primarily, stories of YHWH's faithful deliverance of an unfaithful nation. Its lyrical imperatives to its audience(s) are those of perception and response (vv. 2–3, 9–10), just as its last lines encourage covenant fidelity through faithful (military) action (v. 31). Deborah and Barak's refrain ends the third narrative cycle with hope and finality for the nation—Israel has witnessed YHWH's most decisive victory yet, a prophet has explicitly interpreted for the Israelites its theological significance, and God's people have received a challenge for renewed covenant faithfulness.

Given the optimism of the Kishon account, the way the Midianite oppression under Gideon begins is noteworthy. Following the narrative pattern, the Israelites transgressed their covenant with YHWH. Initially the narrative sets aside descriptions of Israelite transgression for the sake of highlighting the severity of the people's suffering. A description akin to the previous psalmic portrayal of Israel unfolds: the people frantically abandoned their insecure dwellings and agricultural endeavors to seek the relative security of caves and strongholds (6:2–3; cf. 5:6–7). Indeed, they were "brought low": a state of utter helplessness, exhaustion, or poverty.[2] The desperation of God's people,

[2] The verb דלל is relatively rare in the Hebrew Bible, whereas the noun דל is more frequent and helpful for discerning possible connotations of the verb: lacking riches or pos-

war-torn and stripped of their resources, is central to the narrator's description. Their consequent double call for divine intervention strengthens the emphasis on their plight (6:6–7). Significantly, YHWH responds by sending a prophet to highlight the transgressions of the people. Whereas in the previous cycle a divine intermediary addressed the Israelite general with words of direction and clarification (4:6–7), here a prophet addresses the people at large, solely with words of rebuke.³ The people are characterized as those who—despite their covenant God's repeated intervention on their behalf and explicit prohibition of idolatry—have chosen to fear the inhabitants of the land and their gods. Here then, the text has shifted back to an emphasis characteristic of the introduction and the Othniel cycle: the apostasy of Israel.

Despite their transgression, the narrator reports that YHWH raised up a deliverer to lead the people, many of whom are called out according to clan or tribe but are interchangeably referred to as "Israel" or "men of Israel" (7:8, 15, 23). Even though the text records the participation of individual tribes (thereby following a pattern of growing specificity in tribal characterization evidenced in the song), their connection to the corporate body remains clear. However, with Ephraim's complaint regarding Gideon's mustering tactics, intratribal tension surfaces in the macroplot for the first time. The Song of Deborah and Barak had emphasized the notion that certain tribes were more likely to answer the call than others, but only now does the book of Judges explore the ramifications of such mixed responses. The narrator, in chapter 8, again opts for corporate characterization at the end of the Gideon narrative, when the men of Israel (איש־ישראל; v. 22) asked Gideon to serve as their ruler (משל). Moreover, *all* Israel acted unfaithfully with (זנה אחר; v. 27) the idolatrous ephod Gideon constructed in response to their request. The same people divided over Gideon's battle tactics were united in their pagan worship.

In this pericope, the entire people of Israel was culpable for the apostasy that transpired *before* the death of their most recent leader. Only here is Israel's allegiance to YHWH said to fail during a judge's lifetime. Their failure comes to fruition after Gideon's death, in 8:34: "The Israelites did not remember YHWH their God, who had delivered them from the hand of their enemies on every side"—a pattern that began during Gideon's lifetime when the people attributed their salvation to their human ruler, not to God (8:22). The Gideon cycle, then, highlights most emphatically how poorly the people of YHWH respond to the pattern of unearned rescue from dire circumstances;

---

sessions (Exod 30:15; Jer 39:10), battle-worn (2 Sam 3:1), scorned (Isa 53:3), and helpless/extorted (Amos 2:7; 4:1; 5:11).

³ Parallel nomenclature recommends a comparison of the two figures: Deborah, the אשה נביאה in 4:4 and the unnamed prophet, an איש נביא in 6:8.

their apostasy is a direct result of their refusal to acknowledge YHWH's agency in their deliverance. The literary juxtaposition of this account with the Song of Deborah and Barak only heightens the effect of the comparison.

The setting is similar as Abimelek's story begins, but the description of the idolatry of the בני־ישראל departs from the semantic pattern of the first four narrative cycles; instead, the narrator opts for vocabulary similar to the book's introduction. According to 8:33, the people returned (cf. 2:19), acted unfaithfully with (cf. 2:17) the Baals (cf. 2:13), and made Baal-Berit their god. The language of returning (שוב) especially recalls the generational degradation of Israelite faithfulness from the introduction—"whenever the judge died, they turned back and were more corrupt than their fathers" (2:19)—in the context of two main characters from the same family. The characterization of Israel at the transition to the Abimelek narrative is one of heightened, institutionalized corruption.[4] Here the textual accent on Israel's apostasy matches and surpasses the focus on sin that initiated the Gideon narrative. Israelite transgression has reached an anticipated milestone.

Once the text details Abimelek's rise to power, corporate references to Israel all but cease (with two crucial exceptions). The "people of Shechem" interest the narrator most. Unfortunately, as Tammi Schneider notes, "it is not clear who the people of Shechem were presumed to be in this account, and what their relationship was to Israel."[5] Many interpreters have argued that the story casts Shechem as a Canaanite settlement.[6] Sasson has recently questioned this consensus, arguing that "nothing in Hebraic lore about Shechem

---

[4] The collocation ל + שים here connotes an official establishment or installation, not an incidental pattern of apostasy. For other biblical examples of the collocation, see, e.g., Judg 18:31 (gods); 1 Sam 8:5 (king); 2 Sam 7:10 (secure dwelling for Israel); 2 Sam 23:5 (everlasting covenant). See also *HALOT*, 1322. The appearance in Judges 9:4 of the temple of Baal-Berit in Shechem solidifies the connotation.

[5] Tammi J. Schneider, *Judges*, BerOl (Collegeville, Minn.: Liturgical Press, 2000), 135.

[6] Wolfgang Bluedorn (*Yahweh versus Baalism: A Theological Reading of the Gideon–Abimelech Narrative*, ed. David J. A. Clines and Philip R. Davies, JSOTSup 329 [Sheffield: Sheffield Academic Press, 2009], 189) speaks of Gideon marrying a "foreign" woman, assuming that her Shechemite provenance casts her as such. Similarly, K. Lawson Younger (*Judges, Ruth*, rev. ed., NIVAC [Grand Rapids: Zondervan, 2020], 269) argues that her foreign status is a "clear inference" in the text, and would thus render her family—which seems to have significant influence in the city (9:3)—Canaanite as well. That Shechem is never explicitly described as conquered by Israel is noteworthy; however, it is declared a Levitical city and a city of refuge (Josh 20:7, 21:21). In fact, Trent C. Butler (*Judges*, WBC 8 [Nashville: Thomas Nelson, 2009], 196) rightly highlights that "Moses expected Israel to be able to worship near Shechem (Deut 11:29; 27:4). Even with no narrative of conquest there, Joshua took Israel to Shechem for covenant ceremonies (Josh 8:30–34; 24)."

treats it as a Canaanite enclave in Manasseh, especially not after Jacob's children destroyed it (Gen 34).»[7] Five textual cues must be considered in determining the relevance of the portrayal of Shechem for discussing the characterization of Israel.

First, that the settlement was mixed is likely, based on the partial success of Israelite conquest in the period (3:5–6). Given this proclivity, the narrator's lack of clear distinction between the two peoples fits the book's claim that Israel "dwelt among" the Canaanites.[8] The difficulty with which interpreters determine the ethnic makeup of the city reflects the blurred boundaries characteristic of Israel and the nations in the book of Judges.

Second, in 8:33, the narrator explains that *Israel* "made Baal-berith their god." While Baal-Berit is almost certainly a preexisting Canaanite deity, the explicit textual association of Israel with the local Shechemite deity increases the likelihood that Abimelek's maternal relatives could be Israelite, given the financial support that same deity's temple provided them only six verses later (9:4).

Third, the text reports that the leaders of Shechem (9:3; בעלי שכם) made Abimelek their king. However, it also says that he "ruled (שרר) over Israel three years" (9:22).

Fourth, perhaps most importantly, when in 9:16–20 Jotham addresses those who enthroned Abimelek, he reminds them that his father fought for them, risked his life for them, and even delivered (נצל) them from the hand of Midian. The object of God's deliverance in the book of Judges has consistently been the people of Israel, and the Gideon story gives no indication of a break from that pattern. While the exact ancestry of Abimelek's maternal relatives remains shrouded, the collective leaders of Shechem identified in 9:6 and addressed by Jotham are equated literarily with those saved by Gideon, that is, the people of Israel. Jotham either recognizes that the two groups are the same or sees no reason to distinguish between the two groups, as they both saw fit to demonstrate loyalty to Abimelek.[9]

Fifth, in the same way that 9:22 extended Abimelek's reign beyond Shechem to Israel, so also does 9:55 characterize participants in the local conflict as "men of Israel" (איש־ישראל). Consistent with the style of earlier chapters, the text buttresses statements of a tribal or local nature with the

---

[7] Jack M. Sasson, *Judges 1–12: A New Translation with Introduction and Commentary*, AB 6D (New Haven: Yale University Press, 2014), 390.

[8] Robert B. Chisholm Jr., *A Commentary on Judges and Ruth*, Kregel Exegetical Library (Grand Rapids: Kregel Academic, 2013), 313.

[9] So opines Yairah Amit (*The Book of Judges: The Art of Editing*, trans. Jonathan Chipman, BibInt 38 [Boston: Brill, 1999], 107).

narratorial characterization of particular individuals as exemplars of Israel more broadly.[10]

Given these factors, one may reasonably assume that a significant number of the Shechemite people were Israelites and therefore contribute to the characterization of the people of Israel in the book of Judges. Even more directly, the text has signaled that at least a portion of those listening to Jotham were Israelites (9:16–20); therefore, Jotham's fable directed toward Shechem is central in an assessment of the cycle's portrayal of Israel.

Jotham's fable identifies five characters/groups: a group of trees (עֵצִים) who seek to anoint a king over themselves, three plants who reject the offer of kingship—namely, the olive tree (זַיִת), the fig tree (תְאֵנָה), and the vine (גֶּפֶן)—and the bramble (אָטָד), who responds conditionally to the trees' request. Jotham associates the trees with current events by having the conditional clauses of the fable mirror his own interpretive conditional clauses. Parallel syntax associates the trees with those who made Abimelek their king (who is consequently represented by the bramble):

9:15 "If in good faith you [trees] are anointing me [bramble] king over you"

9:16 "If you acted in good faith and integrity when you made Abimelek king"

The fable structure features a repetitious pattern of request and response. Three times—using an identical structure that varies only in terms of gender and accentuation—the trees entreat a variety of plants to act as their king. Their fourth and final request is similar, differing only in the addition of כֹּל to the subject and אֶל to the object.[11] The trees' lack of concern for previous rejections, as well as the disconnect between their stereotypical requests and the responses of the candidates, reflects an obstinate desire for a king that borders on the nonsensical. The pattern of the repetitious petitions, which are put to an end only by the questioning of the bramble and Jotham's

---

[10] Gordon K. Oeste, *Legitimacy, Illegitimacy, and the Right to Rule: Windows on Abimelech's Rise and Demise in Judges 9*, LHBOTS 546 (New York: T&T Clark, 2011), 111–12. The characterization is odd, considering that the text never defines the Shechemites' ancestry or tribal affiliation. Most helpfully, Amit (*Book of Judges*, 110 et passim) observes the parallel between "men of Israel" who showed allegiance to Abimelek during his lifetime and those who set out to anoint Gideon in 8:22.

[11] Such enhancements reflect a general pattern of "progression and intensification" on the level of morphology and grammar. Jan de Waard, "Jotham's Fable: An Exercise in Clearing Away the Unclear," in *Wissenschaft und Kirche: Festschrift für Eduard Lohse*, ed. Kurt Aland and Siegfried Meurer, Texte und Arbeiten zur Bibel 4 (Bielefeld: Luther-Verlag, 1989), 365.

interpretation, gives the impression that the trees' selection of their candidate lacks discernment.[12]

Because Abimelek is the central figure of the chapter, one might expect him to be the main character of the fable. To the contrary, the trees are the central figures in Jotham's speech. Not only are they the most consistent actors in the short vignette but they are also the intended recipients of Jotham's imperatives; the "leaders of Shechem" are the target of Jotham's address (9:7). While Abimelek seeks kingship for himself at the beginning of the chapter (9:2), Jotham presents the trees as relentlessly pursuing a king for themselves. Though Judges 9 does not characterize Abimelek's ascension this way, the wording of the Israelites' request in 8:22 is noteworthy: by seeking the rule of Gideon and his son (and grandson!), technically the Israelites had extended the offer of kingship to Abimelek earlier in the narrative. By characterizing Israel this way, Jotham emphasizes their culpability. *They* rose up against his father, *they* killed Gideon's sons, and *they* made Abimelek king. The effect of such an association is to hold the people responsible for the course of events.

Given the characterization of the Shechemites and the emphases of Jotham's fable, the portrayal of Israel in Judges 9 is internally consistent and programmatically significant: the people of Israel have chosen for themselves a disastrous ruler and have—more directly than ever before—effected their own suffering under an oppressor. Like Gideon at the time of his call, the people of Israel had neglected to credit YHWH with their deliverance and instead turned to human leaders for consolation and security. The people more easily associated victory with a human than the deity (8:22). Their determination to reject YHWH as deliverer and choose for themselves a ruler—a deliverer—begins with their request in 8:22 and is realized in the formal kingship of Gideon's son.

Following Abimelek's tragic end and a reference to two intervening Israelite leaders, the narrator once more remarks on the apostate behavior of YHWH's covenant people. The people fell into a familiar pattern of religious infidelity (they "again" did "the evil"), but with a renewed fervor that constitutes the climax of their literary portrait—they served the Baals and the Ashtaroth (cf. 3:7) alongside the gods of five other hostile territories. Thus, the Jephthah account begins in the pattern of the previous cycles, but with a major development in Israelite infidelity. At the book's midpoint, Israel's worship of Canaanite deities is not only institutionalized—as was emphasized in 8:27–35—but also comprehensive.

---

[12] Hanna Liss, "Die Fabel des Yotam in Ri 9,8–15: Versuch einer strukturellen Deutung," *BN* 89 (1997): 17.

The narrative also highlights Israel's suffering; the oppression of Israel is noted twice (10:8), as is the severity of the peoples' distress (v. 9; cf. 2:15). Given the distinctiveness of the narrative thus far, it is not surprising that Israel's superlative sin and severe suffering are here accompanied by an unparalleled cry for assistance—for the first time in the book of Judges, the narrator provides the content of Israel's cry for help. Moreover, for the first time, the people of Israel repented of their communal sin, using vocabulary that echoes the narrator's portrayal of them (they abandoned [עזב] and served [עבד]; see 10:10, cf. 10:6); the people have accurately interpreted their behavior and expressed a willingness to correct it. Even after YHWH's refusal to assist them, the people reformed their worship and returned to a more orthodox Yahwism (i.e., "they served YHWH"; v. 16). According to the book of Judges, Israel had never—and would never again—respond this way.

Thus at the outset of the Jephthah narrative, Israel's sin had reached its zenith just as YHWH's patience with the people had reached its end.[13] The divine speech culminating in verses 13–14 characterizes the people of Israel as those whom YHWH would rescue no longer. Given this new paradigm, the events of verses 17–18 follow naturally—Israelites assemble to appoint for themselves a new military leader. Like the Shechemites before them, the leaders of Gilead took the initiative to choose their own ruler (whose bramble-like qualities dominate his description). After making Jephthah their leader (קצין), the people are largely absent from the battle narrative. Only in the summary statement of 11:33 are the "people of Israel" relevant, and even here, they are merely beneficiaries of YHWH's action. The narrative mentions Israel corporately only once more—namely, in the explanation that daughters of Israel memorialized (תנה) Jephthah's daughter annually. In 11:40, the verbal root תנה is most often translated "lament,"[14] though the nature of the Israelites' attitude toward the fate of Jephthah's daughter is ambiguous, beyond the fact that the event was embedded in cultural memory. Of greatest relevance is the use of the same verb to describe the way the Israelites responded to the victory at the Kishon; according to Judges 5:11, after Deborah called for the people to tell of the victory (שיח; v. 10), the people responded by recounting (תנה) the righteous acts of YHWH and his militia. The repetition of such a rare root (occurring only five times!) invites comparison of the two texts and measures the degradation of the people's theological perspective. No longer did the people of

---

[13] For a discussion of the statement ותקצר נפשו בעמל ישראל in 10:16 and its contribution to the characterization of YHWH in the cycles section, see below, p. 115.

[14] So, NRSV, ESV, NLT, KJV; cf. Tanakh, "chant dirges." For the translation "commemorate," see NIV, NET.

Israel recount the victories of YHWH; instead, they recounted the devastating choices of a leader (whether in horror or complicity).[15]

The burgeoning tension between Ephraim and Gilead evident in the former's exchange with Gideon (8:1–3) resurfaces and comes to a head with the Gileadite leader, Jephthah, after the death of his daughter. In Judges 12, intratribal tension escalates to a military conflict resembling that of Israel and Ammon in the previous chapter; the narrative parallels cast the Ephraimites as a foreign nation, striving for dominance in a region not apportioned to them by YHWH.[16] Therefore, the words of the leader the Israelites chose for themselves have resulted in inner-Israelite violence on two counts: (1) in the sacrifice of Jephthah's daughter and (2) in the enormous scale of tribal slaughter—forty-two thousand Ephraimites fell at the hands of their Israelite kinsfolk.

Separated only by a short list of intervening leaders, the narrative portrayal of the Israelites shifts considerably between the stories of Jephthah and Samson. Chapter 13 begins with the familiar vocabulary of recurring Israelite transgression and oppression, but the corporate people of Israel is almost entirely absent from the next three chapters. In fact, the Israelites did not even cry out to YHWH as they had in every other instance of oppression. Many commentators opine that the people had accepted their fate at the hands of an occupying nation and implicitly condemn the people's lethargy.[17] Perhaps the people of Israel simply heeded the words of YHWH in the previous cycle; just as they understood that YHWH would not raise up a deliverer to save them from Ammon, so too they might have understood that they should direct their cries elsewhere, as the deity instructed (10:13–14). In either case, the absence of any cry for salvation characterizes Israel as hopelessly occupied by foreign invaders. Only four more times does the text mention Israel and in every case the reference is used for the development of another character: in 13:5, 15:20, and 16:31 the narrative identifies Samson as Israel's protector; in 14:4 the text emphasizes that the Philistines are ruling over Israel during Samson's lifetime. In all cases, Israel is simply a passive agent.

In lieu of references to corporate Israel, it is the Philistine people who dominate the narrative of Samson's personal life. Where an Israelite mate

---

[15] David Janzen, "Why the Deuteronomist Told about the Sacrifice of Jephthah's Daughter," *JSOT* 29 (2005): 348, who argues for complicity.

[16] Janzen, "Sacrifice of Jephthah's Daughter," 351–54, esp. 353.

[17] See, e.g., Daniel I. Block, *Judges, Ruth*, NAC 6 (Nashville: Broadman & Holman, 2001), 395; Robert B. Chisholm Jr., "What's Wrong with This Picture? Stylistic Variation as a Rhetorical Technique in Judges," *JSOT* 34 (2009): 177. This reading takes its exegetical cue from 15:11, in which Judah suggests that Samson's meddling with the Philistines is unnecessary and unhelpful.

is expected, Samson seeks a Philistine wife. The narrator emphasizes the impropriety of his choice through explicit criticism from Samson's parents (14:3) as well as the people of Judah (15:11–12), who received the brunt of Philistine retaliation for Samson's vindictive behavior toward his in-laws. While the Judahite speech does not address Samson's covenantal impropriety explicitly, it does link Samson's initial indiscretion to his vendetta and the raid on the Israelite settlement at Lehi. The narrator hints that YHWH will use Samson's poor choices to preserve his people, but Israel's relationship to Samson—YHWH's instrument of Philistine restraint—is strained throughout his lifetime. The few scenes involving interactions between Samson and Israelites thus contribute to the ongoing pattern of inner-Israelite tension.

Given these developments, the characterization of the Israelites in the cycles section, and the contribution of the Song of Deborah and Barak toward it, may be summarized as follows: The first three narrative cycles emphasize the people's change in circumstances through the mighty victory of YHWH, while the following two narratives (Judg 6–9) are concerned primarily with their apostate response to God's faithful deliverance. Positioned between these two sections, the Song of Deborah and Barak is transitional; it underscores the restoration of Israel by YHWH while introducing the evaluative scheme that dominates the remainder of the book. The song juxtaposes the evidentiary weight of the unprecedented victories of Jael over Sisera and Israel over Canaan (an emphasis characteristic of the first three narrative cycles) with the mixed response of Israel to YHWH's muster, interpreted in the song as a sign of covenant malpractice (an evaluative perspective prominent in the following narratives). The song functions like a linchpin in the characterization of Israel, complicating its otherwise monolithic portrayal and highlighting the budding trend of hesitancy in battle and irreverence for its Sovereign's battle cry. In relation to its near literary context, the song concretizes the evidence that warrants the reproof of the nameless prophet in 6:8–10—it makes abundantly clear that YHWH was Israel's champion and that his recent experiences with the Israelites were as mighty and miraculous as those experienced by past generations. When the ensuing narrative emphasizes Israel's blatant idolatry so soon after the victory over Midian—which the people attributed to Gideon rather than their God—and their disregard for YHWH's most recent salvific activity (8:34), the revelatory and inspirational function of the song for its implied audience is eclipsed by its narrative function as a "witness for [YHWH] against the Israelites" (Deut 31:19), who have evidently disregarded its message.

Israelite inability to recognize and appreciate YHWH's deliverance precipitates the rapid degradation that follows. The people's God gives them over to their covenant infidelity and a growing pattern of self-reliance. That pattern comes to a head in chapters 9–12, in which their attempts to effect deliverance for themselves result in perpetual violence and intertribal hostility. The corporate body of Israel begins to disintegrate, until the character is of little or no importance in the final narrative cycle.

The Saviors

The first narrative dedicated to YHWH's salvific exploits highlights the military campaign under Othniel, the son of Kenaz and younger brother of Caleb. His familial ties are inspiring and hopeful—Caleb's affiliation with the Joshua generation casts him in an approving light from the perspective of Judges, which is echoed and expanded in the broader canon (e.g., Deut 1:36; Josh 14:8). Contrary to popular construal, the Othniel narrative does little more to extol the exemplary characteristics of its deliverer. While interpreters observe correctly that the pericope lacks a negative evaluation of Othniel,[18] few attend to the absence of narrative cues to evaluate the effectiveness of the leader at all. Instead, Judges 3:7–11 mirrors the form, syntax, and vocabulary of 2:11–19, in which *Israel* is evaluated. Ultimately, Othniel is praised neither for his achievements nor his faithfulness to YHWH; instead, Othniel is the efficacious instrument of Israel's deity, who graciously saves his people from their distress. The oscillation between YHWH and Othniel as active agents reflects this: it is YHWH who raises up the deliverer who saves (3:9), YHWH's spirit who empowers the leader who effectively judges and goes to battle (v. 10), and ultimately YHWH who delivers Cushan-Rishathaim into the hands of his agent (v. 10).[19]

The death of Othniel begins the customary cycle in which Israel's apostasy requires punishment and deliverance, the latter at the hand of a leader raised up by YHWH. Like Othniel, Ehud is explicitly designated as that savior (מושיע; v. 15). Unlike Othniel, the text introduces Ehud by more than his redemptive function and tribal affiliation; he is an איש אטר יד־ימינו—a man "bound in his right hand." While some have interpreted the designation as a weakness or physical disability,[20] the phrase more likely emphasizes Ehud's dexterity, skill in battle, and his deftness for the task before him. Twice the Hebrew Bible

---

[18] Robert H. O'Connell, *The Rhetoric of the Book of Judges*, VTSup 63 (Leiden: Brill, 1996), 83, is representative.

[19] Chisholm (*Judges and Ruth*, 167–68, 171) notes the primacy of the deity in the account.

[20] E.g., Jon Alberto Soggin ("'Ehud und 'Eglon: Bemerkungen zu Richter 3:11b–31," *VT* 39 [1989]: 96–97) suggests Eglon seems harmless because he is crippled. Also Schneider, *Judges*, 49; Heinz-Dieter Neef, "Eglon als 'Kälbermann'? Exegetische Beobachtungen zu Jdc 3:12–30," *VT* 59 (2009): 286.

characterizes left-handed (or ambidextrous) warriors from Benjamin as some kind of an elite military force (Judg 20:16; 1 Chr 12:2).[21] Ehud's restraint in using his right hand, then, is not "peculiar and unnatural,"[22] nor a narrative symbol of his inferiority. Ehud's dexterous divergence signals that he is an irregular Benjamite, and consequently, the perfect instrument for Israelite deliverance.

Ehud's encounter with the king is narrated in great detail. His deceptive approach to killing the enemy leader in court (rather than on the battlefield) has turned Ehud into a questionable assassin in recent literature. Wong has most effectively argued for interpreting Ehud's actions negatively, based on the literary parallels between the deliverer's military techniques and those of Joab in 2 Samuel. He concludes that "presenting Joab as a latter-day Ehud" implies that some aspects of Ehud's actions "were also viewed negatively by the author of the Joab accounts," especially in terms of his deception.[23] Sasson, however, highlights the novelty of such readings: "Until recently the story of Ehud was read as yet another account of God motivating his elect to complete his will."[24] Sasson's appraisal of the story's traditional interpretation is in line with the lack of textual evaluation of the deliverer. As with Jael after him, Ehud's struggles and motivations do not interest the narrator, nor is his relationship with YHWH ever tested through prophetic challenge or a narrative complication.[25] To the contrary, Ehud is said to be raised up by YHWH as a savior (a title only shared by Othniel), completed his appointed

---

[21] Baruch Halpern, *The First Historians: The Hebrew Bible and History* (San Francisco: Harper & Row, 1988), 41, was influential in highlighting these parallels. Song-Mi Suzie Park, "Left-Handed Benjaminites and the Shadow of Saul," *JBL* 134 (2015): 701–20, is a more recent proponent of this reading.

[22] Lillian R. Klein, *The Triumph of Irony in the Book of Judges*, JSOTSup 68 (Sheffield: Almond, 1988), 37.

[23] Gregory T. K. Wong, "Ehud and Joab: Separated at Birth?" *VT* 56 (2006): 405, 410. Wong's conclusion requires (1) that both assassinations in 2 Samuel are interpreted as inappropriate, (2) that combining evidence from two assassinations to establish the literary parallel is methodologically sound, and (3) that the literary parallels imply ethical congruence, rather than a contrast or literary foil. In "Ehud: Assessing an Assassin," *BSac* 168 (2011): 280–82, Chisholm addresses the third assumption and argues for a literary contrast between the characters. Mary Conway (*Judging the Judges: A Narrative Appraisal Analysis*, LSAWS 15 [University Park, Pa.: Eisenbrauns, 2020], 98) offers one such (oft-neglected) element of contrast, namely, that Eglon was a foreign oppressor rather than an Israelite.

[24] Jack M. Sasson, "Ethically Cultured Interpretations: The Case of Eglon's Murder (Judges 3)," in *Homeland and Exile: Biblical and Ancient Near Eastern Studies in Honour of Bustenay Oded*, ed. Gershon Galil, Mark Geller, and Alan Millard, VTSup 130 (Leiden: Brill, 2009), 571.

[25] O'Connell, *Rhetoric of the Book of Judges*, 84–85.

task with apparent ease, led his people to military victory, and did so claiming that YHWH was responsible for the victory (3:28). With these last narrative details, the oddities of the Moabite king's death are overshadowed by a straightforward conquest-era battle report: Ehud calls up the Israelite militia (in this case from Ephraim), leads them into battle, successfully repossesses the fords of the Jordan, and completely annihilates the foreboding army of Moab[26]—all in the name of the God of Israel.

After a note about a second deliverer in a separate conflict—that of Shamgar against the Philistines—the narrative turns to the Kishon battle. Two protagonists are cast as deliverers; at different points in the narrative God gives the enemies of Israel "into the hands of" Barak (4:14) and Jael (4:9). Despite the obedient actions of Barak and his participation in the battlefield victory, the textual weight is on Jael's act of deliverance. In fact, the text portrays Jael, like Ehud, as a very effective instrument of YHWH. Like Ehud, Jael accomplishes her task without plot complications or commentary. Moreover, the similarity of the characters' actions is heightened by a series of literary parallels (table 2).[27]

Table 2: Lexical Parallels in the Descriptions of Ehud and Jael

	Ehud	Jael
Deceptive Invitation	3:19–20	4:18
Solitude	3:19	4:18
Sequence of Stabbing	3:21 (יד + לקח + תקע)	4:21 (לקח + יד + תקע)
Aftermath Witnessed	3:25 (הנה + נפל + מת)	4:22 (הנה + נפל + מת)

As I argued in the last chapter, the narrative of Judges 4 construes Jael as one removed from the battle geographically, socially, and politically; she was a civilian and an outsider. The aforementioned semantic parallels between the actions of Ehud and Jael, however, elevate her role as a deliverer of Israel. The literary juxtaposition of the two deliverers then highlights the similarity of their actions despite the disparity in their presumed societal roles.[28] The tent-dwelling wife of Heber the Kenite is just as effective a divine instrument as a Benjamite warrior. Like those of Ehud, the actions of Jael require a witness;

---

[26] On the interpretation of the adjective שמן as "foreboding," see below pp. 101–2.

[27] Chisholm, *Judges and Ruth*, 196–97; Elie Assis, "Man, Woman and God in Judg 4," *SJOT* 20 (2006): 116–17.

[28] In reference to Jael, Richard D. Nelson (*Judges: A Critical and Rhetorical Commentary* [New York: Bloomsbury T&T Clark, 2017], 80) aptly speaks of "deviations from the socially conventional" and YHWH, who "maneuvers ways to use the underdog and the trickster—so beloved of folktales—to deliver Israel."

however, the scene in Jael's tent is witnessed not by two officials of a foreign nation (cf. 3:25) but by a general from Israel—Barak, the second agent of deliverance. Within the narrative world, something in Jael's actions is worthy of observation by an Israelite leader.

Judges 5 testifies to the observational benefit of Jael's actions for the people of Israel. Jael is highlighted as "blessed among women" for her unexpected contribution to the victory. In fact, the psalmic emphasis on Jael's lack of security or military prowess, alongside the societal expectation (voiced by Sisera's household in 5:30) that she would be subdued and treated as plunder, stresses the disparity between perceived weakness and divine empowerment that is thematically central to the song.

The magnitude of Jael's role in Israel's deliverance is heightened by Barak's secondary function in the psalmic presentation of the battle. The song attributed to him twice briefly mentions his military leadership (5:12, 15), but Jael's role is far more prominent. In focusing on the deliverer Jael, rather than the military leader Barak, the song repeats the narrative assertion that Jael's action was the central instrument of YHWH's salvation, thereby distancing the concept of deliverer from the office of judge and military leader, which were associated with deliverance in the previous two narrative cycles (cf. 3:9–10, 15). By the end of chapter 5, YHWH's role as one who enables deliverance—by whatever means—is center stage.

The character development of the early deliverers may be summarized as follows: in the first three narrative cycles, the characterization of the deliverer is relatively flat; the narrator is most interested in the effectiveness with which they complete their task. The Song of Deborah and Barak expounds on this narrative trajectory by highlighting YHWH's providential empowerment of his people and the decisiveness of Jael's victory over Sisera. The prophetic rendition correlates Jael's situation with that of Israel and thus presents her role in deliverance as evidence that the divinely empowered militia is fit to face even the strongest foe. Toward this rhetorical end, the song introduces the first hint of evaluative commentary about a deliverer: Jael is "most blessed." It is good—blessed!—to faithfully act as YHWH's chosen instrument. In contrast to its treatment of those who neglected to come to YHWH's aid, the song celebrates Jael as one who participated in the deity's purposes. Therefore, Judges 5 characterizes the most recent savior as an effective instrument like Othniel and Ehud before her, with the additional note that her effectiveness was societally unexpected.

The simplicity of the portrayal of deliverers in the first three military conflicts stands in sharp relief to that of Gideon, for whom the narrator breaks decidedly from the early pattern of nonevaluative presentation. First, in Gideon the narrator presents a "round" or "full-fledged" character, whose inner life, theological convictions, and point of view are central to the narrative.[29] Up to this point, each deliverer was typified by no more than one or two traits related intricately to major plot developments (e.g., Ehud as left-handed warrior, Jael as non-Israelite civilian), with little attention given to the protagonist's inner life, but the portrayal of Gideon contrasts with the established norm. In the form of narration, chapters 6–7 record Gideon's intentions (6:11), mental perception (6:22), emotions (6:27; 7:10), and religious response (7:15). Through extensive dialogue, the text reveals Gideon's interpretation of YHWH's recent action (or lack thereof) in Israel's history—a perspective opposite to that of the prophet's earlier song. In fact, Gideon's most argumentative interaction with YHWH is literarily so near to the Song of Deborah and Barak that it renders condemnatory Gideon's initial exclamation to YHWH's messenger:[30] "If YHWH is with us, why then has all this happened to us? And where are all his wonderful deeds that our fathers recounted to us, saying, 'Did not YHWH bring us up from Egypt?'" (6:13). Gideon's inability to register God's salvific efforts in history, so recently recounted in Exodus-like imagery by *two* prophets, demonstrates his failure to heed the evidence of divine empowerment provided to him through divine council. Instead, every one of Gideon's exchanges with YHWH or his messengers is marked by incredulity.

Second, whereas the narrator had been content to evaluate unequivocally only Israel's faithfulness in previous narratives, his robust portrayal of Gideon culminates with a negative evaluation of the deliverer himself: Gideon's gold ephod became a "snare" to him and his family (8:27; מוקש). The book's fourth deliverer is thus the first figure to realize the divine messenger's proclamation that the gods of the land's inhabitants would become a "snare" to the people of Israel (2:3; מוקש). The characterization of a man whose inaugural act of leadership was the destruction of pagan altars (6:25–27; cf. 2:3, "you shall break down their altars") concludes with a clear literary indication that he is the prototypical example of an Israelite embarking on the journey of unfaithfulness. Gideon embodies the

---

[29] Adele Berlin (*Poetics and Interpretation of Biblical Narrative*, BLS 9 [Winona Lake, Ind.: Eisenbrauns, 1994], 23, 32) opts for the vocabulary of "full-fledged characters" over against "round characters" to distinguish more clearly between three character types and their respective functions in biblical narrative: full-fledged characters (i.e., round); types (i.e., flat); and agents (flatter still). According to Berlin, rather than being "built around a single quality or trait," as is a type, a full-fledged character is "more complex, manifesting a multitude of traits"—traits "not all belonging to the same class of people."

[30] The narrator attributes speech interchangeably to a messenger and YHWH in the section (6:12, 14, 16, 20–21, 23); both the narrator and Gideon recognize that the conversation is of divine origin and carries divine authority.

downward trajectory predicted by YHWH's messenger: a movement from destroying the strongholds of Canaanite religion to embracing its ensnaring influence.[31] The literary cues of additional character breadth and evaluative detail rhetorically re-center the reader's attention upon the deliverer; for the first time in the book of Judges, the deliverer—in all of his or her complexity, not merely instrumental typification—is the centerpiece of the cycle.

By providing detail about Gideon's theological convictions and inner life, the narrator not only characterizes him as a transitional figure exemplifying Israel's sharp descent into unfaithfulness but also explores the process by which the reversal took place. The budding hesitancy characterizing Barak's response to Deborah's muster is surpassed by Gideon's bold-faced incredulity and unapologetic fear when faced with the challenge to deliver God's people and the assurance of YHWH's empowerment. His initial exchange with the messenger of YHWH ties his unbelief to an inability to recognize the deity's salvific efforts in the generations following Joshua, the very divine exploits underscored by the first three cycles. Thus the narrator's depiction of Gideon connects the introduction's emphasis on religious apostasy with the Song of Deborah and Barak's emphasis on hesitancy in battle as a sign of covenant infidelity. In Gideon readers initially observe an Israelite convinced of his own weakness, unsure of YHWH's strength, and consequently afraid to respond unconditionally; later, they see a leader whose lack of appreciation for (and response to) YHWH's repeated deliverance leaves him vulnerable to misunderstanding his own calling and susceptible to the religious influence of Baalism.

The legacy of Gideon is the institutionalization of Canaanite religion among "all Israel" (8:27), the setting out of which an oppressor arose from within the deliverer's own family and terrorized the nation for three years.[32] Deliverance is hardly the emphasis in the ensuing narrative; instead, the text focuses on YHWH's condemnation of and retribution upon the oppressor. The deliverer is unnamed and her deed summarized in only two verbal clauses: a woman threw an upper millstone on his head and crushed his skull. No name, familial affiliation, or personal details detract from the character's significance as a woman—a noncombatant wielding an instrument of domestication, not war. Like Jael, the typification of the woman as a nonmilitary opponent is essential to demonstrating the ease with which the God of Israel deposes those who oppose him. Unlike the case of Jael, the woman's actions are neither detailed nor presented with attention to their efficacy; to the contrary, Abimelek's armor-bearer must finish the job she began (9:54). Whereas

---

[31] Daniel I. Block, "Will the Real Gideon Please Stand Up? Narrative Style and Intention in Judges 6–9," *JETS* 40 (1997): 365.

[32] On the portrayal of Abimelek as an oppressor of Israel, see below, p. 106.

chapter 4 emphasized YHWH's ability to effect victory through any entity he deems appropriate, chapter 9 emphasizes the negative light such a death sheds upon the oppressor. That the woman's actions would be perceived as shameful to the Shechemite monarch is the culminating element of her character development.[33]

The deliverance of Israel from Abimelek did not bring peace to the land; instead, the men of Israel simply returned to their homes after having witnessed YHWH's judgment upon their most recent oppressor. Tola followed as Israel's next deliverer, who "arose to save Israel" from unspecified subjugation. As is the pattern with noncyclical leaders (see, e.g., 3:31), the narrator does not credit YHWH with Tola's rise to power. The text also mentions Jair the Gileadite, though deliverance is not explicitly part of his brief textual portrait.

YHWH's ensuing rebuke of Israel initiates a new era in the period of the judges, in which the deity would no longer effect decisive victory for his people through the efforts of a deliverer. After YHWH claims as much at the beginning of chapter 10, the textual introduction of Jephthah confirms the pattern—according to the narrator, YHWH did not raise up the next leader of Israel, nor is there any claim (in narration or dialogue) that anyone would save (נצל/ישׁע) Israel. Instead, the Israelites called upon Jephthah to "*begin* to fight" (10:18; לחם + חלל) the Ammonite invaders. By initiating the narrative this way, in its characterization of him the text portrays Jephthah as one whom the people called upon after YHWH refused to provide a deliverer for them. A short note about Jephthah's qualifications for service (11:1; גבור חיל) illuminates why the leaders of Gilead turned to him.[34] The people's initiative in choosing a leader is the first in a string of personal details about Jephthah that recall those of Abimelek. As in the case of the violent Shechemite monarch, Jephthah's matriarchal origins were questionable and eventually led to tension between the individual and his half-brothers. In both episodes, the men surrounded themselves with "worthless" types (11:3, cf. 9:4; ריק).[35] Finally, the goals of both leaders were far removed from (if not contrary to) YHWH's program of deliverance. Despite Jephthah's acknowledgement that salvation comes from YHWH alone, the narrator's detailed introduction of him as an estranged kinsman

---

[33] With this narrative detail, the theme of shame that was (arguably) minimal in chapter 4 is maximal to the retributive motif that drives the narrator's portrayal of Abimelek. To emphasize the perceived shamefulness of a leader's death at a woman's hands is consistent with the emphasis in chapter 9 on retributive justice and the humiliation of the oppressor.

[34] Elie Assis, *Self-Interest or Communal Interest: An Ideology of Leadership in the Gideon, Abimelech and Jephthah Narratives (Judg 6–12)*, trans. Stephanie Nakache, VTSup 106 (Leiden: Brill, 2005), 193.

[35] Schneider, *Judges*, 164–65.

to the Gileadites reveals a secondary motive for his acceptance of their offer, that is, to be reintegrated with them as their leader (11:7–11). The textual suggestion of Jephthah's self-interest recalls Abimelek, who had no interest in saving Israel at all; in fact, he committed violence against fellow Israelites to gain power for himself.[36] Therefore, in personal background and motivation (though certainly not in his military program) Jephthah resembles a recent oppressor of Israel, whom the people of Israel installed over themselves; once more, one might say, in 11:6 the trees approached some bramble: לכה והייתה לנו לקצין (cf. 9:14: לך אתה מלך־עלינו).

Jephthah's first act as leader (ראש) of the Gileadites was to dispatch a diplomatic envoy to the Ammonite king. Their exchange spans sixteen verses (vv. 12–27), the bulk of which contain Jephthah's account of the checkered history of Ammon with Israel. This is the second of four dialogues between Jephthah and another party, wherein the "real dramatic interest of each episode is centered."[37] The clearest element of the characterization of Jephthah is that he is one who speaks. Not only do his words constitute the most significant element of every vignette in which he features but the narrative also highlights the thematic import of his speech through word play and lexical repetition. Webb describes two lexical signals that complement the narrative significance of Jephthah's dialogues: (1) emphasis on the words of Jephthah (11:10, 11, 28); and (2) the description of Jephthah's vow by him and his daughter in terms of "opening (פתח) [his] mouth to YHWH," a clause playing on the verbal root whence the name Jephthah comes (i.e., יפתח, "he opens").[38] The disastrous effects of Jephthah's speech color the remainder of his textual portrait.

Only the narrative cue that YHWH "gave [the Ammonites] into [Jephthah's] hand" (11:32; cf. 3:10; 4:9, 14; 7:9, 15) confirms that his role is comparable to that of previous deliverers—the textual deemphasis on the success of his actions notwithstanding. The Ammonite military skirmish occupies only three verses of two and a half chapters; by contrast, the rest of the narrative surrounds the violence Jephthah carried out against other Israelites—both Ephraim and his own daughter. In both conflicts, the narrative leverages Jephthah's previous words to highlight his role as an agent of violence against

---

[36] This commonality is central to the argument in *Self-Interest or Communal Interest*, 198–99, in which Assis also draws parallels between the calls of Gideon and Jephthah.

[37] Barry G. Webb, *The Book of Judges: An Integrated Reading*, JSOTSup 46 (Sheffield: JSOT, 1987), 73–74. Webb continues, "It follows that if the story has a major theme, these dialogues are likely to bear very directly upon it."

[38] Barry G. Webb, *The Book of Judges*, NICOT (Grand Rapids: Eerdmans, 2012), 341–42.

his own kinsmen. In the case of his daughter, Jephthah attempts to ensure victory for himself through a vow to the deity that results in the sacrifice of his firstborn. While debate persists about the intentions of Jephthah in making the vow and what leeway, if any, the law permitted him in the manner of its fulfillment, the story still portrays an Israelite leader offering a child sacrifice—a custom acceptable only in foreign rites of worship.[39] In the case of his conflict with Ephraim, Jephthah's description of the Ammonite/Israelite conflict (11:15–27) offers a characterization parallel to that of Ephraim/Gilead and provides a narrative lens through which to interpret their actions like those of foreigners. In the midst of the heated exchange with Jephthah, Ephraim's aggressive claims related to Gileadite inheritance provide the grounds for his army's slaughter of forty-two thousand Ephraimites. Thus, the book's sixth narrative cycle portrays Jephthah as a leader befitting the nation who chose him, a nation left to its syncretistic devices. Unlike Jael or Ehud, whose deeds inspired confidence in the power of YHWH, Jephthah's victory over *foreign* oppressors is overshadowed by the tragedy of a pagan child sacrifice and the ensuing battle against *internal* aggressors.

With no mention of rest for the land following deliverance, the text notes only that Jephthah functioned as a judge in Israel for six years. Never credited with achieving complete peace for his people or being raised up by YHWH, once more Jephthah's example distances the office of judge from the theological category of deliverer. The same is true of Ibzan, Elon, and Abdon, each of whom led the people for a relatively short period of time before their death. Their textual portraits lack any reference to military activity or YHWH's deliverance by their hands. The text's silence regarding YHWH's pattern of deliverance does not indicate that the people were not in need of salvation; to the contrary, 13:1 shows that the pattern of apostasy and foreign oppression continued, even when YHWH stopped raising up deliverers.

In contrast to the relatively anthropocentric account of Jephthah's leadership in Israel, the narrative featuring Samson begins under the most auspicious circumstances—a messenger of YHWH visited a barren women, promising her a child who would "begin to save" Israel (ישע + חלל; v. 5). With most interpreters, I read the clause as an explicit indication that the deity would not completely rescue his people from Philistine oppression by the hand of Samson.[40] While this clause, along with the divine pronouncement of 10:11–14

---

[39] By contrast, Solomon Landers ("Did Jephthah Kill His Daughter?" *BRev* 7 [1991]: 28–31, 42) argues that Jephthah never sacrificed his daughter but perhaps dedicated her to ritual service.

[40] Klein (*Triumph of Irony*, 116) is representative when she argues the type scene "raises the highest level of expectation by virtue of the theophanic visit." Her treatment

and the presence of the Philistines in Canaan long into the monarchic period, precludes any expectation of complete military victory, prior to Samson's birth a divine intermediary identifies the Danite as one of YHWH's instruments of deliverance, or, perhaps more accurately, an agent of the people's preservation who would contribute to the security of Israel.

The mode through which Samson will participate in Israel's deliverance differs drastically from that of any of Israel's previous leaders. Despite the repeated notice that Samson judged Israel (15:20, 16:3), he neither led a militia nor mustered the people to his cause; instead, Samson's pursuit of his own affairs utterly alienated him from his kinsmen.[41] Considering this focus on Samson's autonomy, the degree to which he understood himself to be YHWH's agent of deliverance is unclear. In his conversation with Delilah, Samson shows awareness of his Nazirite call, but the only indication that he may have also considered himself a deliverer is his prayer in 15:18, in which Samson identifies himself as the means through which YHWH has effected victory: "You have given by the hand (ביד) of your servant this great salvation (תשועה)." However, his pious words are conspicuous considering Samson's anthropocentric (if not narcissistic) summary of the same slaughter two verses earlier: "With the jawbone of a donkey have I struck down a thousand men."[42]

While the text notes that Samson's exploits have national ramifications beyond the understanding of certain characters (14:4), the account of his aggression toward the Philistines frames the judge's motivations as personal and trivial. Samson's self-centeredness thus eclipses that of Jephthah, whose implied self-interest in accepting the Gileadites' request at least involved his reintegration into tribal life and the preservation of Israel in the midst of an external occupation. By contrast, the narrator explicitly catalogues and highlights the pettiness of Samson's motivations: physical attraction (14:3, 7); vengeance (14:18–19, 16:28); retribution (15:3–5, 7–8, 11); personal welfare (15:18); and annoyance (16:16). His brazen self-indulgence results in his alienation from Philistines and Israelites alike—the very autonomy that gives the story its strange shape.[43]

Given such insight into his inner life and personal relationships, Samson is a full-fledged character, whose personal perspective is as essential to his

---

details the elements of the Judges scene that correspond to those of earlier Israelite matriarchs.

[41] Gerhard von Rad, *The Theology of Israel's Historical Traditions*, vol. 1 of *Old Testament Theology*, trans. D. M. G. Stalker, OTL (Louisville: Westminster John Knox, 2001), 333.

[42] Block, *Judges, Ruth*, 447.

[43] James A. Freeman, "Samson's Dry Bones: A Structural Reading of Judges 13–16," in *Literary Interpretations of Biblical Narratives*, vol. 2, ed. Kenneth R. R. Gros Louis (Nashville: Abingdon, 1982), 156.

character development as his role as the deity's instrument of provocation. Interpreters have long perceived these details as an indictment of Samson's inability to deliver (or judge) effectively, focusing especially on his failure to uphold his Nazirite vow.[44] Surely this negative assessment is warranted; however, this reading of the narrative overlooks one key narrative element: Samson accomplishes everything YHWH claimed he would; he provoked a conflict with the Philistines and "began" to save Israel (13:5; 14:4).[45] While Samson did not deliver Israel in the manner of the earlier judges, according to the divine pronouncement of 10:13, YHWH—not Samson—was responsible for this outcome. Moreover, how consistently the text emphasizes Samson's failure to uphold his Nazirite status is unclear, with the exception of the scene in which his hair is cut.[46] The narrator more consistently correlates Samson's incredible abilities and divine empowerment: (1) the Spirit facilitates the majority of Samson's extraordinary feats (13:25; 14:6, 19; 15:14), (2) YHWH answers Samson's prayers for his preservation (15:18–19, 16:28–30), and (3) Samson's strength is associated with ceremonial dedication to YHWH (i.e., as a Nazirite; 13:5, 16:17–20). Samson's great strength is consistently and emphatically of divine origin.[47] To attend to YHWH's strengthening on the one hand, and Samson's moral failings on the other (especially the stereotypical Israelite sin of marrying foreign women; cf. 3:6), is to highlight the disparity between the Israelite's inherent ability to accomplish divine purposes and that supernaturally given by YHWH. Assis articulates this dynamic well:

> Samson's power is extraordinary, and the dependence of this power on his hair is extraordinary. But what happens if his miraculous power is taken away? Who is Samson now? Samson himself, without his special divine power, is not an ordinary man; he is an extraordinarily weak one.[48]

In short, in the last narrative cycle, the text portrays Samson as an agent of preservation who is entirely useless without the direct and constant control of YHWH. Through Samson, YHWH successfully instigates a conflict with

---

[44] E.g., von Rad, *Theology of Israel's Historical Traditions*, 333–34; Klein, *Triumph of Irony*, 117–18.

[45] Observed by Elie Assis, "The Structure and Meaning of the Samson Narratives (Jud. 13–16)," in *Samson: Hero or Fool? The Many Faces of Samson*, ed. Erik Eynikel and Tobias Nicklas, TBN 17 (Leiden: Brill, 2014), 2.

[46] Robert B. Chisholm Jr., "Identity Crisis: Assessing Samson's Birth and Career," *BSac* 166 (2009): 147–62.

[47] J. Cheryl Exum, "The Theological Dimension of the Samson Saga," *VT* 33 (1983): 37–40.

[48] See Assis, "Structure and Meaning of the Samson Narratives," 10, who builds his argument on Exum's insights.

Philistia whose resolution is delayed until the time of the monarchy; through his portrait of Samson, the narrator reiterates that all power to save is YHWH's.

With this final assessment of Samson, we may summarize a consistent trajectory in the characterization of the deliverers, of which the Song of Deborah and Barak is a crucial part. Judges 3:7–16:31 includes accounts of various military conflicts between Israel and the surrounding nations that YHWH instigated and carried out through agents of oppression and deliverance. The central portion of Judges does not simply evaluate the effectiveness of each military leader and document a downward turn in Israelite leadership. Arguably, the trajectory of characterization is more sophisticated and serves broader theological concerns. The first three deliverers are relatively flat characters whose faithfulness is not the narrative's primary interest; by contrast, they are cast as perfect instruments of YHWH, uniquely suited and empowered to complete conquest-related directives. In the prophetic song concluding the third narrative cycle, through the example of Jael, the deliverers' fitness for battle is leveraged to inspire confidence in the deity's ability to work with an inferior militia.

The introduction of Gideon as a full-fledged character breaks from this pattern; the narrative explores his inner life and theological perception. Gideon's incredulity regarding YHWH's salvific action in recent history—juxtaposed with the theological assessment of the recent prophetic song—demonstrates the inability of the Israelites to respond appropriately to their own salvation and explains the means by which the nation misunderstood the nature of military victory and came to reject YHWH. Through an increasingly unfavorable portrayal of Gideon and the entirely negative depiction of Abimelek, chapters 6–9 emphasize how the Israelites turned to their own strength and the gods of the other nations for deliverance, rather than to their covenant partner. This pattern of degradation precipitated a change in the divine program; as a result, the narratives of the next two judges highlight not their role in ensuring Israel's survival in Canaan but the fact that Israel and its leaders are only as effective as their divine endowment. What is clear positively in the portraits of Othniel, Ehud, Barak, and Jael, the narrator demonstrates negatively through the portrayal of Jephthah and Samson: an individual's—or an army's—abilities are negligible and irrelevant; their fidelity to YHWH is paramount. It is the Song of Deborah and Barak—particularly in its juxtaposition with the Gideon and Abimelek narratives—that initiates this shift in characterization.

The Oppressors

Judges 2:14 promises that YHWH's unfaithful people would be plagued by plunderers (שֹׁסִים) and enemies from the surrounding nations, whom Israel would be unable to withstand. Cushan-Rishathaim (king of ארם נהרים) is the first in this series of formidable opponents. Given the abbreviated style of Othniel's encounter with the foreign king, the text offers no further description, other than Othniel's triumph over him. The characterization of Cushan-Rishathaim, then, is entirely dependent upon his name (invoked four times in a pericope of five verses) and geographical affiliation. In reference to the former, commentators have consistently noted that the king is named "Cushan of Double Wickedness" or "Cushan the Doubly Wicked One," and most have claimed that the title is likely humorous, if not a pseudonym or contrived for the sake of caricature.[49] Younger extends the pejorative expression to the first half of the foreigner's name and renders it "dark, doubly wicked!"[50] This move toward abstraction, in which an antagonist is flattened into a representative of a particular category, is fitting for the narration style of the Othniel account. By such methods the abbreviated narrative effectively draws parallels between the particulars of this foreign occupation and the types of actions summarized in the similarly constructed introduction. With as few words as possible, the narrator has effectively identified Israel's opponent as a cruel and threatening oppressor.

The doubly wicked king challenging Othniel hailed from ארם נהרים—literally, Aram of the two rivers, or Mesopotamia (cf. Gen 24:10; Deut 23:4). The designation seems relatively straightforward. On one hand, interpreters have questioned the historical plausibility of a Mesopotamian king extending his influence as far as the land of Canaan, just as others have balked at the suggestion that an Israelite tribal leader could defeat such a formidable ruler.[51] It is this very unbelievability that makes the narrative so effective in its context; the overwhelming might of the enemy—represented by a military leader—is thematically central to the initial chapters of the book of Judges. With such an introduction, Cushan-Rishathaim has both set a thematic trajectory and provided evidentiary weight for the textual affirmation that Israel's militia—when acknowledging its covenant commitment to and empowerment by YHWH—is unbeatable.

The defeat of Cushan-Rishathaim gives way to rest and resurgent apostasy after the death of Othniel. Eglon, king of Moab, is the next oppressor whom YHWH brought against Israel. In 3:12, Eglon was "strengthened" (חזק) by

---

[49] See, e.g., Block, *Judges, Ruth*, 153; J. Clinton McCann Jr., *Judges*, IBC (Louisville: Westminster John Knox, 2002), 42.

[50] Younger, *Judges, Ruth*, 137.

[51] To the first, the strategic location of Palestine as an access point to Egypt strengthens the likelihood of Mesopotamian efforts in the area. Abraham Malamat ("Cushan Rishathaim and the Decline of the Near East around 1200 B.C.," *JNES* 13 [1954]: 231–42) uses this logic to associate Cushan-Rishathaim with a Syrian ruler who took power in Egypt at the end of the nineteenth dynasty.

YHWH for the task of invading Jericho and was thereby enabled to draw to his cause the Ammonites and Amalekites. The text thus presents Eglon as a well-allied opponent, well-suited to wreak havoc on a crucial Israelite holding. The degree to which the name "Eglon" sets an exegetical key for the remainder of the narrative has divided scholars in their reading. Robert Alter's description of Eglon represents an interpretive trend:

> The writer's imagination of the event is informed by an implicit etymologizing of Eglon's name, which suggests the Hebrew *'gel*, calf. The ruler of the occupying Moabite power turns out to be a fatted calf readied for slaughter, and perhaps even the epithet *bari*, "stout," is a play on *meri*, "fatling," a sacrificial animal occasionally bracketed with calf. Eglon's fat is both the token of his physical ponderousness, his vulnerability to Ehud's sudden blade, and the emblem of his regal stupidity.[52]

If Eglon's portrayal is comical and satirical as Alter contends, the narrator would have shifted his characterization of the enemies of Israel considerably from that of the formidable Mesopotamian opponent of the last cycle. In fact, the function of Eglon as YHWH's agent of testing Israelite fidelity is far less intimidating (and arguably, narratively ineffective) if the king's portrayal is so blatantly pathetic. The potential tension caused by the juxtaposition of such formidable opponents (including not only Mesopotamia but the well-armed Canaanites and innumerable Midianites) with a hilariously impotent one should give the reader pause; at this point, one must consider that animal names are not uncommon in the ancient Near East (for people and places) and may lack any pejorative nuance.[53]

After the brevity of the Mesopotamian king's description, Eglon's is surprisingly detailed. In verse 17, the narrator reports that the king was receiving tribute from Israel and was, consequently, healthy and well-fed (i.e., ברִיא). The adjective rendered "fat" in most English versions is the chief element of characterization lending credence to the aforementioned interpretation of Alter and others; however, to be well-fed does not necessarily signify "fattened" or "a perfect creature for sacrifice."[54] By contrast, the context of Eglon's "strengthening" by YHWH (v. 12) and the scene of tribute-offering suggests that he "is a successful king, grown healthy and prosperous on other

---

[52] Robert Alter, *The Art of Biblical Narrative* (New York: Basic Books, 1981), 39. In questioning whether עֵגֶל so straightforwardly connotes "fattened calf" without an additional modifier, Lawson G. Stone ("Eglon's Belly and Ehud's Blade: A Reconsideration," *JBL* 128 [2009]: 654) raises a pertinent objection.

[53] Consider Caleb: "dog." Interestingly, according to Josh 10:34–35, 12:12, Eglon is the name of a conquered Canaanite city.

[54] Phrases from Butler, *Judges*, 70.

people's offerings."⁵⁵ The king is—quite seriously—imposing, as are those in his army, who are described as robust and healthy (v. 29) in contrast to the presumably weaker Israelite rebels.⁵⁶ In short, Eglon and his forces are characterized as *strengthened*, both by regional alliances and tributary offerings. Eglon is living off the fat of the promised land.

Aside from noting Eglon's prime alliances and well-nourished frame, the narrator's portrayal of the Moabite monarch centers entirely on his death at Ehud's hand. Eglon presented no challenge to the deliverer's subterfuge; with every move he unknowingly facilitated Ehud's efforts to assassinate him. The murder itself is detailed and grisly—the assassin's knife was thrust so forcefully into Eglon's abdomen that the knife was lost altogether and only gore remained.⁵⁷ While the detail that "fat" closed over the blade has lent itself to the suggestion of Eglon's comic obesity, Stone rightfully notes that חלב is standard vocabulary for the internal mess that is spilled on the battlefield.⁵⁸ Decisively defeated and splayed upon the ground, Eglon's last appearance in the narrative is as a mutilated corpse. The unqualified defeat of the Moabite king is the first in a string of equally decisive victories by the Israelite militia over his forces, in which every single (strong and imposing) soldier is subdued (vv. 28, 29).

A brief note about Shamgar ben Anath mentions the defeat of another oppressor of Israel—namely, the Philistines. The text recalls no details of the conflict, save one—that six hundred of Israel's foes were defeated with a simple makeshift weapon. Like the narrative that precedes it, this short aside depicts an enemy of Israel as a victim of unexpected military force from an unbelievable source—one man with a nontraditional weapon.

Ehud's death in 4:1 once more precipitated Israelite infidelity met by YHWH's swift action. In the Kishon conflict, it was Jabin, king of Canaan, and his general, Sisera, who acted as YHWH's agents of oppression. The repeated

---

⁵⁵ James K. Aitken, "Fat Eglon," in *Studies on the Text and Versions of the Hebrew Bible in Honour of Robert Gordon*, ed. Geoffrey Khan and Diana Lipton, VTSup 149 (Leiden: Brill, 2012), 146. That the LXX (A–B) renders the king αστειος—"handsome"— supports such an interpretation.

⁵⁶ So also Sasson, "Ethically Cultured Interpretations," 575; Neef, "Eglon als 'Kälbermann'?" 288–89; and Stone, "Eglon's Belly and Ehud's Blade," 651. The description of Moabite soldiers—כל שמן וכל איש חיל—connotes able-bodied and strong men (*HALOT*, 1567). Jodi Magness, "Toilets and Toilet Humor in the Story of Eglon's Murder by Ehud (Judges 3:15–26)," *JBL* 142 (2023): 85, however, argues that these soldiers should *also* be considered obese.

⁵⁷ Michael L. Barré ("The Meaning of *pršdn* in Judges 3:22," *VT* 41 [1991]: 6–7) observes that the enveloping of the dagger by Eglon's insides shows the "physical force and determination with which Ehud acted."

⁵⁸ See, e.g., 2 Sam 1:22. Stone, "Eglon's Belly and Ehud's Blade," 652.

reference to Jabin recalls a similar opponent of days gone by, whose same iron chariots proved imposing to a previous generation in northern Canaan. Despite the prominence of the Canaanite king in the frame of Judges 4, Sisera embodies the role of Israel's cruel and well-armed oppressor for much of the Kishon battle account. While the Mesopotamian king was known for his wickedness, and the Moabite king for his military alliances and physical condition, Sisera and the forces of northern Canaan are characterized by their harsh tactics and superior weaponry. Given this strategic advantage, Sisera managed to oppress Israel longer than both Cushan-Rishathaim and Eglon (twenty years [4:3]; cf. eight [3:8] and eighteen years [3:14], respectively).

When Sisera relinquishes his chariot in 4:15, the text begins systematically to defy battlefield expectations and reveal the overturning of Jabin's regional dominance. His armament neutralized, Sisera's flight by foot provided the unprecedented occasion for Israel's God to use a civilian woman to take down Israel's most effective opponent. In a manner reminiscent of Eglon's death at Ehud's hands, Sisera presented no challenge to Jael's unimpeded acts of aggression. With no apparent struggle, Jael extinguished Sisera's life and his corpse became the central piece of evidence for the efficacy of YHWH's promise through Deborah. By this means, God subdued Jabin and empowered Israel to destroy utterly (כרת) the forces of northern Canaan.

This victory gives way to a responsive song in the voices of the prophet and the general. The initial verses of the Song of Deborah and Barak name the past and potential political rivals of Israel as witness to the prophet's message (5:3; מלכים . . . רזנים). While the psalm eventually identifies alternate addressees (cf. v. 10), the initial stanza reflects the expectation that a theologically astute exposition of the battle is useful to any who would challenge Israel. The bulk of the song characterizes the opposing army with the abstract terminology of "the mightiest of the people" (v. 13a) and the "warriors" (vv. 13b, 23). Here the song speaks of specific opponents using abstracted character traits that are consistent with the characterization of the oppressors in the first three narrative cycles: they are truly formidable foes. Even the specific designation "kings of Canaan" in verse 19 reinforces the abstracted, and thereby paradigmatic, quality of the depiction of the enemy in the first five stanzas. With the exception of its final section, the song recasts Israel's foes in terminology reminiscent of the book's introduction. Verse 19d is especially important in terms of the macroplot: "spoil of silver they did not take." The plunderers of Israel (cf. 2:14) are stripped of their most characteristic feature.

The sixth and seventh stanzas break from this pattern of abstraction by recounting the murder of Sisera and its aftermath. The poetic recounting of the tent scene and the havoc wreaked on Sisera's household capitalizes on gritty detail to highlight the decisiveness of Jael's unexpected victory over the Canaanite general. The lack of abstract vocabulary does not signal a compositional shift away from the archetypical quality of the oppressor's characterization; instead, the song uses commentary to convey the paradigmatic import of Sisera's detailed defeat in verse 31: "In this way, may all your enemies perish." One expects the pattern of military deliverance YHWH enacted through Jael over all enemies (v. 31) of Israel—enemies being any who refuse to show covenant loyalty (אהב) to Israel's God.

Therefore, the first three narrative cycles portray the oppressor du jour as a formidable opponent. In the skirmishes with Eglon and Jabin (Sisera), the text semantically emphasizes the initial fortitude of the foe and the systematic reversal of his power grip over Israel. In both narratives, the skill and effectiveness of his killer is of some interest to the narrator, but the slain foreign leader is more important; both narratives devote a scene to the slain corpse being witnessed by characters in the narrative world, first by officials of the foreign nation and subsequently by an Israelite general. Despite the readers' knowledge of events, the narrator provides certain characters an opportunity to process the death of a powerful leader within the narrative. In both cases, the death and defeat of the foreign monarch functions literarily as evidence of YHWH's ability to save: first to foreigners, and then to YHWH's own people. It is the Song of Deborah and Barak that solidifies and capitalizes on this narrative pattern. Fundamentally, the song offers the general and the prophet an opportunity to reflect on the theological significance of Israel's victory over an oppressor. These authoritative voices identify the manner of Sisera's demise as paradigmatic of YHWH's decisive defeat of Israel's enemies on the one hand and faithfulness to those committed covenantally to him on the other. Therefore, in the first three narrative cycles, the oppressors of Israel provide evidence of YHWH's power and dedication to deliver his people from any sort of foe: one wicked and threatening, another well-allied and well-fed, and one well-armed and geographically advantaged.

Given such a decisive statement of YHWH's ability to deliver his people from the mightiest of foes, the description of new Midianite oppressors is significant on two counts: First, the primary agent of destruction is the Midianite raiders, but the text mentions also the Amalekites and the "people of the East" (בני־קדם). Once more Israel met the Amalekite army who joined forces with Eglon; twice YHWH has used this historical foe of Israel to reinforce the occupying army (and thereby, the imposing nature of their literary portrayal).[59]

---

[59] The people of Amalek are descendants of Esau from the land of Edom (Gen 36:16), whom the Hebrew Bible consistently characterizes as Israel's most hostile enemy during the Exodus and wilderness wanderings (Exod 17:8–18; Num 14:39–45; Deut 25:17–19).

Second, while the period of Midianite occupation was much shorter than that of Israel's previous foes (seven years; 6:1), the account uses the imagery of locusts to show that the vast camel-riding host was not only innumerable but also exerted a devastating impact upon the landscape. No less than five verses (6:2–6) detail the agricultural and economic hardship exacted upon the starving Israelites—the most literary emphasis thus far dedicated to an enemy's occupation. The absence of singular Midianite rulers from these introductory statements reinforces the narrator's preoccupation with the size of the invading army. It is the abundance of Midianites, rather than their leader's cruelty (Cushan-Rishathaim), strength (Eglon), or weaponry (Sisera), that primarily characterizes the present foe of Israel.

A second prophet answers the cry of the people and offers further characterization of recent oppressors (לחציכם): they have been defeated and driven out in the manner of the Egyptians (6:10).[60] YHWH's message here juxtaposes the paradigmatic deliverance of the people's forefathers with the deliverances experienced in their own time and, significantly, in close literary proximity. The prophet's characterization of Israel's foes in 6:9 matches that of the narrator in the first three cycles: the oppressors of Israel are evidence of YHWH's power to save—exemplars in a pattern of the deity's might over the most formidable surrounding armies, beginning with the exodus. Whereas the prophet of the last cycle challenged the people through her song to view their oppressors as those defeated by YHWH, and respond to him with covenant fidelity, the next prophet rebukes them for not having done so.

The accounts of Gideon's call and preparation for battle focus on the Israelites and their leader. However, a short description of the waiting Midianite army recalls their earlier introduction by newly emphasizing their locust-like

---

That the severity of their opposition had particular theological (and historical) significance is implied by passages such as Exod 17:14–16 and 1 Sam 15:2–3. Gerald L. Mattingly, "Amalek (Person)," *ABD*, vol. 1, 169–71.

[60] Statements similar to that of the prophet envelop the Exodus narrative. Semantic and syntactical similarity draws the Exodus and Judges statements into comparison and highlights the deliberate addition of "all who oppressed you" (cf. 2:18) to the statement in 6:9, thus highlighting their most recent deliverances:

> Exod 3:8   "I have come down to deliver them from the hand of Egypt."
> Exod 18:9 Jethro rejoiced over all the good that YHWH had done for Israel, in that he had delivered them from the hand of Egypt.
> Exod 18:10 "Blessed be YHWH, who has delivered you from the hand of Egypt, and from the hand of Pharaoh, and has delivered the people from under the hand of Egypt."
> Judg 6:9   "I delivered you from the hand of Egypt *and from the hand of all who oppressed you*."

abundance (7:12). In short order these oppressors were defeated, down to the leaders of the army, who had been of little importance to this point. Just as the death of the enemy leader underscored the decisiveness of the earlier victories in the book, here two were captured, killed, and beheaded (7:25). Two additional heads of state—namely, the kings Zebah and Zalmunna—persisted in their flight and provided the inciting incident for the ensuing tension between Gideon and Ephraim that occupies the next chapter. While Judges 8 details the eventual defeat of these kings, the external oppressors become background to a more significant internal conflict. In fact, the priority of Gideon and his interactions with the Israelites throughout the narrative cycle is the first of several significant factors that suggest a larger narrative transition.

The ensuing narrative featuring Gideon's progeny presents an even more significant perspectival shift in the standard cyclical structure of the book's central section. While certain formal features hint that chapter 9 consists of its own narrative cycle,[61] the compositional move to highlight a figure who was clearly not a judge (i.e., Abimelek) puzzles interpreters. Moreover, the thematic foregrounding of YHWH's retributive justice contrasts with the patience and dedication the deity had shown to his people previously.[62] Assuming that the chapter is consistent with its present context and constitutes its own microplot (distinct from that of Gideon), Abimelek functions neither as a judge, a deliverer, nor a prophet; instead, the text characterizes Abimelek as oppressor of Israel.

To illustrate: after an extended description of the depths of Israelite idolatry after Gideon's death, at the narrative moment normally reserved for YHWH's agent of oppression, the text instead documents Abimelek's rise to power in Shechem.[63] In a move that privileges the perspective of the oppressor, a more extensive description of the events leading to Abimelek's crowning replaces the succinct statement of YHWH's facilitation of foreign occupation (i.e., "he sold [מכר] them into the hand of"; cf. 3:12). The most curious detail of the early characterization of Abimelek is the number of his murdered siblings, documented five times in the story—Gideon's son killed all seventy of his brothers (8:30; 9:2, 5, 18, 24, 56). While seventy may function simply as a round, symbolic number, it also opens an avenue of comparison between Abimelek and Adoni-Bezek, the first and paradigmatic Canaanite oppressor of

---

[61] On which, see p. 122.
[62] Webb, *Integrated Reading*, 158–59.
[63] In fact, the narrator explains Abimelek's relationship to Gideon in 8:29–31 and thereby avoids interrupting the sequence of (1) notice of sin (8:33–35) and (2) the rise of a king to rule over Israel (9:1–6), which is the pattern of the last four narrative cycles (cf. 3:7–8, 12; 4:1–2; 6:1–5).

the book of Judges, known for mutilating seventy kings.[64] This verbal parallel draws attention to a broader thematic one: divine retributive justice enacted upon the antagonist. Adoni-Bezek interpreted his mutilation by Judah as retribution for his own actions (1:7); similarly, the narrator interprets the fate of Abimelek as evidence that "God returned the evil of Abimelech, which he committed against his father in killing his seventy brothers" (9:56). Such explicit retributive vocabulary is consistent with the implicit retributive divine action enacted upon the book's earlier oppressors: the "hand" of Othniel prevailed over Cushan-Rishathaim, into whose "hand" YHWH had previous sold the people of Israel (3:8, 10); Israel "struck" (נכה) ten thousand Moabites, just as Eglon had "struck" them (3:13, 29); and finally, the "hand" of the people pressed severely upon Jabin's forces in the same way that they had suffered under his "hand" (4:2, 24). The Song of Deborah and Barak also brings retribution on Sisera to the fore through the juxtaposition of the general's victimization by a woman and the expectation of his household to have brought home women as plunder. Retributive justice, then, is present in each narrative cycle, but it merely serves a general theme of reversal. By contrast, in the Abimelek story the theme is developed into a full-throated, divinely facilitated, and perfectly appropriate revenge; the oppressor's demise in chapter 9 is more detailed and narratively justified than that of his literary forbears. Abimelek's death comes across as especially decisive.

YHWH's chosen medium of retribution for those who follow Abimelek derives from the fable uttered by Jotham, the sole survivor of his half-brother's fratricidal massacre: "All the evil of the men of Shechem God made to return on their heads, and the curse of Jotham the son of Jerubbaal came upon them" (9:57). While the fable ultimately criticizes the undiscerning trees, the fact that Abimelek was but one in a line of candidates—and clearly the worst candidate—casts him in a particularly dubious light. Many have noted a progression from the productive, prized olive tree to the lowly, thorny bramble, which is best suited as kindling for cooking (Ps 58:10[9]). That the esteemed plants of the ancient world wanted nothing to do with ruling over the trees suggests that the worthless bramble lacks wisdom that the other plants possess.

---

[64] For an account of the parallels between the narratives, see Gregory T. K. Wong, *The Compositional Strategy of the Book of Judges: An Inductive, Rhetorical Study*, VTSup 111 (New York: Brill, 2006), 204–6, though Wong is not the first to notice the similarities. See, e.g., Webb, *Integrated Reading*, 85, n. 14. For the argument that "seventy" is symbolic, see F. C. Fensham, "The Numeral Seventy in the Old Testament and the Family of Jerubbaal, Ahab, Panammuwa and Athirat," *PEQ* 109 (1977): 113–15. That the number may be symbolic does not rule out its potential broader narrative function.

As in the cases of Ehud and Sisera, the narrator's concluding description of Abimelek highlights YHWH's mastery over him (9:56); however, this account also includes a restatement of the deed for which the oppressor earned retribution—namely, the slaughter of his brothers. Whereas earlier cycles simply depicted Israel's external oppressors as pawns of YHWH, strengthened and disposed of according to his purposes, the text repeatedly highlights Abimelek's wrongdoing. Presumably this addition is related to the oppressor's identity as an Israelite. His transgression of familial and covenantal standards through inner-Israelite violence is directly relevant to the overarching narrative.

According to 9:53–57, YHWH removed another oppressor from Israel with swift retributive justice and a housewife's millstone. Following Abimelek's demise, Tola alleviated an undefined threat, before the text names the Philistines and Ammonites as the next regional powers to dominate Israel. For eighteen years foes from Israel's eastern and western borders put pressure on both the Cis- and Transjordanian settlements. The geographical breadth of Israel's occupation in chapter 10 thus matches the theological breadth of the nation's burgeoning religious apostasy. The account involving Jephthah focuses on the latter of the two oppressors—Ammon—and its threat to the Gileadites. In contrast to the narrative descriptions of YHWH's previous agents of persecution, that of Ammon is surprisingly succinct, offering little depth of characterization. The narrator attributes two personal details to the Ammonite leader: (1) his warped theological perspective (11:13) and (2) his refusal to heed Jephthah's words (11:28). These brief textual details function only to provide Jephthah an opportunity to recount and engage the ongoing Ammonite-Israelite conflict. The text depicts Ammon as no more than the nation subdued by the efforts of the people's flawed champion.

After noting the brief tenures of Ibzan, Elon, and Abdon, who may or may not have addressed any element of foreign occupation, the narrator returns to the nation's aforementioned conflict with the Philistines. The years of Philistine oppression (forty) extend beyond those overlapping with Ammonite control (eighteen) and constitute a threat under which YHWH will intervene to preserve (but not deliver) his disobedient people. Like the initial description of the Ammonites, that of the Philistines involves no abstract elements of characterization. They are simply the most recent threat to Israel. In the following three chapters, however, the Philistines feature prominently as a power firmly entrenched in Israel and involved in its daily affairs (i.e., the Israelites "lived among" them; cf. 3:5). When the personal conflict of Samson with a contingent of Philistines has military ramifications for Lehi, the small-scale skirmish highlights that the Israelites were not actively seeking to revolt against their oppressors (15:11).

A more official delegation of Philistine leaders (סרני פלשתים) features in the story surrounding Delilah. While YHWH's coordination of events is conspicuous in the narrative (e.g., 14:5), the focus in chapter 16 is not on the Philistines as divine agents, or even enemies of Israel, so much as the enemies of Samson, trying to remove a destructive force from their area of governance. Their success became an occasion for a victory song in praise of their deity: "Our god has given our enemy into our hand, the ravager of our country, who has killed many of us" (16:24). For the first time, the book of Judges permits the invaders of Israel their own cry of victory, albeit short-lived. Ultimately, the text emphasizes the inferiority of the Philistines and their deity when Samson's God empowers the captured Danite to smite more than three thousand of their most noteworthy citizens. The chapter concludes with a notice of Samson's death, not the ousting of Israel's oppressors. At the close of the cycles section, the Philistines have yet to be overthrown.

In a series of narrative cycles, the central section of Judges describes the experience of the Israelites under nine oppressors. The textual portraits of Mesopotamia, Moab, Canaan, and Midian are imposing and (with the exception of the first) detailed. In each case the narrator emphasizes the key to their ruler's superiority, whether it be his legendary cruelty, robust armies, superior armament, or innumerable, destructive forces. The most substantive contribution the Song of Deborah and Barak makes to the character arc of Israel's oppressors is to reinforce the might of these early enemies through the paradigmatic example of Canaan. With the closure of the Gideon narratives, the text focuses little on Israel's foreign foes; instead, in the final stories of Gideon, along with those of Jephthah and Samson, the oppressors of Israel are the background against which the people's (or a person's) relationship to YHWH might be evaluated. An anomalous narrative cycle that highlights the deeds of an oppressor who is *also* an Israelite eases this transition. This indicting narrative emphasizes Israel's culpability before initiating a change in divine response, after which YHWH no longer offers decisive deliverance. By the end of the cycles section, the Philistines were comfortably ruling over Israel, with little to no resistance from Israel. Only through YHWH's prodding did an impulsive young Danite have (self-centered) reason to upset the status quo and thereby initiate a slow shift in regional power.

The Deity

The portrait of YHWH in the Othniel cycle follows the contours laid out in the introduction: YHWH was the agent who determined Israel's transgression (3:7), allotted and arranged for their oppression under a foreign ruler (v. 8), heeded the cry of his suffering people (v. 9), and rescued them by the hands of a deliverer

(vv. 9–10). The simplest and most straightforward narrative in the cycles section highlights YHWH's coordination of history according to his aims, defined contextually as testing Israel's covenant faithfulness (2:21–22; 3:1, 4).

In much the same way, the narrative of Ehud highlights divine initiative at the outset. The narrator speaks from the deity's perspective and attributes to him the instigation and resolution of the present military conflict—the pronouncement of Israel's sin, the preparing (lit. "strengthening") of a Moabite ruler, and the rescue of his people through a deliverer, in response to the cries of his people. In contrast to the divinely saturated Othniel account, the narrator leaves divine action inexplicit; after the introduction of Ehud in 3:15, YHWH's agency is only implied by cyclical expectations and the speech of Ehud, who attributes to him Israel's defeat of Moab (v. 28). This attribution is unmatched by the narrator, who neglects to mention the deity in his own summative statement: "So Moab was subdued that day under the hand of Israel" (v. 30).[65] Scholars have argued that the silence of God in these fifteen verses is deafening; some have interpreted the silence as disapproval and distance from the questionable actions of the deliverer, while others have judged the simplicity of the story and the paucity of plot complications as a mark of YHWH's agency in the narrative.[66] A third and preferable option is to assign the absence of explicit divine action to a shift in narrative emphasis. The story of Moabite oppression highlights how circumstances have changed for the Israelites and their effectiveness in carrying out their military endeavors. The narrative relies upon the reader to recall the divine initiative in the opening verses to temper any possible judgments based upon that anthropocentric literary focus. In highlighting what YHWH empowered the Israelites to accomplish, the story of Ehud presents

---

[65] While one might argue that the *niphal* verbal form is a "divine passive," the stylistic choice to utilize a passive verbal form—rather than introduce YHWH as a verbal subject—contributes to a pattern of emphasizing the reversal of circumstances. Moreover, the passive formula is hardly a striking anomaly; in fact, the text expresses verbal agency in a regularly alternating pattern:

3:10	"YHWH gave Cushan-Rishathaim into his hand . . ."	— Active: Deity
3:30	"Moab was subdued on that day under the hand of Israel."	— Passive
4:23	"God subdued on that day Jabin King of Canaan . . ."	— Active: Deity
8:28	"Midian was subdued before the Israelites."	— Passive
9:56	"God returned the evil of Abimelek . . ."	— Active: Deity
11:33	"The Ammonites were subdued before the Israelites."	— Passive

[66] For the former, see, e.g., Block, *Judges, Ruth*, 171; for the latter, see Yairah Amit, "The Story of Ehud (Judges 3:12–30): The Form and the Message," in *Signs and Wonders: Biblical Texts in Literary Focus*, ed. J. Cheryl Exum, SBLSS (Atlanta: Society of Biblical Literature, 1989), 98–99.

literary evidence that serves as background characterization for the several chapters that follow: the militia had nothing to fear; they were equipped to accomplish their divine military directives.

The deity initiates military conflict once more in response to Israelite apostasy. As in the last two narrative cycles, the text emphasizes YHWH's agency in positioning Israel's oppressor; however, in Judges 4, YHWH does not explicitly raise up a savior. Instead, the deity speaks and acts through his prophet Deborah, who was entrusted with the task of positioning Israel's military leader. YHWH's indirect activity recalls the Ehud account in which the speech of the deliverer had attributed the victory to YHWH, not the narrator. In the same way, the actions and intentions of Israel's God at the beginning of the Canaanite skirmish are communicated only through a divine intermediary. Despite this similarity, the fact that Deborah was an official spokesperson of YHWH heightens the reader's sense of the deity's agency in the battle, especially compared to the silence of the previous chapter. This shift climaxes in 4:15, when the narrator attributes to YHWH decisive military action: "And YHWH routed Sisera and all his chariots and all his army before Barak by the edge of the sword." In the Battle of Kishon, the narrator leaves no question as to whom honor is due. The chapter's conclusion reiterates YHWH's agency by stating that God subdued Jabin before the people of Israel (v. 23).

The manner of depicting the deity in the reports of the Moabite and Canaanite occupations continues in the Song of Deborah and Barak. Like chapter 4, the song that concludes the Kishon battle sequence is theocentric (though not exclusively so)—YHWH was Israel's Divine Warrior, who strode forth in battle, equipping and mustering his human troops to follow willingly. Despite his call to Israelite soldiers, his supernatural forces did the real work on the people's behalf. Ultimately, the prophet and the general of Israel explained to the people that YHWH was Israel's champion and used that theological truth to challenge a troublingly hesitant militia.

The first three narrative cycles, then, increasingly underscore YHWH's agency, with the song epitomizing this pattern. Following the contours of the introduction, divine activity that is consistently echoed by human activity saturates the Othniel account. In this way, the initial cycle reinforces narrative expectations set in the previous chapter and strengthens the textual portrayal of YHWH as the initiating and delivering agent in the period's military conflicts. This pattern plays out as the overarching narrative proceeds; according to the emphases of all three cycles, the deity is consistently responsible for the infiltration of Israel's settlements by outsiders. The text never claims that Israel's oppressors challenged God's people on their own accord. This pattern develops and shifts between the second and third cycles. In the story of

Ehud, the text highlights the initiating elements of divine deliverance; God arranged and prepared all appropriate players who—the story shows—were able to accomplish his directives with ease. By contrast, in the account of Deborah, Barak, and Jael, the narrative emphasizes YHWH's consistent agency in every stage of battle: initiation, muster, execution, and dénouement. Moreover, the cycle's final prophetic pronouncement—the Song of Deborah and Barak—declares that the ability of Israel's militia to succeed is ultimately based on YHWH's ability, not their own.

In his work on Judges 4, Assis also contrasts the textual portrayal of divine action in the second and third narrative cycles. He argues that in the Ehud account, the deliverer's image "overshadows the concealed actions of God. . . . In [the Deborah story] the aim is to avoid dependence on a leader and to see God's hand at work instead."[67] Assis' view of Judges 4–5 as a corrective to the previous account too readily dismisses as negative the narrator's emphasis on the success of human agents in 3:12–30 (i.e., Ehud and the Israelites). In reality, the two prose accounts present complementary theological truths whose relationship is explicated by the prophetic interpretation of the Kishon battle in Judges 5. Like the Ehud narrative (and the Jael portion of the Kishon narrative), the song demonstrates that YHWH uniquely equipped Israel to succeed in battle. Like the Kishon narrative, the song emphasizes that the aforementioned Israelite success is ultimately initiated, facilitated, and ensured by YHWH.

The fresh apostasy of Israel after a prophetic declaration of deliverance and challenge prompted YHWH once more to hand Israel over to an opponent—this time the Midianites, allied with the Amalekites and eastern nomadic tribes. Once more the deity responded to the cries of his people, but this time with a prophetic rebuke (6:7–10). Through the prophet, YHWH characterized himself as Israel's deliverer par excellence, who rescued the people from Egypt, as well as from any other army that had since threatened them. In reiterating a standard injunction reminiscent of several earlier covenantal contexts,[68] he repeated for the people the foundational statement whence his relational demands derive—"I am YHWH your God"—and does so only here in the book of Judges.

The explicit and covenantal nature of YHWH's revelatory characterization in the prophet's speech continues throughout the Gideon account. Given the frequency with which YHWH speaks and interacts in Judges 6–7, along with the literarily adjacent song emphasizing divine intervention in recent history,

---

[67] Assis, "Man, Woman and God," 114–18.
[68] E.g., Deut 6–7. Assis (*Self-Interest or Communal Interest*, 23–24) argues that the language of the censure derives from the Decalogue.

here YHWH's self-disclosure reaches its narrative zenith. First, having issued a prophetic challenge in the previous cycle and a warning through a second prophet, YHWH enters into a robust exchange in which his presence with the judge (and thereby his troops) is central. As Cheryl Exum has observed, "No character in the book receives more divine assurance than Gideon and no one displays more doubt."[69] Second, God acts repeatedly in the account. In contrast to the Battle of Kishon, in which YHWH acted explicitly only once (4:15), according to Judges 6:11–7:25, God spoke or acted twelve times,[70] and the dialogue of every character involved in the military skirmish—even the Midianites!—highlights divine activity. The narrator confirms the deity's battlefield intervention through two statements: one related to the muster (6:34: "The spirit of YHWH clothed Gideon") and another to execution (7:22: "YHWH set every man's sword against his comrade and against all the enemy"). In the midst of the fray, the agency of YHWH in Midian's defeat is sufficiently clear that even the hard-hearted son of Joash surrenders to him in worship (7:15).

As many interpreters have noted, a discernible shift in narrative emphasis divides the Gideon account in two.[71] A decided change in divine activity contributes to that narrative shift. On one hand, after 7:22 the narrator recounts no divine acts or words; on the other, Gideon's human conflicts take center stage. Juliana Claassens rightly observes that, in the Zebah-Zalmunna episode, "the focus exclusively falls on Gideon and God is largely absent. In this juxtaposition, the question remains whether Israel will remember who God is. Or will they choose Gideon over God?"[72] Gideon, whom Israel credits entirely with the victory over Midian (8:22: "for you have saved us from the hand of Midian"), eclipses YHWH, the definitive savior of Israel, whose agency was emphasized in dialogue and narration throughout the last two chapters.[73]

---

[69] J. Cheryl Exum, "The Centre Cannot Hold: Thematic and Textual Instabilities in Judges," *CBQ* 52 (1990): 416.

[70] אלהים or יהוה is the subject of an active verb twelve times in the narrator's reports: 6:14, 16, 23, 25, 34 (רוח יהוה as subject), 40; 7:2, 4, 5, 7, 9, 22. In Judg 8, the deity appears as a subject only in dialogue; the narrator neither confirms nor denies the validity of the characters' statements about him.

[71] David W. Gooding, "The Composition of the Book of Judges," *ErIsr* 16 (1982): 74; followed and adapted by J. Paul Tanner, "The Gideon Narrative as the Focal Point of Judges," *BSac* 149 (1992): 160–61.

[72] L. Juliana M. Claassens, "The Character of God in Judges 6–8: The Gideon Narrative as Theological and Moral Resource," *HBT* 23 (2001): 58.

[73] The text may anticipate this shift in 7:20 with a battle cry naming YHWH and Gideon. Block makes this observation in "Will the Real Gideon Please Stand Up?" 360. Jotham makes a similarly problematic statement when he argues that it was his father who delivered Israel from the hand of Midian (9:17).

While it is possible that the absence of divine activity signals judgment upon the characters, it demonstrates more straightforwardly that the characters have less to say about, or give less to credit to, the deity. The narrator confirms this reality in 8:34: "And the Israelites did not remember YHWH their God, who delivered them from the hand of all their surrounding enemies." At the close of Gideon's judgeship, the people have misidentified the true agent of their deliverance, thereby sacrificing the theological narrative undergirding their relationship to YHWH and exposing themselves to the allure of other national deities.

While the Abimelek cycle commences with another account of Israelite apostasy, God does not initiate Israel's oppression. The narrative emphasis on the people of Israel and their response to the deity's past self-disclosure carries over from the previous chapter; the account highlights instead their agency in the ensuing conflict. Nevertheless, references to Israel's God appear in both dialogue and narration. While God is not a character in Jotham's fable, Jotham claims to be his spokesperson:[74] "Listen to me, you leaders of Shechem, that God may listen to you" (9:7). Jotham explicitly aligns himself with the God of Israel, but he only does so in terms of the generic noun אלהים; he does not invoke the covenant name of YHWH. Although faithful Israelites have long referred to God as אלהים rather than YHWH—the narrator did so as recently as 6:40 (cf. 5:8)—Bluedorn argues the pattern in the present text reflects conflict between YHWH and Baal. Because the generic noun may refer to either deity, he argues that to invoke only the designation אלהים is to leave room for interpretation.[75] Further, in the application of the fable, including the historical account of the deliverance from Midian, Jotham attributes victory not to YHWH (or אלהים) but rather to Jerubbaal. By neglecting to acknowledge the deity's agency, Jotham perceives history like his kinsmen do (cf. 8:22), not from a perspective of divine omniscience or prophetic clarity.

The references to divine activity in the rest of the chapter, however, caution against too quickly dismissing Jotham's use of the generic noun as idolatrous accommodation or pandering by a theological minority. The narrator speaks of Israel's God using only the noun אלהים in 9:23, 56, and 57—each of which describes the deity's intervention to bring ruin upon Abimelek and his followers and thereby to neutralize his people's most recent oppressor. His pattern of designation aside, the narrator emphasizes throughout the Abimelek

---

[74] While the repeated phrase אלהים ואנשים may refer to Israel's God, the fable's more generalized language makes a merism—namely "mortals and deities alike"—more likely. See, e.g., NRSV: "'Shall I stop producing my rich oil by which gods and mortals are honored, and go to sway over the trees?'" (v. 9 et passim).

[75] Bluedorn, *Yahweh versus Baalism*, 271–72.

account that YHWH enacts retributive justice against Israel's oppressor, as he has done consistently in the book of Judges.

After disposing of the Shechemite king with a housewife's millstone and a young soldier, YHWH observes Israel's plummet into the most diverse and extensive stage of brazen apostasy. According to 10:6, the covenant God of Israel is abandoned (עזב). YHWH introduces two agents of oppression, on account of whom the Israelites repent and request deliverance. Rather than raising up a deliverer or sending a prophet in response, the deity rebukes the people directly, accentuating the breadth of their apostasy, the nature of their transgression, and most importantly, the consequence: YHWH vows that he will save Israel no longer (10:13).

One of the most challenging statements about the deity in Judges follows YHWH's declaration that he would no longer rescue his people from oppression. The narrator asserts, ותקצר נפשו בעמל ישראל (v. 16). Translations of the ambiguous phrase in English versions and commentaries range from "and he could no longer bear to see Israel suffer" (NRSV) to "he lost patience with Israel's behavior."[76] This critical statement not only describes YHWH's general disposition toward his people but contributes to the discussion of whether the deity changed his mind after his pledge of nondeliverance. Certain elements of the phrase are less ambiguous than others; surely the root קצר ("to be short") idiomatically indicates that "a limit of tolerance has been reached, leading to an explosive response."[77] The crucial interpretive difficulty is the referent of the construct phrase עמל ישראל—whether the suffering/misery experienced by Israel or the evil committed at their hands.[78] Swayed by YHWH's previous pattern of deliverance, English translations imply not only that the suffering of Israel was the object of the deity's impatience but also that his disposition precipitated an immediate course correction—with NRSV, NIV

---

[76] Sasson, *Judges 1–12*, 407.

[77] Lawson G. Stone, "From Tribal Confederation to Monarchic State: The Editorial Perspective of the Book of Judges" (PhD diss., Yale University, 1988), 322. Elsewhere the root קצר describes the state of the grumbling Israelites in the desert (Num 21:4), Samson's displeasure with Delilah's persisting questioning (Judg 16:16), and Job's disposition in complaint (Job 21:4). See also Mic 2:7; Zech 11:8; and *HALOT*, 1126–27.

[78] Given its comparable context, the most relevant example is Deut 26:7, in which God notices the עמל of the Israelites, alongside their affliction (עני) and oppression (לחץ), before he intervenes to save them. Throughout Job, עמל designates something semantically adjacent to affliction or suffering (3:10, 5:7, 11:16). By contrast, in Isa 10:1 and Hab 1:3, עמל denotes the transgression that causes trouble for another and is therefore conceptually parallel to און. In Ps 7:17[16], עמל seems to denote harm (// חמס). Janzen ("Sacrifice of Jephthah's Daughter," 347) argues emphatically for the latter, just as Stone ("Tribal Confederation to Monarchic State," 323) suggests the noun "could well denote Israel's sinfulness."

emphasizes that he could "no longer bear" the misery of Israel; NET renders, "Finally the LORD grew tired of seeing Israel suffer so much." Still, even if the statement emphasizes divine compassion, there is no narrative indication that YHWH goes back on his word.[79] Never again in the book of Judges does the deity raise up an agent who delivers his people from oppression or grant rest to the land. Jephthah is chosen by his kinsmen to attack Ammon, but his divinely facilitated battlefield victory does not bring peace to the region. Similarly, Samson is raised up by YHWH only to instigate, not terminate, a conflict with the Philistines. A more plausible interpretation of 10:16 is that it explains why YHWH does not respond to Israel's repentance by saving them—his forbearance for the behavior of Israel (which involved both transgression and suffering) had reached its limit.[80]

In keeping with his declaration, YHWH did not raise up a deliverer for his people. Instead, the people chose their own leader, through whom YHWH acted twice on the battlefield: the Spirit of YHWH moved the general to confront the Ammonites (11:29), and the deity himself "gave them into his hand" (11:32). As in the narratives involving Ehud and Gideon, the narrator's summary of the divinely facilitated victory is passive, highlighting a narrative condition, rather than divine causality: "The Ammonites were subdued before the people of Israel" (v. 33). Unfortunately, the account lacks any indication that the land achieved rest (and thereby qualifies the degree to which the Israelites experienced deliverance); perhaps 10:7 implies that at YHWH's instigation, the Philistines had already begun to exert pressure at the land's western border. In either case, the brief victory over Ammon recedes quickly into the background, along with the action of the deity. The God of Israel was silent as Jephthah sacrificed his daughter in God's name and slaughtered fellow Israelites. The narrative centers instead on the degradation of Israelite societal structures in a period when God had promised to leave the people to their own devices.

The decisiveness of YHWH's withdrawal from the business of deliverance is matched by the miraculous quality of his intervention in Samson's birth. That he had not changed his plans is clear; YHWH declared that Samson would not deliver his people but only *begin* to save them from Philistine oppression. Even so, the deity separated him from birth, calling him to Nazirite service and preparing him from infancy for his participation in Israel's safekeeping. The literary accent on divine intervention that characterizes Samson's birth account

---

[79] Lee Roy Martin belabors this point in *The Unheard Voice of God: A Pentecostal Hearing of the Book of Judges*, Journal of Pentecostal Theology Supplemental Series 32 (Blandford Forum: Deo Publishing, 2008), 212–13.

[80] So also Block, *Judges, Ruth*, 348–49.

permeates the entire narrative. Exum rightly observes that "the pivotal theological principle in the saga is that Yhwh is the guiding force behind events."[81] The Samson narrative is so rife with YHWH's presence and empowerment that it disambiguates the nature of the deity's statement in 10:13—God did not abandon his people to their fate nor withdraw himself from their care. To the contrary, he interrupted an unsuccessful cyclical pattern by preserving his people without, however, decisive military deliverance. He would no longer save them, but he would not abandon them, either.

As early as 14:4, the narrator draws attention to a discrepancy between human perception and divine omniscience that undergirds the entire Samson cycle. Perhaps the height of this theological tension surfaces in the celebration of Dagon hosted by the Philistine officials at the time of Samson's capture and eventual demise. In contrast to the Ehud episode, in which the climax of the narrative was the moment the king's slain corpse was witnessed by Moabite government officials (3:25), and the Song of Deborah and Barak, in which foreign kings were called to witness YHWH's exploits (5:3), 16:23–24 features a host of Philistines declaring that *their* god had conquered *their* enemy. Their deaths at the hands of that same enemy in the verses that follow highlight their ignorance. By emphasizing that more Philistines died at Samson's hand at this point than any other, the narrator reveals that this moment of apparent Israelite failure is the moment of the Danite's most significant contribution, and thereby, the fulfillment of YHWH's intentions for him. While this narrative closure underscores the futility of Samson's efforts during his lifetime, it also reinforces the deity's determination to use Samson to limit the power of the Philistines, at their moment of greatest hubris. The limits of Philistine perception are matched by Samson's own physical, emotional, and spiritual limits. At every narrative turn, the strength, ability, and knowledge of God contrasts with the insufficiency and desperation of the humans under his superintendence. Samson was powerless to save Israel, as had been any figure whom YHWH did not empower. In the conclusion of the cycles section, the ignorance of Israel and the haughtiness of its oppressors reinforce a portrait of YHWH that emphasizes *his* saving power, a power effectively wielded regardless of human allegiance or understanding.

In 3:7–16:31, the characterization of YHWH is neither confined to mere repetition nor reflective of an internal conflict between graciousness and jealous rage.[82] By contrast, the cycles section highlights a deity acting according

---

[81] Exum, "Theological Dimension of the Samson Saga," 36.

[82] Contra Lee Roy Martin ("Yahweh Conflicted: Unresolved Theological Tension in the Cycle of Judges," *OTE* 22 [2009]: 356), who speaks of "a deep theological tension within the character of Yahweh himself, an irreconcilable conflict between his anger and his compassion."

to one overriding purpose and developing his relationship with Israel to advance his objective. We may summarize the narrator's development of his character as follows:

(1) *Evidence* (3:7–4:23): Emphasizes YHWH's power to overcome Israel's enemies and his faithfulness in equipping his people to accomplish the task.
(2) *Challenge* (5:1–31): A prophetic account of YHWH's miraculous deeds in recent history and challenge to the people to recognize and respond to divine activity with covenant fidelity (especially military involvement).
(3) *Rebuke and Warning* (6:1–7:25): Highlights the inability of the people to heed the evidence of YHWH's deliverance through prophetic rebuke and initial exchange with Gideon. The deity responds with (significantly) heightened self-disclosure.
(4) *Failure* (8:1–9:57): Divine self-disclosure ceases. The narrative highlights the characters' inability to acknowledge divine agency and its idolatrous consequences.
(5) *Censure* (10:1–16): YHWH pledges to save Israel no longer.
(6) *Aftermath* (10:17–12:15): While preserving the safety of his people, God does not intervene to protect them from the disastrous results of their own immorality.
(7) *Negative Demonstration* (13:1–16:31): YHWH continues to sustain his people, but the narrator highlights their inability to effect military victory through any means other than his direct empowerment.

In regard to the characterization of YHWH, the first half of the cycles section emphasizes that the Israelites had no need to fear the inhabitants of the land or their own insufficiency. The might of YHWH was superior to any worldly power and he was willing and able to muster and prepare the perfect instrument of salvation. This portrayal culminates with the Song of Deborah and Barak. The second half of the cycles section demonstrates a correlating principle: the power to save—to ensure the safety and prosperity of the people—was YHWH's, and his alone. Not only did his people have no reason to fear but they had no room for inappropriate self-confidence either. Their flourishing in the land depended entirely upon their covenant dedication to YHWH, the God of Israel.

Conclusion

The core of the book of Judges tells the story of YHWH, Israel, those who occupy their land, and the agents through whom YHWH saves his people. As a set, the first three conflict accounts highlight the vulnerability of the Israelites and the effectiveness of YHWH's agents of deliverance; these accounts do not herald the judges as praiseworthy heroes but highlight the means by which YHWH effected such a mighty salvation for his people. This pattern of characterization shifts in the Gideon episode, which emphasizes the impropriety of Israel's response to YHWH, as evidenced by the actions of the people and their leader Gideon (as well as by the collective's response to Gideon's role in the victory). Under the leadership of Gideon and Abimelek, the people's faithfulness to YHWH took a decisively downward turn. The might of the oppressors of Israel—highlighted so prominently in the early chapters—transitions from being a prominent element of the narrator's accounts to serving as a backdrop to stories more concerned with the futility of Israel's efforts to save itself through the power of entities other than YHWH—whether it be the work of the Israelites' own hands or the gods of the surrounding nations.

The Song of Deborah and Barak reinforces the crucial transition from the first three narrative cycles to the last four. The song underscores and makes explicit that YHWH is mighty to save and has effectively done so for his people in recent generations. By demonstrating the humiliation of overwhelming opponents and the strengthening of an underwhelming army, the song matches the narrative emphases of the first three cycles but then supplements that familiar material with two stanzas dedicated exclusively to YHWH's supernatural strength and deliverance. The song juxtaposes this divine portrayal with a stanza evaluating the response of Israelites to that victory and thereby provides a theologically astute appraisal of the narrative's major players that effectively challenges the self-perception of the song's audience and, consequently, their behavior. Thus, the refrain of Judges 5 advances a shift in the book from presenting evidence of YHWH's mighty deliverances to evaluating Israel's response to that action.

4
Plot and Themes in the Song and the Savior Stories

In his essay on characters in the book of Judges, P. J. Nel is right to observe that the "richest form of story is formed when plot, character and theme are fused and balanced. But when the characters are but recurrent types in a great cyclic plot pattern, there must be something very special in the design of plot and theme."[1] Having already addressed character development in the cyclical core of Judges, this chapter will focus on the remaining two elements of narrative: plot and theme.

Plot Development

A close reading of the deliverer stories in the core of Judges reveals a colorful narrative detailing the woes of the generations after Joshua who lacked an intimate knowledge of their covenant God and the mighty deliverances experienced by previous generations. According to this macroplot, the people who lived under the leadership of the judges suffered from the allure of pagan influence among them and, at every opportunity to prove faithful to their Sovereign, refused to acknowledge their saving history and, consequently, abandoned the God of their fathers. From beginning to end, the book of Judges marshals historical detail and literary artistry to highlight the degradation of Israel's relationship to YHWH in its historiographic enterprise. The contribution of Judges 5 to the development of that plot is the focus of this section.

While the narrator identifies the narrative's trajectory in 2:19, the exact shape of that narrative movement and its consequent plot must be addressed to properly discern the role of the Song of Deborah and Barak in it. This "narrative structure"—to borrow language from Berlin[2]—focuses on the formal

---

[1] P. J. Nel, "Character in the Book of Judges," *OTE* 8 (1995): 202. Nel's assertion that the characters in Judges are "but recurrent types" is only partially true; as the last section argued, certain characters are exceptionally dynamic (e.g., YHWH).

[2] Adele Berlin, *Poetics and Interpretation of Biblical Narrative*, BLS 9 (Winona Lake, Ind.: Eisenbrauns, 1994), 101–2.

features of the book's core, rather than simply the series of events. Three sets of formal features strike me as integral to the narrative's structure and, therefore, informative to plot development.

Cyclical Divisions

The section consisting of 3:7–16:31 is formally cyclical, following the pattern provided in the book's introduction. The presence of these formal elements delimits the central section from the concluding narratives beginning in chapter 17, which feature their own distinct refrain. The number of cyclical elements identified and the vocabulary used to describe them varies, but scholars generally recognize between four and seven repetitive elements, including (1) Israel's sin, (2) foreign oppression, (3) cry of distress, (4) raising of a judge, (5) the subduing of the enemy, (6) the land's rest, and (7) the judge's death.[3] By analyzing the presence (or absence) of these features, most scholars divide the intervening narratives into six cycles with interspersed lists of six noncyclical "judges."[4] This consensus has been challenged. The Abimelek narrative in Judges 9 complicates the otherwise straightforward internal organization. To count six cycles is to assert that the events surrounding Abimelek belong formally to the so-called Gideon cycle.[5] Roy Heller argues most thoroughly for a formal division between the accounts, asserting the latter is "separate from what follows, formally separate from what precedes, and thematically different from the Gideon story."[6] Heller highlights textual features that set off

---

[3] See, e.g., Yairah Amit, *The Book of Judges: The Art of Editing*, trans. Jonathan Chipman, BibInt 38 (Boston: Brill, 1999), 36–37 (five elements); Frederick E. Greenspahn, "The Theology of the Framework of Judges," *VT* 36 (1986): 385–96 (five elements); Daniel I. Block, *Judges, Ruth*, NAC 6 (Nashville: Broadman & Holman, 2001), 146–47 (six to seven elements); Mark J. Boda, "Recycling Heaven's Words: Receiving and Retrieving Divine Revelation in the Historiography of Judges," in *Prophets and Prophecy and Ancient Israelite Historiography*, ed. Mark J. Boda and Lissa Wray Beal (Winona Lake, Ind.: Eisenbrauns, 2013), 388 (seven elements, including a "divine intermediary" element).

[4] Note that only five of these explicitly "judge" (שׁפט). Judg 3:31 says that Shamgar saved (ישׁע) Israel—a feat credited only to him and Othniel (and by inference, Ehud, who is called a "savior"; 3:15).

[5] Barry G. Webb (*The Book of Judges*, NICOT [Grand Rapids: Eerdmans, 2012], 34) represents those who champion this approach. Assuming that each narrative cycle is defined predominantly by the presence of a judge, Webb calls these events a "sequel" to the preceding chapters, based on the fact that Abimelek "is not a judge at all in terms of the way that office has been described in the introduction."

[6] Roy L. Heller, "What Is Abimelek Doing in Judges?" in *Raising Up a Faithful Exegete: Essays in Honor of Richard D. Nelson*, ed. K. L. Noll and Brooks Schramm (Winona Lake, Ind.: Eisenbrauns, 2010), 226. Heller's more extensive observations are similar to those made earlier in Amit, *Book of Judges*, 40–44, in which Amit's primary concern is to demonstrate how Judg 9 serves the "thematic axes" of the book's editing.

the Abimelek narrative from its context, including the presence of standard cyclical features.⁷ Moreover, the portrayal of Abimelek as a new oppressor of Israel suggests a formal break between the two stories; whereas contemporary interpreters tend to see each narrative cycle defined by the presence of a judge, the oppressors are the instigating element in the cyclical pattern described in 2:14.

If the narratives surrounding Abimelek constitute an independent episode in the drama of the judges period, the cycles section features seven narrative cycles, the third of which contains the Song of Deborah and Barak. At the very least, the portrayal of the Israelites in 2:19 raises the expectation that the cycles will demonstrate increasingly pagan activity among the Israelites, as is recognized by almost all scholars of Judges.⁸ Twice in the book, however, significant variations to these patterns occur that preclude an overly simplistic account of a simple downward trajectory.

First, of pivotal importance is the rendering of the first element of Israel's behavioral pattern: their repeated apostasy. When in 3:7 the Israelites commit apostasy for the first time, the text straightforwardly reports their transgression as "doing [the] evil": ויעשו בני־ישראל את הרע. The corresponding notice in the next two battle narratives is retrospective and adds the auxiliary verb יסף to emphasize each pericope's association with the previous: ויספו בני ישראל לעשׂית הרע ("did the evil *again*" or "*continued* to do the evil"; 3:12, 4:1). This pattern breaks in 6:1, where the narrator opts for the original verbal clause from 3:7. Lawson Stone argues that the grammatical shift signals a literary shift, that is, an editorially designed "new departure" at the start of the narratives involving Gideon, which implies a brief respite after the events of Judges 4–5 from rampant, cyclical apostasy.⁹ Observing the same phenomenon, one early Jewish

---

⁷ Two major cyclical features—the statement of rest closing the Gideon account (8:28) and renewed apostasy after Gideon's death (8:33)—appear between the accounts of Gideon and Abimelek. Assuming a new narrative begins in 8:33, Heller ("What Is Abimelek Doing?" 233) argues that the length of Abimelek's reign recorded in 9:22 is comparable to passages relating the length of foreign oppression in 3:8, 14; 4:3; 6:1; and 10:8. Amit (*Book of Judges*, 43) makes similar claims.

⁸ On which, see, e.g., J. P. U. Lilley, "A Literary Appreciation of the Book of Judges," *TynBul* 18 (1967): 94–102; J. Cheryl Exum, "The Centre Cannot Hold: Thematic and Textual Instabilities in Judges," *CBQ* 52 (1990): 410–31. Exum's work on deteriorating patterns (matching deteriorating morality) in Judges has been especially influential in recent decades.

⁹ Lawson G. Stone, "From Tribal Confederation to Monarchic State: The Editorial Perspective of the Book of Judges" (PhD diss., Yale University, 1988), 302; observed also by Wolfgang Bluedorn, *Yahweh versus Baalism: A Theological Reading of the Gideon–Abimelech Narrative*, ed. David J. A. Clines and Philip R. Davies, JSOTSup 329 (Sheffield: Sheffield Academic Press, 2009), 57; and noted briefly by Lilley, "Literary

interpreter mused that the "song had wiped out all that went before"; indeed, Israel's slate had been wiped clean.[10] After this literary reset, the remaining cycles return to augmented descriptions of Israel's apostasy that imply a heightened level of (con)sequentiality (8:33 [שוב rather than יסף; cf. 2:19], 10:6, 13:1).[11]

Reports of the land's rest constitute a second variation in the cyclical delimiters. The final two narrative cycles depict a rest-less land. At the end of Gideon's questionable tenure, a note about the land having rest appears for the final time (8:28).[12] This shift in the narrator's summary emphasizes that YHWH uses neither Jephthah nor Samson (and certainly not Abimelek!) to bring the people to the level of security and sociopolitical stability that he did for their predecessors; the outcome of YHWH's intervention is decidedly different in these narratives. This element of narrative structure suggests a plot development that precedes the end of the Jephthah cycle (i.e., before 12:7). The implications of both variations in the cyclical pattern will be addressed below.

Divine Self-Description

The introduction to the book of Judges identifies a pattern of behavior, a divine purpose statement, and an expectation of deterioration, but it also includes a word from YHWH—through a divine intermediary—about his action going forward. According to both Joshua and Judges 2:17, the settlement efforts under Joshua's leadership were marked by divine empowerment and Israelite obedience. Within this scheme, YHWH drove out the nations before Israel, thereby guarding them from any occupation or subjugation. The

---

Appreciation," 98. This change to the narrative pattern coincides with the death notice missing from the narrative involving Deborah, Barak, and Jael, which functions in the book to highlight the cyclical nature of Israelite apostasy after the pattern provided in 2:18. Its absence lends credence to a formal and narratorial break between the chapters.

[10] *Midrash Song of Songs Rabbah* (4:3), quoted in David M. Gunn, *Judges*, Blackwell Bible Commentaries (Malden: Wiley-Blackwell, 2005), 55.

[11] Others have made similar observations. For example, in "The Literary Structure of Judges Revisited: Judges as a Ring Composition," in *Windows to the Ancient World of the Hebrew Bible: Essays in Honor of Samuel Greengus*, ed. B. T. Arnold, N. L. Erickson, and J. H. Walton (Winona Lake, Ind.: Eisenbrauns, 2014), 253, Kenneth Way notices several shifts in the cyclical vocabulary of Abimelek's narrative that are "likely employed by the narrator for intensified rhetorical effect (characterizing the second half of the book by apostasy)."

[12] The Abimelek cycle also lacks a notice of the land's rest; however, that episode does not foreground a deliverer. Deprivation of the land's rest is more significant in light of YHWH's military intervention through a judge (an element present in the last two cycles and missing from the Abimelek cycle); the statement's absence highlights that YHWH intervened but did not bring a decisive victory to his people.

disobedience of the generations after Joshua (summarized in 2:10ff) provides the point of departure for the Judges narrative and the occasion for YHWH to declare through his messenger a change in his behavior: "So now I say, 'I will not drive them out before you, but they shall become thorns in your sides, and their gods shall be a snare to you'" (2:3). Therefore, one may define the Judges period as a new stage in divine conquest activity, in which the deity provides an opportunity to test the level of obedience that Israelites are able to demonstrate in a partially dispossessed land. The introduction asserts that YHWH will save his people, but he will not drive out the land's inhabitants. The episode initial description in 3:5 is the formal setting of the cycles section: "The Israelites settled among the Canaanites, Hittites, Amorites, Perizzites, Hivites, and the Jebusites."[13] Therefore, YHWH's initial declaration (2:3, repeated in 2:21–22), with its consequent narrative fulfillment (3:1–6), provides the backdrop for the first five conflicts of the book of Judges—namely, those involving the rulers of Mesopotamia, Moab, Canaan, Midian, and Shechem.

In 10:6–10, the narrator introduces YHWH's second declaration with a summary of Israel's egregious apostasy, severe oppression, and repentance—a pattern that had in the past been met with YHWH's deliverance of his people. Instead, in 10:13, YHWH declares his intent to save them no more. Thus, a third stage of divine activity begins, in which YHWH neither drives out the nations from the land of promise nor saves his people from their oppressors. This declaration provides the theological foundation for the final two external military conflicts (featuring Jephthah and Samson), as well as the series of events highlighting Israel's internal chaos in chapters 17–21. These stages of divine activity may be plotted as follows according to the book's chapter divisions (fig. 1):

Figure 1: Stages of Divine Activity in Judges

1	2	3	4	5	6	7	8	9	10	11	12	13	14	15	16	17	18	19	20	21
1	Stage 2 (2:1–5; 2:20–10:5)								Stage 3 (10:6–21:25)											

Stage 1:	YHWH drives out the land's inhabitants.	
Stage 2:	YHWH does *not* drive out the land's inhabitants.	
	YHWH *does* save his people from oppression.	
Stage 3:	YHWH does *not* drive out the land's inhabitants.	
	YHWH does *not* save his people from oppression.	

---

[13] For an analysis of the syntactical relationship between 3:1–6 and 3:7, see Marvin A. Sweeney, "Davidic Polemics in the Book of Judges," *VT* 47 (1997): 522–23.

Speeches of Divine Intermediaries

Spokespersons of YHWH address Israel twice in addition to the two speeches in which YHWH announces a change in the divine program (discussed above).[14] Both utterances are prophetic—the first in the form of a song from the perspective of Deborah (5:2–31; אשה נביאה) and the second on the lips of an unnamed male prophet (6:10–12; איש נביא). Taken together with the speeches in chapters 2 and 10, four orations by YHWH or those who speak for him punctuate the book of Judges. Their distribution in reference to the cyclical core of the book is represented visually in figure 2.

Figure 2: Speeches of Divine Intermediaries

מלאך		נביאה		נביא		יהוה	
Oth.	Ehud	Deb.	Gideon		Abi.	Jephthah	Samson
Stage Two: YHWH Saves					Stage Three: YHWH Does Not Save		

Speech 1: Declaration of YHWH through מלאך יהוה; see 2:1–5, reiterated in 2:20–22

Speech 2: Song of Deborah and Barak; see 5:1–31

Speech 3: Rebuke from YHWH through איש נביא; see 6:10–12

Speech 4: Direct declaration of YHWH; see 10:11–14

The second and third speeches end and begin the Barak and Gideon narrative cycles, respectively. At the start of the Gideon cycle, the unnamed prophet delivers a rebuke reminiscent of YHWH's other declarations—he contrasts YHWH's covenant faithfulness with the unfaithfulness of his subjects. Through his prophet, YHWH repeats the assertion of the מלאך יהוה in 2:2 that the Israelites "have not obeyed my voice" (6:10), despite the continuing revelation of the deity in act and word (most recently, that of Deborah). The transgressions of which the messenger (and again YHWH in 2:20–22) accused previous generations in 2:1–5 are assigned now to a later generation (6:10–12).[15]

---

[14] I distinguish formal speeches from short dialogues with divine intermediaries: 5:23 (the curse of Meroz, embedded in the Song of Deborah and Barak); 6:11–26 (the call of Gideon); and 13:3–20 (Samson's birth narrative). Moreover, YHWH speaks to characters directly at several points in the book in a less formal capacity.

[15] This is an example of the distinctive themes and vocabulary the Gideon narratives borrow from the opening chapters. Way ("Literary Structure of Judges Revisited," 254) demonstrates that the presence of language from the introductory and concluding chapters of the book of Judges in this (central) cycle mark it as a "transitional pivot for the entire book"; his argument thereby lends credence to my own.

Like the other three speeches, Judges 5 declares the mixed faithfulness of the Israelites and emphasizes YHWH's faithful deliverance of his people; however, its similarity to the other formal divine messages ends here. In contrast to speeches 1, 3, and 4, whose structure and vocabulary are similar, the celebratory song is formally distinct. Moreover, its reflection on the actions of both covenant partners is particular and occasional rather than abstract and summative. Finally, the narrator credits the song *not only* to the divine intermediary but also to another Israelite leader. These stylistically distinct elements render the song a concrete application of the other more general divine pronouncements. Rather than to declare that YHWH delivers, the Song of Deborah and Barak describes the tangible means through which he does so and the degree to which his mighty acts transform the experience of the semi-settled Israelite people. The structural import of the song is thus distinct from that of the other three speeches, which provide definitive markers relating to the current state of the covenant between YHWH and Israel and, thereby, the structure of the overarching narrative. By contrast, the song is largely explanatory; its pedagogical orientation is reflective and, therefore, ideal for reinforcing the subtle evaluative content of previous narratives. The song is best described in terms of concluding the narrative segment that precedes it. Together with the immediately following prophetic pronouncement of 6:8, the Song of Deborah and Barak marks a formal break in the narrative.

Synthesis

As indicated by the statements of YHWH and his intermediaries, the preceding discussion identified three stages of divine activity, the second and third of which include the episodes of the cycles section. Moreover, two speeches by prophets combined with variations in the pattern of cyclical elements suggested not only a general pattern of degradation but also a break between the third and fourth cycles (5:31–6:1), as signaled by the unaugmented statement "Israel did [the] evil" at the beginning of the Gideon narrative. By overlaying the structural patterns suggested by these data, the following narrative structure for the cycles section emerges (fig. 3):[16]

---

[16] This diagram resembles Stone's in "Tribal Confederation to Monarchic State," 469. Stone also identifies three stages in the cycles section, acknowledging the same major structural breaks. His scheme differs from my own in that he identifies Othniel as the "paradigm" and the stories of Ehud and Deborah as triumphant, even though they constitute the first stage of "progressive decay." Elie Assis (*Self-Interest or Communal Interest: An Ideology of Leadership in the Gideon, Abimelech and Jephthah Narratives [Judg 6–12]*, trans. Stephanie Nakache, VTSup 106 [Leiden: Brill, 2005], 130) recognizes a similar structure, highlighting judges he considers positive (i.e., Othniel, Ehud, and Deborah) and negative (i.e., Abimelech, Jephthah, and Samson), with Gideon occupying the central (and transitional) position.

Figure 3: The Narrative Structure of the Core of Judges

Oth.	Ehud	Deb.	Gideon	Abi.	Jephthah	Samson
Unit 1			Unit 2		Unit 3	
Stage Two: YHWH Saves					Stage Three: YHWH Does Not Save	

The structural breaks provided by the two major YHWH speeches also explicitly identify their relevance to plot development: they mark shifts in divine activity during the judges period. The absence of notices describing the land's rest at the conclusion of the narratives of Jephthah and Samson suggest a narrative shift that coincides with these stages of divine activity; the land's rest-less-ness is a natural consequence of YHWH's decision to deliver his people no longer. The plot development constituted by YHWH's second programmatic declaration thus accounts for the variation to the cyclical delimiters in the final two narrative cycles. By contrast, the significance of the shift at 6:1 (i.e., the unaugmented statement that the Israelites "did the evil") is less clear. Four factors deserve consideration:

First, as described above, the return to the language of the first narrative cycle (3:7; and that of the introduction, 2:11) implies that 6:1, while syntactically (con)sequential to 5:31, hints at a break in the cyclical pattern of the section. To label 6:1 a "new beginning" might overstate the case, but this varied syntax, alongside the absence of a death notice at the end of the third cycle (which tends to trigger a new moment of apostasy), implies a brief respite in the circular pattern of Israel's unfaithfulness, as Stone has argued.

Second, the rebuke of the prophet who appears in 6:8 bolsters the structural import of the Gideon cycle and suggests that the unfaithfulness of Israel had undergone a significant enough shift to warrant divine address, though not complete enough to necessitate a change in divine action, as will transpire after the reign of Abimelek.

Third, several related events occur between 6:1 and the next cyclical pattern variation in 10:6. These include (1) the fulfillment of YHWH's warning in 2:3, that the people of Israel would prove unfaithful in response to their Sovereign's test, when the nations God brought to rest in the land had influenced Israel and thereby became a "snare" (8:27); (2) national infidelity to YHWH during a judge's lifetime (8:28, 33); and (3) the institutionalization of pagan religion in Israel (8:33, 9:4). In short, the Gideon and Abimelek narratives depict a sharp decline in the faithfulness of Israel.[17] The religious

---

[17] Many speak of Gideon in this way. See, e.g., David W. Gooding, "The Composition of the Book of Judges," *ErIsr* 16 (1982): 74–75; Paul Tanner, "The Gideon Narrative as the Focal Point of Judges," *BSac* 149 (1992): 156.

disintegration at which the introduction hinted was not as gradual as some have claimed; the formal establishment of syncretistic worship under the leadership of Gideon and Abimelek constitutes a significant development.[18] The religious faithfulness of Israel thus diminishes substantially during this period, resulting in the initiation of a new pattern of divine activity in the next stage.

Fourth, elements of character development reflect a change that transpires after the break suggested by the varied syntax of 6:1: (1) in the narrator's depiction of Israel, the accent begins to fall more heavily on Israelite unfaithfulness than it does Israel's distress (though both are present throughout) and (2) narratorial attention refocuses on the leader and the propriety of his actions (and thereby, the propriety of Israel's support of him).

Given these considerations, the plot development associated with these structural realities is summarized in figure 4 in reference to the section's narrative cycles:

Figure 4: Plot Development in the Core of Judges

Oth.	Ehud	Deb.	Gideon	Abi.	Jephthah	Samson
Stories of salvation: Emphasize YHWH's power to save by empowering the weak			*Transitional stories:* Highlight institutional rejection of YHWH as savior		*Stories of an unsaved people:* Accentuate the inability of the strong to save without YHWH's power	
Stage 2: YHWH saves						Stage 3: YHWH does not save	

The earliest stories in the cycles section highlight the superiority of the enemy and the ability of YHWH to address the threat of the surrounding nations through appropriate deliverers. YHWH's ability to save his people from the mightiest opponent is emphasized consistently in these narratives and is the hallmark of the Song of Deborah and Barak. The song underscores the miraculous quality of a paradigmatic battle and calls Israel to heed the mighty acts of YHWH and respond appropriately. The song focuses on the response of Israel, both retrospectively (by evaluating how the militia volunteered) and prospectively—rhetorically challenging Israel to respond to this latest salvation with enduring faithfulness.

The syntactical reset of 6:1 suggests a break from what precedes, the import of which the speech of the prophet in 6:8 clarifies: Israel failed to

---

[18] Exum ("Centre Cannot Hold," 412) makes a similar claim, contra Heller, "What Is Abimelek Doing?" 231–32, who represents those who too neatly trace such degradation. He speaks of a literary cycle that "slowly dissolves" through the tales of the deliverers that "parallels the progressive brokenness of Israelite society as the people continue to worsen their sinful infidelity with each successive cycle." This interpretive tendency requires a far more negative view of the leaders and the people in the episodes featuring Ehud and Barak than I have set forth.

heed the challenge most recently articulated by Deborah and Barak and has proven to be even more unfaithful than previous generations. The remainder of the narratives surrounding Gideon and Abimelek highlight the culpability and increasing depravity of the nation and its leaders as they failed to embrace YHWH as their covenant partner and, therefore, deliverer.

This sharp downturn occasions a change in YHWH's response to the nation: he would no longer save them as he had previously. Thus, the last two cycles feature stories of military conflict in which Israel is preserved but is not decisively victorious; their exploits bring no peace to the land. Instead, their flawed leaders demonstrate how even the mightiest human hero is powerless to act with integrity or secure lasting military victory without the support of YHWH; the power to bring salvation to Israel belongs to God alone. The cycles section thus consistently documents the refusal of the Israelites to heed this fundamental truth.

Thematic Emphases

The introduction to the cycles section frames the following stories in terms of a relationship between three characters or groups of characters: YHWH, his covenant partner Israel, and the inhabitants of the land. According to 2:19, the trajectory of the overarching narrative is the deterioration of the relationship between YHWH and his people and the increasing influence of the pagan nations upon Israel. The narrator frames the subsequent cycles in terms of three interconnected themes that contribute to that trajectory: (1) a tendency to forget the work of YHWH on Israel's behalf (2:10), (2) the testing of Israel's covenant fidelity through serial plundering (2:22; 3:1–2, 4), and (3) the generational degradation of Israel's disposition toward the covenant (2:10, 2:17–19).[19] As we will see, the song makes important contributions to the development of each of these themes.

Forgetting YHWH

The introduction to the cycles section attributes one characteristic to the generation(s) of Israelites who succeeded Joshua: they "did not know YHWH or the work that he had done for Israel" (2:10). Before enabling them to possess the land of promise, through Moses YHWH had insisted that each generation recall and recount the dynamics of Israel's election by YHWH (e.g., Deut 4:9–14, 6:6–15) to experience a life of blessing in Canaan. It is noteworthy

[19] For the vocabulary of "trajectory," see above, pp. 9–10. Here I differentiate themes from elements of plot (i.e., events, developments; 2:11: "the Israelites did [the] evil") or characterization (2:15: "they were in terrible distress").

that the prohibition against forgetting (שׁכח) YHWH, his deeds, and his covenant is frequent in the book of Deuteronomy.[20] Deuteronomy 8:11–20 concretizes the injunction with two possible scenarios in which Israel would forget: (1) that Israelites would credit themselves with its good fortune: "My power and the might of my hand have effected for me this prosperity" (v. 17) or (2) attribute their salvation to foreign gods (v. 19). Ultimately, the effect of forgetting YHWH is to attribute his work to another entity. The song of Deuteronomy 32:1–43 perfectly anticipates this pattern in Israel's subsequent history. YHWH commands the people to internalize and teach these verses, which detail how he chose the nation as his "portion" (32:9), to ensure that they would successfully possess the land of promise (32:47). The hallmark of the characterization of the new generation in Judges 2 is their failure to live up to that Deuteronomic ideal.[21] The textual focus on this singular trait identifies its foundational importance for the ensuing narrative.

It is then fitting that the Othniel narrative, which opens with a notice that Israel had committed the evil of apostasy, associates the transgression with forgetting YHWH (שׁכח) and serving the deities of Canaan (3:7). At the beginning of the cycles section, the consequence of the people's neglect of their saving history is a susceptibility to the religion of the land's inhabitants. "The evil" that the Israelites repeated in 3:12 and 4:1 is the same; Israel's disregard for YHWH's past actions, including his forging a covenant with them, undermines their allegiance to him and facilitates the worship of other deities.

In contrast to the prose preceding and following the song, Judges 5 does not address apostasy forthrightly; nowhere does the prophet condemn the worship of foreign deities or attribute Israel's distress to the people's religious malpractice. Instead, the song heralds the miraculous intervention of YHWH to rescue his people from Canaanite oppression using terms reminiscent of the foundational moments of Israel's relationship with YHWH—the exodus from Egypt and the theophany at Sinai. God's storm-like appearance in verses 4–5 recalls the departure of YHWH from the south after the covenant ceremony of a previous generation (cf. Deut 33:1–4), just as the deadly surge of water from the Kishon in verse 21 resembles the victory over Pharaoh's army in Exodus. This prophetic rendition not only recalls the mighty acts of God in Israel's history but also identifies the militia's recent victory over Canaan as another event in kind. The song emphasizes that it was *YHWH* who acted on Israel's behalf and that such intervention was *wondrous*. In short, the prophet depicts the Kishon battle as another of YHWH's wonderful deeds, like those recounted to the post-Joshua generations by their fathers.

---

[20] Deut 4:9, 23, 31; 6:12; 8:11, 14, 19; 9:7; 25:19; 26:13. Cf. 31:21, 32:18.
[21] An eventuality YHWH foretold in Deut 31:19–21.

The thematic importance of casting the Kishon battle as one of YHWH's mighty works is evident from the correlative question posed by Gideon in the following chapter—namely, "Where are all his wonderful deeds that our fathers recounted to us, saying, 'Did not YHWH bring us up from Egypt?'" Given the song's position in its context, Gideon's negligence to recognize the literarily adjacent victory over Canaan as evidence of YHWH's commitment to Israel is indicting.[22] The juxtaposition of Gideon's incredulity with the prophetic assurance of the Song of Deborah and Barak casts the deliverer as an exemplar of a forgetful generation who knew neither YHWH nor his mighty acts. Given this contextual effect, the song functionally addresses the foundational issue of the judges period: an unfamiliarity with YHWH marked by a tendency to forget his deeds.[23] Whereas interpreters often consider Judges a chronicle of Israelite infidelity, it is crucial to recognize it is also (and perhaps more importantly) an exploration of the ways in which the generation(s) after Joshua came to be characterized as such.

YHWH's Test

The programmatic statements in 2:21–22 speak of a "test" associated with the continued presence of nations other than Israel in the land of promise. Their syntax is not entirely clear. According to the most common interpretation of the verses, the clause beginning with למען נסות is subordinate to לא אוסיף להוריש ("I will no longer drive out"; v. 21), rather than עזב יהושע ("Joshua left"; v. 22).[24] Thus, in verses 21–22, YHWH asserts that he will no longer help the Israelites dispossess the land's inhabitants—those whom Joshua had failed to

---

[22] Within a narrative context, literary adjacency often implies temporal adjacency. Even when a text's arrangement is not strictly chronological, an episode's position in a plot that develops linearly is definitive for its temporal association with the unfolding narrative (assuming the absence of explicit chronological notices to the contrary). In this case, the (con)sequentiality of the Gideon narrative with that which precedes is implied by the continuation of *wayyiqtol* forms from 5:31 to 6:1.

[23] Gregory T. K. Wong (*The Compositional Strategy of the Book of Judges: An Inductive, Rhetorical Study*, VTSup 111 [New York: Brill, 2006], 253) makes a similar observation in passing: "Moreover, the reason for this readiness to forsake YHWH also seems to be hinted at in 2:10 as a lack of knowledge of YHWH and what He has done for the nation."

[24] Robert B. Chisholm Jr. (*A Commentary on Judges and Ruth*, Kregel Exegetical Library [Grand Rapids: Kregel Academic, 2013], 159–60) has mapped these views, noting that the latter has been popularized recently in the work of Barry G. Webb (e.g., *The Book of Judges: An Integrated Reading*, JSOTSup 46 [Sheffield: JSOT, 1987], 114, esp. n. 110; following Moshe Weinfeld, "The Period of the Conquest and of the Judges as Seen by the Earlier and the Later Sources," *VT* 17 [1967]: 93–113]). Though Webb attempts to explain it, the notice of Joshua's death in verse 22 is syntactically awkward if one adopts his interpretation.

drive out during his lifetime—in order to test (נסה) his people. The test is thus experienced by present and future generations, including those living under the leadership of the judges.[25]

YHWH explains that the test determines "whether or not they will keep (שמר) the way of YHWH, to walk in [it]," a state of affairs the narrator later associates with "obeying the commands of YHWH, that he commanded their fathers by the hand of Moses" (3:4). The lexical contrast of testing (2:22; 3:1, 4) and teaching war (3:2) leads some commentators to speak either of two purposes or distinct agendas for each generation (i.e., under Joshua YHWH *taught*; under the judges YHWH *tested*).[26] By contrast, Webb and Block represent those who equate the two purposes, asserting that to learn war is to conduct חרם war according to Deuteronomic standards and thereby demonstrate loyalty to YHWH.[27] The latter interpretation is probable given the structure of the passage. The fact that 2:22 and 3:1 both assert that YHWH caused certain nations to settle in the land for the purpose of testing Israel suggests that נסה is the overarching purpose of his action. Thus, 3:2 consists of two restrictive clauses that qualify the objective of the test and its intended audience: to confer knowledge of war to the Israelites, specifically those who lacked previous experience in the wars of Canaan (v. 2; cf. v. 1).[28] Therefore, in the introduction to the book of Judges, to be tested by YHWH involves experiencing the wars of Canaan and thereby receiving divine instruction in them. To pass that test is to embrace the divine imperative to show "total fidelity to Yahweh, total

---

[25] By contrast, the alternate view restricts the period of "testing" to the generation under Joshua; the occupations of the Judges period would then serve as punishment for a previous generation's failing the test. Webb (*Integrated Reading*, 115) explains, "The nations which were originally left as a test are now to be left as a punishment."

[26] The latter is the perspective of Chisholm, *Judges and Ruth*, 159–60. Other commentators speak of a dual purpose. See, e.g., Trent C. Butler, *Judges*, Women's Bible Commentary 8 (Nashville: Thomas Nelson, 2009), 60.

[27] Webb, *Book of Judges*, 114–15; Block, *Judges, Ruth*, 136–37; so also Lawson G. Stone ("Judges," in *Joshua, Judges, Ruth*, ed. Philip W. Comfort, Cornerstone Biblical Commentary [Carol Stream, Ill.: Tyndale House, 2012], 233), who adds that experiencing the Canaanite conquest teaches "total confidence in [YHWH's] power." Nathan Stemmer ("The Introduction to Judges, 2.1–3.4," *JQR* 57 [1967]: 239) briefly mentions a similar interpretation (i.e., "that the younger generations may see the wonders which God performs during wars").

[28] Syntactically speaking, the restrictive purpose clause in v. 2a modifies the verb נסה in v. 1 and the relative clause of v. 2c modifies the substantive דרות בני־ישראל: "These are the nations YHWH left to test Israel by them . . . only so that the generations of Israelites—only those who had not formerly known—might experience, and thereby he might teach them, war."

obedience to his instructions, and total confidence in his power."[29] YHWH's remedy for the generation that "did not know (ידע) YHWH or the work that he had done for Israel" (2:10; cf. 3:1) was to "know" (ידע) war (3:2) and thus address this theological deficit.[30]

Judges 3:1 provides a syntactical break that, when coupled with the uninterrupted chain of *wayyiqtols* extending from 3:4 into the Othniel narrative, designates 3:1–6 as the proper launch of the cycles section. The location of these verses frames the remainder of the book as a description of how through these nations YHWH tests his people directly (i.e., the Canaanites and the Philistines oppress Israel) and indirectly (i.e., the nations influence Israel to respond unfaithfully when oppressed). In 3:3, four specific threatening nations are identified as now inhabiting the land: the Philistines, Canaanites, Sidonians, and Hivites—a list roughly matching that of Joshua 13:1–7.[31] While the book of Joshua emphasizes that YHWH would eventually drive out these nations (13:6), the introduction to the cycles section in Judges emphasizes that YHWH would delay the fulfillment of that promise, thereby measuring Israel's fidelity when settled among other people groups. An elderly Joshua anticipated this Judges-era struggle in Joshua 23:6–13, where he warned that to associate closely with Canaanite nations, primarily through intermarriage, would result in YHWH's refusal to facilitate the completion of the conquest and leave the people in danger of religious compromise. What the Judges period shows is that God's test involved not only leaving the conquest unfulfilled but also bringing in outside nations to complicate the task even further.

Through this lens, the following cycles constitute opportunities for the people of God to demonstrate their loyalty through fidelity to their covenant

---

[29] Lawson G. Stone, "Judges, Book of," in *Dictionary of the Old Testament: Historical Books*, ed. Bill T. Arnold and H. G. M. Williamson (Downers Grove, Ill.: InterVarsity Press, 2005), 233. So also Block, *Judges, Ruth*, 136–37, who speaks of learning "the nature and significance of this war" and consequently "accept[ing] their sovereign and their responsibilities in fulfilling his agenda."

[30] The collocation "to learn/teach war" (למד + מלחמה) denotes acquiring skill in warfare (Song 3:8; 1 Chr 5:18). It is the context—not the lexemes—that imbues the collocation in this text with the sense of divine empowerment. For an example of the collocation with a similar connotation, see Ps 18:35 = 2 Sam 22:35. See also my argument in "The Prophet's Song of Victory: Judges 5 within a Trajectory of Theological Training in the Book of Judges," *BBR* 33 (2023): 287–303.

[31] Stone, "Judges, Book of," 230–31. This list differs from that offered in 3:5, which more closely resembles the stereotypical list of the land's inhabitants, with whom the people were not to intermarry (e.g., Deut 7:1). While the phrasing of the first list ties these verses to YHWH's declaration in Josh 13, the phrasing of the second underscores that Israel defied specific instructions given by Moses.

with YHWH.³² Each narrative begins with the assertion that the people compromised their religious integrity, but each encounter with an opposing army provided the people with another opportunity to demonstrate their loyalty to, and confidence in, YHWH: to "experience the wars of Canaan" or to fulfill his command to inherit the land fully. More straightforwardly than any prose in the cycles section, the Song of Deborah and Barak assesses the willingness of the people to respond to YHWH's muster. Each narrative describes the action of God's people in war, but only the song thoroughly evaluates their military response. The occasion for the song is evaluative in and of itself: that the people offered themselves willingly (5:2, 9) and acted righteously (5:11). The fourth stanza provides a more nuanced assessment of the response of individual tribes, contrasting those who "went down" and "were sent" with those who "stayed," "remained," and "sojourned." Moreover, Jael—depicted as a crucial agent of YHWH in the Kishon battle—is blessed, while the reluctant settlement Meroz is cursed for its lack of participation in the conflict with Canaan. Like the book's introduction, the song juxtaposes the language of military engagement with that of covenant fidelity. The military exploits of Israel's downtrodden militia are "righteous" (v. 11), just as it is those who "love" (אהב; show covenant dedication to) YHWH whom Deborah expects to be empowered by YHWH for victory (v. 31).³³ Despite its theological perspective, the song does not directly promote orthodox Yahwism or condemn Israel's apostate behavior; in contrast to the rest of the cycles section, the people's culpability in the Kishon conflict is entirely absent. Instead, the criterion by which Israel is being evaluated is its willing participation in battle—an action contextually interpreted as obedience to the commands of YHWH.

The narratives of the cycles section record the involvement of certain tribes in military conflicts, but only two emphasize the response of a particular character to a divine muster as part of the narrative mainline: the summonses to Barak (4:6, 14) and Gideon (6:14), the accounts that flank the Song of Deborah and Barak. Their literary proximity is surely no accident. By emphasizing the response to YHWH's imperatives, these narratives highlight more explicitly the testing of Israel and its leaders to be faithful to their Sovereign's agenda in conquering the land. YHWH's testing of Israel, then, is thematically

---

³² See also Robert H. O'Connell, *The Rhetoric of the Book of Judges*, VTSup 63 (Leiden: Brill, 1996), 77, who asserts that the individual battle stories in their current context "serve a scheme that shows how each new cycle functions as a 'test' of Israel's loyalty to YHWH."

³³ On the connotation of אהב as fidelity to covenant, see above, p. 44, n. 28.

concentrated in the launch of the cycles section (2:22–3:4) and in Judges 4–9, the cycles on either side of the major cyclical break at 6:1.[34]

While the initial responses of Barak and Gideon are similarly hesitant, in the aggregate their narrative portrayals differ drastically. Barak's initial hesitancy was met by divine corrective through a prophet. He obediently led the militia to battle and responded to the victory that he witnessed privately by sharing it with the people publicly. The battle in which he participated is framed in celebration. By contrast, Gideon's incredulity pervades the entire narrative of the Midianite conflict. While at one point he worshiped YHWH for Israel's deliverance (7:15)—the sincerity of which the text does not question—his more consistent doubt regarding divine empowerment left him vulnerable to a misunderstanding of his own calling, prone to the religious influence of Baalism, and father to Israel's next oppressor. By embodying contrasting responses to YHWH's imperatives and subsequent deliverance, these characters embody contrasting outcomes to divine testing. Barak and Gideon demonstrate the thematic import of the plot developments in the transitional portion of the cycles section (chapters 6–9): with the prophet, Barak relayed divine instruction to the Israelite people regarding warfare (i.e., through him and Deborah, YHWH "taught Israel war"; cf. 3:2); as a representative of his generation, Gideon proved unreceptive to that instruction and ultimately failed "to walk in the way of YHWH" and "obey the commandments of YHWH" (2:22, 3:4).

Generational Degradation

The deterioration of Israel's religious character figures significantly in the cycles section. In 2:19, the narrator raises the expectation of the people's spiritual deterioration by speaking of each successive generation being more corrupt (שחת *hi.*) than the previous.[35] The previous section (related to plot) argued that several specific events under the leadership of Gideon and Abimelek demonstrated this narrative trajectory. In addition, elements of familial degradation surface in these interrelated episodes—specifically in terms of the son's treachery toward his father (8:34–35, 9:16–19).[36] By framing the accounts in terms of dynastic succession and highlighting the unfaithfulness of the successor, the narratives surrounding Gideon and Abimelek provide a

---

[34] On which, see the section describing "Cyclical Divisions" above.

[35] Wong, *Compositional Strategy of the Book of Judges*, 249–54, identifies the progressive deterioration of the post-Joshua generations as the central theme of the entire book, not simply the cycles section.

[36] The motif of fractured interclan relationships is prevalent in the remainder of the cycles section and demonstrates moral degradation in general. See further Gordon K. Oeste, "Butchered Brothers and Betrayed Families: Degenerating Kinship Structures in the Book of Judges," *JSOT* 35 (2010): 307–9.

concrete example of one son—a representative of the Israelite people—who has turned (8:33 שוב; cf. 2:19) and been disloyal, with the result of corruption surpassing that of the previous generation.

The contribution of the Song of Deborah and Barak to the development of this theme is modest. The prophetic declaration never speaks of generations, nor explicitly or implicitly compares the faithfulness of present and past Israelites. Instead, Deborah and Barak reflect on one conflict—only hinting at an awareness of other conflicts[37]—and the faithfulness of God and the people in that conflict. Insofar as the song is the backdrop against which Gideon's incredulity is portrayed, its chief effect in terms of portraying generational degradation is to act as a foil against which to measure Gideon's theological awareness. The statement that the land had rest for forty years in 5:31b marks the passing of a generation and thereby depicts the events of 6:1 and the subsequent Midianite conflict as belonging to another. Within this scheme, the song characterizes the Kishon conflict as an exemplary moment in Israelite covenant fidelity and provides a measure by which the faithfulness of future Israelites may be measured.

Conclusion

The past two chapters have drawn together the function of the Song of Deborah and Barak on at least three levels: characterization, plot development (especially in terms of narrative structure), and thematic emphases. We may synthesize this information to speak of the song's contribution as follows:

In its literary location, the song closes the first of three units in the cycles section, here termed the "Stories of Salvation." The song presents a fitting conclusion to the section. Reiterating the primary issue of the macroplot (i.e., the faithfulness of the Israelites to their Sovereign, YHWH), the text provides interpretive clarity to the battle at the Kishon, yet its paradigmatic quality renders its insights relevant to the cycles that precede. Moreover, the degree to which trends in characterization and plot development culminate with the song signals its broader contextual import. In terms of characterization, the song completes and highlights an otherwise subtle transition: while these cycles mention the punishment of Israel for its infidelity, the narratives increasingly emphasize the suffering from which YHWH consistently and

---

[37] To speak of Shamgar ben-Anath in 5:6 implies contextual awareness that extends beyond the Kishon battle. Considering his introduction before Ehud's death (3:31) and his association with Jael in the song, Shamgar's tenure likely overlapped with that of Ehud, Deborah, and Barak. Mark J. Boda, "Judges," in *Numbers–Ruth*, vol. 5 of *The Expositor's Bible Commentary*, ed. Tremper Longman III and David E. Garland, rev. ed. (Grand Rapids: Zondervan, 2017), 1110.

effectively rescued the nation. In these cycles, most characters are relatively flat and serve only as instruments of YHWH. The song is the culmination of this narrative trend; it highlights the might of YHWH to empower the weakest instruments to defeat the mightiest foes. Given the evaluative slant of its fourth and fifth stanzas, the song simultaneously offers theological instruction and indicts those who have been unresponsive to previous revelation—to the instructions of YHWH to execute faithfully his purposes in the land of promise. In so doing, the song recalls the introduction's assertion that the encounters with foreign nations in this period were tests of Israelite faithfulness, not simply accounts celebrating (or indicting) Israelite heroes. Thus, in content the song is both revelatory and evaluative, reiterating the theological truths of previous accounts and introducing an element of evaluation anticipated by the introduction.

The song has a similar binary effect in its wider literary context. As the concluding declaration in a series of salvation-oriented stories, which highlight the decisiveness of Israelite victory and the ease with which YHWH accomplished it, the song underscores YHWH's power to save. At the same time, the song indicts those who forget YHWH and his miraculous deeds, and therefore unnecessarily fear the inhabitants of the land and offer fealty to their gods. This dynamic is clearest when considering the subsequent call of Gideon. Immediately following the Song of Deborah and Barak and the rebuke of a second prophet, Gideon refused to acknowledge YHWH's recent miraculous activity and doubted the deity's ability to empower him for service, based on his perceived weakness. The precision with which the song had so recently addressed Gideon's insecurities indicts the Israelite as unreceptive to divine revelation. He thereby becomes a representative of a generation who had "forgotten YHWH" and failed to heed his instruction; in short, Gideon failed the test of 2:22 and 3:4. Although instructed by YHWH and enabled to experience the wars of Canaan, Gideon and his generation neglected to walk in the way of generations past.

Given this contextual dynamic, the Song of Deborah and Barak facilitates a shift in the cycles section from primarily declarative texts to evaluative ones—from stories that provide evidence of YHWH's mighty deliverance to those that evaluate Israel's response to that action and thereby demonstrate the trend already described in the introduction: that Israel would fail with escalating depravity. As a text that catalogues the first signs of this downward trajectory, the song highlights the insecurity that proves to be budding apostasy. In its present literary context, especially in relation to the Gideon narratives, the Song of Deborah and Barak demonstrates what the narrator had already claimed: that the post-Joshua generations were willfully ignorant of the work of YHWH and had thereby abandoned the theological narrative undergirding their relationship with (and faith in) YHWH. Bereft of this theological foundation, the people exposed themselves to the allure of other national deities and consequently neglected to walk in the way that their fathers had. In a devastatingly predictable pattern, the covenant people had failed YHWH's test.

5
The Narrative Function of the Song of Deborah and Barak in the Book of Judges

> And what more shall I say? For time would fail me to tell of Gideon, Barak, Samson, Jephthah, of David and Samuel and the prophets—who through faith conquered kingdoms, enforced justice, obtained promises, stopped the mouth of lions, quenched the power of fire, escaped the edge of the sword, were made strong out of weakness, became mighty in war, [and] put armies to flight.
>
> Heb 11:32–34

In contrast to the book of Hebrews, I have devoted significant time to recounting the deeds of Gideon, Barak, Samson, and Jephthah, not to mention Deborah or Jael. Hardly a catalogue of Israel's heroes, the book of Judges relays the exploits of men and women who—in the words of the New Testament— "conquered kingdoms," "became mighty in war," and "put armies to flight" but did so only through the explicit empowerment of YHWH. Consequently, to describe these leaders as those "made strong out of weakness" is the simplest and most appropriate characterization of the judges one could offer. With clarity and uniformity, the central section of Judges has emphasized the weakness of its titular characters in construing the history of the pre-monarchic period with one overriding purpose: to indict the people of Israel for their inattention to their Sovereign's saving power and the covenant transgression fostered by such willful ignorance. The Song of Deborah and Barak plays a crucial role in that indictment.

The book's introduction frames the ensuing narratives in terms of a test whose results the remainder of the book reports—an opportunity for the people of YHWH to respond appropriately to the revelatory experience of participating in the battles of Canaan. Following Joshua's death, the generation of the elders who outlived him was comparatively faithful to YHWH, walking in his ways and repenting when confronted with its own covenant failures (2:4–5, 7). Despite this generalization, the Northern tribes failed to take possession of their allotted territories in Canaan, allowing the land's inhabitants to remain and even entering into covenant with them (1:22–26, 2:1–2). In response, YHWH declared (2:3; and reiterated to the next generation, 2:20–22) that he would delay the fulfillment of his promise (through Joshua; 13:6) to dispossess the nations and would instead test the obedience of the generations under the judges through serial military occupation.

The context of the core of Judges is the failure of the Northern tribes, with the Canaanites (and their religious influence) thoroughly entrenched in Israelite society (3:1–5).[1] Each narrative in the book's cyclical center documents the cultic influence of the land's inhabitants on Israel, who continually abandoned YHWH and served pagan deities. Despite their transgressions, YHWH did not abandon them. The first three narrative cycles highlight the extraordinary ability of Israel's God to deliver the nation from the mightiest of foes through the weakest of instruments. With growing intensity, each of these early cycles reinforces the severity of Israel's subjugation and the precise and exhaustive reversal of their circumstances through the deity's perfectly equipped agent(s) of deliverance.

The Song of Deborah and Barak demonstrates that this construal of history is not simply for the readers' benefit; through the song the prophet interpreted the Battle of Kishon for the Israelites in exactly these terms "on that day." Given its pedagogical orientation and its prophetic quality, Judges 5 is the culmination of God's revelatory activity in the early cycles. In the voice of YHWH's spokesperson, the song's mythic imagery and graphic detail emphasize that God empowered his hopelessly occupied people to overcome a mighty enemy, in the same way a vulnerable civilian woman was able to slay a powerful Canaanite general. Moreover, the song celebrates the faithful execution of חרם by those Northern tribes who responded to the muster.[2] Notably, the tribes whom the fourth stanza addresses are the

---

[1] Andrew Tobolowsky ("The Problem of Reubenite Primacy: New Paradigms, New Answers," *JBL* 139 [2020]: 35) postulates that the tribal list in Judg 5 is "*particularly representative of northern imaginations*" because the Jacob tribes appear at its head and the Southern tribes do not appear at all. In my view, however, given this narrative context, the absence of the Southern tribes from the Song of Deborah and Barak is not surprising. Moreover, one need not conclude that Judah and Simeon constituted a political entity separate from pre-state Israel (as has been claimed by, e.g., Volkmar Fritz, "Das Debora-Lied Ri 5 als Geschichtsquelle," in *Studien zur Literatur und Geschichte des alten Israel*, Stuttgarter Biblische Aufsatzbände 22 [Stuttgart: Katholisches Bibelwerk, 1997], 184), or that the tribal list is corrupted or incomplete.

[2] Admittedly, the root חרם does not appear in the song; however, the portrayal of warfare depicted therein—against the mightier Canaanites, in a tribal allotment, directed and enabled by YHWH, and complete (i.e., leaving no survivors)—corresponds to the destruction associated with חרם in key texts (e.g., Deut 7:1–2, 20:16–18).

same ones singled out for their conquest-related failures in the introduction. In Judges 5, five of these prove faithful; the other two are censured along with the Transjordanian tribes.[3] The paradigmatic quality of the battle heightens the significance of the faithfulness of the Northerners—YHWH's people are victorious over Israel's archetypal enemy, the Canaanites, whom they destroy decisively, despite the chariots of iron brandished by its troops, which had proven insurmountable for even the most faithful of Israel's (Southern) tribes (1:19). On this day, the plunderers of Israel (2:14) took no plunder (5:19, 30). Deborah's rendition of the battle does not simply reflect theologically on the events near Mount Tabor; rather, the prophet uses YHWH's most recent exploits to confront her increasingly battle-wary people with one fundamental theological truth: neither their weakness nor the strength of the opponent du jour is a match for the might of the God of Israel. The song's negative evaluation of the tribes who failed to participate reveals that Deborah (with Barak) communicates a second correlative truth: to hesitate in battle is to doubt YHWH's power and Israel's saving history—a theological misstep whose consequence is the rampant apostasy emphasized in the remainder of the book. Within the narrative world, the prophet's song offered to the generation who "did not know YHWH or the work that he had done for Israel" (2:10) an opportunity to correct this theological deficit and embrace the God of their fathers anew.

The launch of the Gideon cycle dashes the hopes of the optimistic reader and thereby highlights the devastating consequences of the Israelites' failure to separate themselves from the land's inhabitants. Despite the uncharacteristic faithfulness of the Israelites at the Battle of Kishon and the prophet's impassioned lyrical challenge to the people, the next two cycles document a sharp downturn in Israel's relationship with YHWH. Gideon's characteristic blindness to YHWH's salvific work functions as a precise foil to a faithful response to the Song of Deborah and Barak. While in the narrative world the song is revelatory (and of course corrective), at the level of literary function, the song is condemnatory. As the culmination of YHWH's revelation, in which the prophet highlights YHWH's characteristic faithfulness and concretizes his repeated promises and warnings to a hard-hearted generation, the song concludes the "Stories of Salvation" and presents the ultimate test to God's

---

[3] Those who are faithful include Ephraim and Manasseh [Machir] (or, "the house of Joseph"), Benjamin, Zebulun, and Naphtali. While Issachar is not mentioned in Judges 1 as either a failure or a success, the tribe is likely implicated in the report of its closely related tribe, Zebulun (1:30). In the blessing of Deut 33:18–19, Issachar is folded into the lines addressing Zebulun in just this way. The remaining tribes listed in the introduction—Asher and Dan—are among those censured for their nonparticipation in the song.

people. The Gideon and Abimelek cycles demonstrate just how emphatically the Israelites failed that test.

When the people of Israel started explicitly rejecting YHWH in favor of human leaders, and the echoes of the Song of Deborah and Barak proved powerless to convince them that YHWH was their faithful deliverer, the patience of their Sovereign came to an end. In 10:13, YHWH pledged to save Israel no longer. The remaining cycles—"Stories of an Unsaved People"—demonstrate that the most promising human leaders are powerless to decisively bring rest to Israel without YHWH's explicit empowerment. With the failure of Samson, the final judge and YHWH's agent of preservation, mention of the judges or the nations who oppress Israel disappears. Instead, the conclusion highlights the precise reversal of the conditions of Israel in the introduction. In these chapters, it is Israelites who are facilitating the worship of false deities (17:11–13), Israelites settling in lands *not* apportioned to them by YHWH (18:27–30), Israelites who are committing sexual violence (19:23–26), and Israelites who are slaughtering their own people (20:14–18). At this point, readers see in horrifying detail the consequences of "forgetting YHWH." The early signs of hesitancy in battle that the song attempted to address, which grew into full-fledged self-reliance and apostasy under Gideon, have by this point blossomed into a rejection of the moral imperatives and life-sustaining virtues embodied in Israel's covenant with their Sovereign. The Israelites' abandonment of YHWH's kingly claim to their loyalty and submission had societal repercussions; their faithlessness threatened not only the benefits of the covenant (e.g., divine protection) but also the basic dignity of humanity before God. The last chapters of Judges chronicle the days when Israel had failed the test of covenant faithfulness and found itself left by its Sovereign to its own devices. In those days, there was—emphatically—no King in Israel.

Appendix: Lexical and Text Critical Analysis

The text of Judges 5 has been the object of significant critical inquiry for centuries. Accordingly, the following analysis will address two different types of interpretive difficulties: (1) those that arise from variant readings among ancient texts—both true variants (reflecting different underlying source texts) and variant interpretations of a difficult source text and (2) those that scholars have identified in cases of textual uniformity.[1] In instances of the former, the text critical method I apply adheres to the following commitments about the nature of the biblical text: (1) the more difficult reading is not necessarily the better reading; (2) the longer reading is not necessarily secondary; (3) where there is repetition of substantial portions of the text, consideration should first be given to poetic technique rather than dittography;[2] (4) the ancient texts (especially the primary versions) are likely to preserve a more authentic reading than any scholar's educated guess;[3] emendation is, therefore, a last resort; however, (5) the Masoretic text should be given priority over the LXX not

---

[1] Walter Groß and Erasmus Gaß, *Richter: Übersetzt und ausgelegt*, HTKAT (Freiburg: Herder, 2009), 294, hypothesize that the ancient versions rarely help to reconstruct the Hebrew *Vorlage* of Judg 5 and instead preserve interpretations of a text that was already difficult for early translators.

[2] This commitment is specifically in reference to Judg 5. Its distinct style of parallelism (attested in other nonbiblical sources from, e.g., Ugarit) involves significant repetition.

[3] The versions with which I most frequently interact are Targum Jonathan (TJon), the Syriac Peshitta (Syr.), Codex Alexandrinus (LXXA), Codex Vaticanus (LXXB), and the Latin Vulgate (Vulg.). The LXX (especially LXXA in Judg) is most helpful for textual criticism, because it deviates from the Masoretic tradition more frequently than the rest of the versions (thus most likely witnessing to a prestandardized Hebrew text). The *kaige* features of LXXB reflect a revision of the Old Greek to more readily conform to the Hebrew texts (Natalio Fernandez Marcos, *Judges*, vol. 7 of *Biblia Hebraica Quinta* [Stuttgart: Deutsche Bibelgesellschaft, 2011], 8*). Syr. reflects a fairly literal translation of the proto-MT, to which TJon and Vulg. also witness (Emmanuel Tov, *Textual Criticism of the Hebrew Bible*, 4th rev. and exp. ed. [Minneapolis: Fortress, 2022], 29). TJon's translation also features "occasional glosses and midrashic expansions," most heavily in

because of any supposed intrinsic superiority but because in Judges 5 the LXX has preserved readings that make little sense.[4] The preceding translation reflects careful attention to the details of the text and an attempt to identify the most likely reading based on the song's context, poetic form, and thematic emphases. In instances of confusing cola, where ancient versions are broadly uniform, precedence is given to intertextual links and canonical attestation of given forms over comparative evidence, although the latter was carefully considered.

Verse 1

Then Deborah sang. The use of a compound subject with a 3ms verbal form is common (cf. Exod 15:1). In these cases, the verb tends to agree in gender and number with the first noun of the compound subject.[5] A similar construction employing a 3fs verb occurs here. While Deborah may be the agent whose role is emphasized grammatically, the song's attribution to both leaders is noteworthy.[6]

Verse 2

At the unbinding of hair in Israel. The meaning of the phrase בִּפְרֹעַ פְּרָעוֹת בְּיִשְׂרָאֵל remains one of the most difficult to determine in the song. The phrase consists of (1) a בְּ preposition (here circumstantial) prefixed to the infinitive construct of פרע, normally meaning "to loosen" or "cast off"; (2) a plural substantive of the same root; and (3) an adverbial prepositional phrase. The connotation of פרע remains the interpretive crux. Assuming that the grammatical parallelism of 2a and 2b is accompanied by synonymous semantic parallelism,[7] the

---

Judges 5 (Marcos, *Judges*, 12*). Similarly, Vulg. reflects the proto-MT but incorporates stylistic and paraphrastic alterations (Marcos, *Judges*, 10*).

    [4] Regarding Judg 5, Philip Satterthwaite (introduction to Judges, NETS, 197) acknowledges that "some of the LXX translations in these verses seem little short of nonsense. The translator has made his best guess at the meaning of individual words . . . , but these guesses taken together do not yield coherent sense. In most cases it is rare Hebrew words that have caused the problem. . . . But it is impossible to read a modern, philologically informed translation of Judges 5 such as NRSV without feeling that it has come closer to what the Hebrew likely meant." Similarly, Tov ("The Textual History of the Song of Deborah in the A Text of the LXX," *VT* 28 [1978]: 225) opines that "within the complicated text history of the Greek texts of Judges, the text of the Song of Deborah suffered more than any other chapter."

    [5] *BHRG*, §35.9.
    [6] For this reason certain Greek MSS and Vulg. use a plural verb.
    [7] While it is statistically likely that the lines exhibit semantic parallelism that complements the evident grammatical equivalence, it is by no means "required." Contra Barnabas

meaning of בִּפְרֹעַ פְּרָעוֹת should correspond in some way to בְּהִתְנַדֵּב עָם, "at the volunteering of the people."

Of the various proposed translations, "the unbinding of hair" seems to be the most plausible.[8] The root פרע is used most frequently in the Hebrew Bible to indicate "casting off" or "turning away"—negatively with the sense of rejection or unfaithfulness (Exod 5:4; 32:25; Ezek 24:14; Prov 1:25; 13:18; 15:31; 29:18; 2 Chr 28:19),[9] or positively as in avoiding sin (Prov 4:15). The Pentateuch, however, uses the root more frequently to describe the untying of bound hair (Lev 10:6; 13:45; 21:10; Num 5:18), an action that in each case is prohibited or associated with uncleanliness. Nowhere is the noun פֶּרַע collocated with the root פרע; only four times (Num 6:5; Deut 32:42; Judg 5:2; Ezek 44:20) does the noun appear at all. In Numbers 6 and Ezekiel 44, פֶּרַע, "loosely hanging hair," designates either the uncut hair of the Nazirite or the free flowing hair prohibited to the priest. As in Judges 5, the meaning in Deuteronomy 32 is debated; many have recommended "princes."[10]

Lindars, *Judges 1–5: A New Translation and Commentary*, ICC (New York: T&T Clark, 1995), 225.

[8] For a summary of possible translations, see Lindars, *Judges 1–5*, 225–27. Robert Miller builds on Lindars' summary and adds an interpretive option of his own in "When Pharaohs Ruled: On the Translation of Judges 5:2," *JTS* 59 (2008): 650–54. Still favored by contemporary interpreters, the translation adopted here is attributed to W. Robertson Smith by C. F. Burney, *The Book of Judges: With Introduction and Notes*, 2nd ed. (London: Rivingtons, 1920), 107–8.

[9] So the first of two juxtaposed translations in the Targum: "When the House of Israel rebelled against the law." Willem F. Smelik, *The Targum of Judges*, OtSt 26 (New York: Brill, 1995), 392–93. פרע is subsequently interpreted in the sense of retaliation (a meaning derived from postbiblical Hebrew): "because of the retribution of Sisera's shattering and that of his army." For an argument in support of the Targum's second reading, see Chaim Rabin, "Judges 5:2 and the 'Ideology' of Deborah's War," *JJS* 6 (1955): 132–33, who translates "when duty was done."

[10] Following *HALOT*, 970, which points to the Ugaritic *prʿ*, meaning "prince" or *prʿt* meaning "princess"; however, the text on which this gloss is based (KTU 2.31) is fragmentary and enigmatic. With a variety of contemporary scholars, Charles L. Echols (*"Tell Me, O Muse": The Song of Deborah (Judges 5) in the Light of Heroic Poetry*, LHBOTS 487 [London: T&T Clark, 2008], 18) follows T. Kronholm ("פֶּרַע," *TDOT*, 2:98), who suggests that the Ugaritic parallel *prʿ* means "prince" based on KTU 2.31.16, 37, 15?—whose ambiguous nature is frequently overlooked—and KTU 1.8.9 (so also *HALOT*, 971). However, given the recent association of KTU 1.8 with 1.3 (rather than 1.4), the problematic root *prʿ* is even less likely to mean "lofty one" or "princess." On which, see Mark S. Smith and Wayne T. Pitard, *Introduction with Text, Translation and Commentary of KTU/CAT 1.3–1.4*, vol. 2 of *The Ugaritic Baal Cycle*, VTSup 114 (Leiden: Brill, 2009), 373–74. For similar doubts regarding the applicability of Ugaritic *prʿ*, see Groß and Gaß, *Richter*, 297–98.

With the paucity of biblical evidence, translators have long turned to comparable Semitic roots for clarification. Assuming a common derivation, the Ugaritic word pr', "prince" and the Arabic root *fara'a*, "to excel" (or *far'u*, "chief") have led many to translate פְּרָעוֹת as "leaders."[11] The parallel is tempting on thematic grounds; indeed, such a translation makes good sense of the bicola—"leaders taking the lead" parallels the "volunteering of the people"—and what seems to reiterate similar concepts in verse 9. There, פְּרָעוֹת is replaced by חֹקְקֵי יִשְׂרָאֵל, a similarly debated phrase (discussed below) that likely should be read as "leaders of Israel." Neither the Ugaritic nor the Arabic parallel is persuasive. Peter Craigie argues for a slightly different nuance based on the Arabic *fara'a*, which he argues provides evidence for the reading "devote exclusively."[12] His suggestion provides an even tighter semantic equivalence with the parallel root נדב in 5:2b but relies on a less chronologically proximate linguistic parallel.[13] While the translation selected here—"unbinding of hair"—is preferable to these alternatives based on attestation of the relevant lexemes within the Hebrew Bible itself, the phrase still seems to *connote* something like "leaders leading" or individuals demonstrating exclusive devotion, such as that demonstrated by a Nazirite.

Verse 3

I, to YHWH, I will sing. Verse 3 introduces a pattern of textual variance among the ancient translations. LXXA (ᾄσομαι) and Vulg. (*canam*) lack the second independent personal pronoun, while a few Greek manuscripts lack the first. Because the poem so frequently uses this kind of repetition,[14] and the ancient

---

[11] "(Or *far'u*, 'chief')": Lindars, *Judges 1–5*, 225. "Have led many to": The translator of LXXA seemed to understand the text in this way: Ἐν τῷ ἄρξασθαι ἀρχηγοὺς ("when chiefs take the lead," NETS). Echols, *"Tell Me, O Muse,"* 19, finds the comparative evidence convincing in the thematic context of the poem and translates "when the leadership leads."

[12] Peter C. Craigie, "A Note on Judges V 2," *VT* 18 (1968): 397–99. This translation is preferred by John Gray, "Israel in the Song of Deborah," in *Ascribe to the Lord: Biblical and Other Studies in Memory of Peter C. Craigie*, ed. Lyle Eslinger and J. Glen Taylor, JSOTSup (Sheffield: JSOT, 1988), 421–55, and Daniel I. Block, *Judges, Ruth*, NAC 6 (Nashville: Broadman & Holman, 2001), 220, though the latter bases his argument on a likely "ritual act of dedication" (comparable to that of the Nazirite; Num 6:5) that involved loosing hair before battle.

[13] On the connotation of נדב in this context, see Rabin, "'Ideology' of Deborah's War," 128–30, who argues for the meaning "to go to war in answer to a call." While his argument is based in part on a textual variant in a single LXXA MS (*proeleusis*), the resulting thematic consistency offered by his reading warrants further consideration.

[14] Burney, *Book of Judges*, 171, attributes the scholarly tendency to emend and remove such phrases to a lack of attention to the poem's unique style of parallelism. His

versions tend to omit repeated words, the absence of the pronouns in the translations likely reflects on the translators' techniques rather than variant sources. Such pronominal variance does not provide sufficient grounds for emending the MT.

Verse 5

The mountains quaked. The verb of which הָרִים is the subject would either be vocalized as נָזְלוּ (MT, Vulg.), a *qal* perfect from נזל ("to flow"), or נָזֹלּוּ (LXX, Syr., TJon), a *niphal* perfect from זלל ("to quake").[15] By following LXX, Syr., and TJon in their interpretation, the text of verses 4–5 presents a chiasm:[16]

אֶרֶץ רָעָשָׁה	4c	The earth shook, (A)
גַּם־שָׁמַיִם נָטָפוּ		even the heavens poured, (B)
גַּם־עָבִים נָטְפוּ מָיִם		even the clouds poured water. (B′)
הָרִים נָזְלוּ מִפְּנֵי יְהוָה	5	The mountains quaked before YHWH (A′)

In the Hebrew Bible, mountains are known both to quake (Isa 5:25, using רגז) and to melt (Mic 1:4, using מסס); thus, both morphological options are *conceptually* plausible. Moreover, YHWH's theophanies are associated with

---

designation of this style as "climactic" has been influential. Climactic parallelism involves a certain colon partially paralleling the preceding colon but adding an element to the sense of the cola together. For his list of examples, see Burney, *Book of Judges*, 170. Cf. the designation "staircase parallelism" in Wilfred G. E. Watson, *Classical Hebrew Poetry: A Guide to Its Techniques*, JSOTSup 26 (Sheffield: JSOT, 1984), 150.

[15] ("To flow"): So also the rabbinic tradition. Rashi is representative of this when he explains the text by saying, "Like flowing water (נחלים) they melted away." See Schmuel Fishelis and Avraham Shelomoh Fishelis, *Judges: A New English Translation of the Text, Rashi and a Commentary Digest*, ed. A. J. Rosenberg, Judaica Books of the Prophets (New York: Judaica, 1983), 36. For a description of the section's logic and an analysis of the issues, see Alexander Globe, "The Text and Literary Structure of Judges 5,4–5," *Bib* 55 (1974): 168–78.

[16] See Globe, "Text and Literary Structure," 174–75, though Globe wonders if this is a "case of poetic counterpointing," in which the reader is denied the gratification of an expected form. A similarly playful poetic interchange is inferred by Jack M. Sasson, *Judges 1–12: A New Translation with Introduction and Commentary*, AB 6D (New Haven: Yale University Press, 2014), 287. The use of these lines in Ps 68 is potentially significant: Judg 5:4c–d (with אַף replacing גַּם) and 5b–c are repeated almost verbatim (with אֱלֹהִים replacing יְהוָה), while lines 4e and 5a (B' and A' in the proposed chiasm) are missing. Such an omission may suggest that these lines are semantically repetitive to an extent that the first two lines were sufficient to communicate meaning. This would seem to support the proposed chiasm (or, in the opinion of many scholars, require a shortening of the Judges version).

thunderous quaking as well as flowing rain (cf. Ps 68:8–9, which parallels Judg 5:4–5 almost verbatim), so both lexical possibilities are also *contextually* appropriate.[17] The MT of Isaiah 63:19–64:2 [64:1–3] uses the form נָזֹלּוּ (*niphal*) to describe the quaking of the mountains in a similar theophany, thereby making the *niphal* form recommended here marginally more plausible.[18]

This one, Sinai. The phrase זֶה סִינַי in 5:5b appears only here and in Psalm 68. Most scholars understand the phrase to be an "appellation of deity" introduced by the demonstrative pronoun and best translated "the One of Sinai."[19] The consensus since Albright has been that the phrase is a divine epithet; yet some prefer to delete it as a gloss, either to the mountain(s) or the entire theophany.[20] If one accepts the scholarly consensus, the parallel structure of 5:5a–b would equate זֶה סִינַי with יהוה and construe the phrase as parallel to "the God of Israel," rather than to the mountains or the theophany:[21]

---

[17] In "La Théophanie de Jud 5:4–5," *ETL* 43 (1967): 528–31, Joseph Coppens attempts to bring together the elements of pouring and quaking by retaining the MT and understanding נזל to mean "descend" (*descendre*). He imagines the text's motif to be a torrential downpour (described in 5:4–5 and accentuated in Ps 68) that leads to the dislodging of large chunks of mountainside that "descend" into the valley (531).

[18] The vocalization in Isa 63 is debated; LXX and Syr. read נָזְלוּ. However, "quake" makes better sense in the context of ch. 63, where the mountains and the nations react similarly to the theophany—note the formal equivalence of מִפָּנֶיךָ הָרִים נָזֹלּוּ and מִפָּנֶיךָ גוֹיִם יִרְגָּזוּ—and the nations "tremble" (רגז).

[19] William F. Albright, "The Song of Deborah in the Light of Archeology," *BASOR* 62 (1936): 30. Albright bases his argument on the fact that "in North Canaanite, just as in later North Arabic, appellations of deity were sometimes formed with the demonstrative pronoun *d*." Since Albright's time, scholars have compared the genitive function of זֶה to Ugaritic *dū* (on which, see John Huehnergard, *An Introduction to Ugaritic* [Peabody, Mass.: Hendrickson, 2012], 145), Amorite *zu*, and Old Sinaitic *ḏ*. See *HALOT*, 265. For examples of Amorite names using *zu*, see Sasson, *Judges 1–12*, 287, who lists Zu-ḥadnim, Zu-dādi, Zu-baḥli, and Zu-dIšḫara. For a short explanation of the Nabatean parallel "Dushara," see H. Niehr, "He-of-the-Sinai," *DDD*, 387.

[20] The former seems to be the meaning of the TJon, which reads, "This [is] Sinai [which] was stirred up." For this translation and a thorough discussion of the text's "disputing mountains" motif, see Smelik, *Targum of Judges*, 413–30. Assuming the phrase glosses the theophany in its entirety, Lindars (*Judges 1–5*, 233–34) provides the amplified translation, "the mountains quake before Yahweh—(and here I'm referring to the Sinai theophany)," following the LXX and Michael Fishbane, *Biblical Interpretation in Ancient Israel* (New York: Oxford University Press, 1985), 54–55.

[21] See also Globe, "Text and Literary Structure," 172, which identifies the structural parallel in v. 3.

מִפְּנֵי יְהוָה זֶה סִינַי Before YHWH, the One of Sinai
מִפְּנֵי יְהוָה אֱלֹהֵי יִשְׂרָאֵל׃ Before YHWH, the God of Israel

Robert Holmstedt has argued that the grammatical function of זֶה in the phrase requires reassessment. Rereading the comparative evidence, Holmstedt asserts that the demonstrative *never* serves as a "genitive" marker in biblical Hebrew or other Semitic parallels.[22] Instead, the normal function of זֶה as a deictic demonstrative applies also here: "this (mountain), Sinai" identifies more specifically *which* mountain was said to quake. Rather than a gloss in need of deletion, the phrase זֶה סִינַי provides a poetic parallel to הָרִים.[23] The parallelism should thus be construed as follows (acknowledging the poet's use of ellipsis and the customary "climactic" parallelism):

נָזֹלוּ מִפְּנֵי יְהוָה הָרִים   The mountains quaked before YHWH
מִפְּנֵי יְהוָה אֱלֹהֵי יִשְׂרָאֵל זֶה סִינַי This one, Sinai, [quaked] before YHWH, God of Israel.

Verse 6

Roads fell into disuse. The introduction provided by verse 6 includes the statement that אֳרָחוֹת "ceased" or "refrained" (חדל)[24] in Israel. Ancient and modern

---

[22] Robert D. Holmstedt, "Analyzing זֶה Grammar and Reading זֶה Texts of Ps 68:9 and Judg 5:5," *JHS* 14 (2014): 16.

[23] Holmstedt ("Analyzing זֶה Grammar and Reading זֶה Texts of Ps 68:9 and Judg 5:5," 12, esp. n. 14) notes also that the Masoretic notation accords with his proposal. Mark J. Boda ("Judges," in *Numbers–Ruth*, vol. 5 of *The Expositor's Bible Commentary*, ed. Tremper Longman III and David E. Garland, rev. ed. [Grand Rapids: Zondervan, 2017], 1124) concludes the same.

[24] There is no need to read חדל II here or in v. 7. Contra D. W. Thomas, "Some Observations on the Hebrew Root *ḥdl*," in *Volume du Congrès: Strasbourg, 1956*, VTSup 4 (Leiden: Brill, 1957), 8–16; P. Calderone, "ḤDL-II in Poetic Texts," *CBQ* 23 (1961): 451–60; Marvin Lee Chaney, "ḤDL-II and the Song of Deborah: Textual, Philological, and Sociological Studies in Judges 5, with Special Reference to the Verbal Occurrences of ḤDL in Biblical Hebrew" (PhD diss., Harvard University, 1976). Norman K. Gottwald follows Thomas in *The Tribes of Yahweh: The Sociology of the Religion of Liberated Israel, 1250–1050 B.C.E.* (Maryknoll, N.Y.: Orbis, 1979), 504. For an opinion similar to mine and a summary of Chaney's argument (which expands on the earlier research of Thomas and Calderone), see Theodore J. Lewis, "The Songs of Hannah and Deborah: HDL-II ('Growing Plump')," *JBL* 104 (1985): 105–8. Lewis also argues convincingly that, when devoid of complement (as here), the nuance of חדל is better expressed as "to refrain from doing something" rather than "to cease" (107). Followed by J. David Schloen, "Caravans, Kenites, and *Casus belli*: Enmity and Alliance in the Song of Deborah," *CBQ* 55 (1993): 24 and Richard S. Hess, "Judges 1–5 and Its Translation," in *Translating the Bible: Problems and*

interpreters give a variety of translations for אֳרָחוֹת. The versions generally follow the MT, though most translators emend the text to אֹרְחוֹת, "caravans," to provide a more personal subject or to avoid a word that is often used metaphorically.[25] This emendation is unnecessary for two reasons:

First, in arguing for the semantic flexibility of the word אֳרָחוֹת, Sasson notes that the Akkadian *ḫarrānum* may refer to a road, a caravan, or a military campaign.[26] Assuming the Hebrew root has the same semantic range, to suggest that the historical referent was "caravans" does not require emendation of the MT. This seems to be the reading of TJon, which retains the MT's "roads ceased" but adds the word "travelers" for interpretive clarity.[27]

Second, the repetition of אֳרָחוֹת in 6d—where the lexeme is parallel to נְתִיבָה, "path"—commends a lexeme with the connotation "road." While many commentators omit this second appearance of the term, LXX, Syr., TJon, and Vulg. include it. Retaining the Masoretic vocalization thus provides lexical and thematic continuity (cf. vv. 6d, 10c).[28]

Verse 7

Villagers. Appearing in the Hebrew Bible only here and in 5:11, this rare lexeme פְּרָזוֹן has generally been understood to refer to either (1) unwalled settlements, including their inhabitants (i.e., "villagers") or (2) some type of leader, military or otherwise. The first option is commended by the lexemes פְּרָזוֹת and פְּרָזִי, which very clearly denote "unwalled cities" or "villages" (in Deut 3:5; 1 Sam 6:18; Ezek 38:11; Zech 2:8; and Esth 9:19).[29] In the Esther text, residents of those settlements are designated as הַפְּרוֹזִים (*qere* הַפְּרָזִים).[30] The rendering

---

Prospects, ed. Stanley E. Porter and Richard S. Hess, JSNTSup 173 (Sheffield: Sheffield Academic, 1999), 152.

[25] "Generally follow the MT": A noteworthy exception is LXXA, which opts for "kings were lacking" (NETS; ἐξέλιπον βασιλεῖς). "To avoid a word that is often used metaphorically." See Jan Alberto Soggin, *Judges: A Commentary*, trans. John Bowden, OTL (Philadelphia: Westminster, 1981), 85. אֹרַח is generally used to describe a standard way (cf. דֶּרֶךְ) or behavior. E.g., Gen 18:11; Isa 2:3; Ps 19:6; Job 22:15; and Prov 1:9.

[26] Sasson, *Judges 1–12*, 288. Sasson translates 6c–d, "Trails are unused, wayfarers take twisting trails" (277).

[27] Smelik, *Targum of Judges*, 431.

[28] Admittedly, in the translation provided, this lexical continuity is sacrificed in the interest of the personal nature of the noun.

[29] The Ezekiel text is especially salient, since it describes settlements as being insecure due to a lack of walls, bars, or gates: בְּאֵין חוֹמָה וּבְרִיחַ וּדְלָתַיִם אֵין לָהֶם.

[30] The ן ending in Judg 5 is normally termed a "collective." See *HALOT*, 965, for bibliography. Contra Israel Knohl, "The Original Version of Deborah's Song, and Its Numerical Structure," *VT* 66 (2016): 47, and the assertion that חָדְלוּ פְרָזוֹן indicates the Israelites' transition away from un-walled settlements characteristic of the monarchic period.

of TJon and Syr. recommends understanding the noun פְּרָזוֹן similarly here. By contrast, with LXXB (δυνατοί) and Vulg. (*fortes*), some have rendered MT's פְּרָזוֹן as "leaders," either reconstructing רוֹזְנִים or assuming a derivation shared with Arabic *faraza*.[31] Argued by William F. Albright, the latter was accepted by a variety of commentators and readdressed by Peter Craigie, who recommends translating "warriors" on philological, intertextual (cf. Hab 3:14, *qere*), and thematic grounds.[32] Lawrence Stager offers the most convincing argument against the translation "warriors."[33] After exposing the weakness of Albright's earlier argument and emphasizing the correlation of פְּרָזוֹת with פְּרָזוֹן, Stager demonstrates convincingly that the motif of the "the urban élite and the rural population"[34] is used throughout the poem to "epitomize the hostilities between Israel and Canaan."[35]

Until I arose, Deborah. The morphology of the form שַׁקַּמְתִּי is less difficult to discern. Composed of the temporal adverbial construction שֶׁ + עַד ("until") and the root קוּם, the MT preserves either the standard first-person perfect form or an archaic second-person spelling.[36] TJon and Syr. use a first-person verb and make their choice explicit with a pronominal subject.[37] By contrast, the Greek versions (with Vulg.) unanimously render the verb as a *third*-person form (ἀνέστη). While assuming a narrating third-person perspective is reasonable, and the MT's spelling is formally equivalent to that of the second person, invocation of the first-person voice is a "conspicuous feature" of the Song of Deborah and Barak.[38] Although the second-person perspective is also used in

---

[31] Because δυνατοί is used to render רוֹזְנִים in 5:3, the presence of δυνατοί here may signal a repetition of the Hebrew word in the LXX's *Vorlage*. See *BTAT*, 79.

[32] William F. Albright, *Yahweh and the Gods of Canaan: A Historical Analysis of Two Contrasting Faiths*, JLCRS 7 (London: Athlone, 1968), 49. Albright's argument is based principally upon the Egyptian transcription *prt* in Papyrus Anastasi—a text that does little to clarify the meaning of the word. See also Peter C. Craigie, "Some Further Notes on the Song of Deborah," *VT* 22 (1972): 349–53. Note that Craigie does not associate his argument with Albright.

[33] Lawrence E. Stager, "Archaeology, Ecology, and Social History: Background Themes to the Song of Deborah," in *Congress Volume: Jerusalem, 1986* (Leiden: Brill, 1988), 221–34.

[34] Stager, "Archaeology, Ecology, and Social History," 224.

[35] Stager, "Archaeology, Ecology, and Social History," 225.

[36] ("Until"): The collocation עַד (adverb) and שֶׁ/שׁ (relative pronoun) occurs also in Ps 123:2; Song 2:7, 17; 3:4, 5; and 8:4. While these texts are generally considered later than the Song of Deborah and Barak (and normally associated with *late* biblical Hebrew), the relative pronoun שׁ is comparable to Akkadian *šu/ša*, which would suggest a much earlier attestation. For a theory of its development, see *HALOT*, 1365. Cf. *GKC* §36. "And the root קוּם": see *GKC* §44h.

[37] Smelik, *Targum of Judges*, 435; Marcos, *Judges*, 56*.

[38] Smelik, *Targum of Judges*, 435.

the song (e.g., in the next stanza), this stanza gives no comparable indication of a shift in voice,[39] so the first-person reading is preferable.

Verse 8

God chose new ones. The syntax of 8a is notoriously ambiguous. Echols has remarked that "the meaning of v. 8a is obscure, and remains so after generations of scholarship."[40] The clause either introduces the idea of apostasy, which is otherwise absent from the poem—an element highlighted by the book's cyclical framework—or emphasizes the agency of the deity in providing assistance through Deborah and Jael, a theme that is consistent with the narrative account in the previous chapter (cf. 4:23). Three principal translations are possible:

First, he [Israel] chose new gods. In this construal, חֲדָשִׁים is an adjective modifying אֱלֹהִים and the subject is implied by the immediately preceding context.[41] TJon clarifies that the text describes apostasy by choosing the pejorative term "idols." By way of associative translation, TJon includes a direct quotation from Deuteronomy 32:17 in rendering Judges 5:8.[42] LXX also preserves this reading, using a plural form of the verb to designate the implied subject.[43]

Second, he [YHWH] chose new leaders [אֱלֹהִים]. Assuming the same syntax, some argue that אֱלֹהִים is a designation for leaders, based on certain pentateuchal texts.[44] Unfortunately, this interpretation derives from unlikely translations of other difficult passages that consequently offer limited interpretive

---

[39] In the third stanza, the song describes the people of YHWH recounting the mighty deeds of YHWH and his army and thus marks the shift in perspective that is realized with the people's address to Deborah and Barak. No such indication of direct quotation is evident here. While this is not *required* in poetry, the first-person form offers a more convincing alternative.

[40] Echols, *"Tell Me, O Muse,"* 28.

[41] The previous line ends with the prepositional phrase בְּיִשְׂרָאֵל. For the construction in v. 8a as an "impersonal passive," see *GKC* §144b. While I prefer a different translation, Brian Tidiman (*Le Livre des Juges* [Vaux-sur-Seine: Édifac, 2004], 136) helpfully articulates the logic of this rendering in its context: "C'est l'absence de foi, et non celle de 'fabricants d'armes' (Burney), qui explique le manque de résistance, symbolisée par le *bouclier* et la *lance*."

[42] For translation and further discussion, see Smelik, *Targum of Judges*, 435–37. Rashi follows TJon.

[43] LXXA, ἥρέτισαν θεοὺς καινούς; LXXB, ἐξελέξαντο θεοὺς καινούς.

[44] These leaders are designated as "the mouthpiece of Divine sentence" by George A. Cooke, *The History and Song of Deborah: Judges IV and V* (Oxford: Horace Hart, 1892), 35, whose century-old summary of the issues confirms Echols' suggestion that significant interpretive advances toward understanding this text have not been made in the last hundred years. Cooke's summary is adopted by Sasson, *Judges 1–12*, 291.

assistance.⁴⁵ This reading is the least likely, given that the deity is never mentioned in the stanza and is thus an unlikely implied subject.

Third, God chose new ones [i.e., leaders]. According to this syntactical appraisal, אֱלֹהִים is the subject and חֲדָשִׁים (substantival adjective meaning "new [leaders]") is the object. In this rendering, the clause reflects the standard pattern of V-S word order, but the interpreter must assume the conjunctive *mûnaḥ* is designating חֲדָשִׁים as something other than an attribute adjective modifying אֱלֹהִים. Further, Israel's deity is designated in the poem exclusively as יהוה (and only twice amplified with the appellation אֱלֹהֵי יִשְׂרָאֵל; cf. 5:3, 5).⁴⁶ A switch to the generic designation אֱלֹהִים creates an impression of theological inconsistency.

While the accentuation of the MT (as well as the versions and subsequent medieval Jewish interpretation) appears to support the first option, and despite the objections just enumerated, the final option is marginally more plausible given the line's context. The present stanza focuses on leaders lexically and formally, while blatant apostasy is completely absent from the Song of Deborah and Barak. The degree to which the rest of Judges emphasizes covenant infidelity presents the possibility that ancient and contemporary commentators want to find it here, despite its thematic peripherality in the stanza. Moreover, the immediately preceding line describes the installation of at least one new leader and thus moderately commends the third option.⁴⁷

Then fighting was at the gates. The word לָחֶם is another interpretive crux, here translated as "fighting," but easily mis- or reinterpreted as לֶחֶם, "bread." Consequently, Syr. agrees with LXXA's ὡς ἄρτον κρίθινον, "like barley bread." Presumably to avoid such a reading, the MT indicates that the final syllable is accented rather than the first (as would be the case with the segolate noun לֶחֶם).⁴⁸ Following the MT, the form should be considered a *piel* infinitive construct from לחם, "to fight." While some have offered creative reconstructions

---

⁴⁵ The references used by interpreters to support this reading vary. Most list Exod 21:6 and 22:8[9].

⁴⁶ Primarily for this reason the third option is rejected by Heinz-Dieter Neef, "Deboraerzählung und Deboralied: Beobachtungen zum Verhältnis von Jdc. IV und V," *VT* 44 (1994): 32–33.

⁴⁷ So also Richard D. Nelson (*Judges: A Critical and Rhetorical Commentary* [New York: Bloomsbury T&T Clark, 2017]), 96–97; Echols, *"Tell Me, O Muse,"* 28; and Hess, "Judges 1–5 and Its Translation," 153, who follows Craigie, "Some Further Notes," 350–51. Sasson, *Judges 1–12*, 291, "gingerly" makes the same recommendation, just as Mark S. Smith and Elizabeth Bloch-Smith (*Judges 1: A Commentary on Judges 1:1–10:5*, Hermeneia [Minneapolis: Fortress, 2021]) do so "most tentatively."

⁴⁸ For a thorough discussion of accentuation and manuscript evidence, see Marcos, *Judges*, 56*.

of the text,[49] significant evidence to prefer a reading other than the MT is lacking; "fighting" is consistent with the context in which the phrase is found.

Certainly no shield was seen. While few contest the text or the meaning of verse 8c, the syntax is challenging.[50] Here the אִם functions asseveratively, meaning "certainly not."[51]

Verse 9

My heart is for the leaders of Israel. As suggested above regarding 5:2, the word חוֹקְקֵי is related semantically to the root נדב (see 5:2b, 9b) and פרע (see v. 2a). Words derived from חקק appear three times in the Song of Deborah and Barak: verses 9 (מְחֹקְקִים), 14 (לְחוֹקְקֵי), and 15 (חִקְקֵי־לֵב). The root חקק is generally associated with "engraving," whether concretely (e.g., Isa 22:16) or abstractly, meaning "to decree" or "enact." The latter meaning is especially clear when the verb is collocated with the related noun חֹק, "portion," "law," or "prescribed task" (e.g., Isa 10:1).[52] TJon and Syr. interpret the text in terms of "teachers of the law" or "lawgiver."[53] However, such a narrow legal reading is not required by the lexeme's use in the Hebrew Bible, nor does it suit this context. The *poel* subst. ptc. מְחֹקֵק (so also the *qal* חֹקֵק) more generally refers to some sort of commander, ruler, or the staff associated with the leader (e.g., Gen 49:10; Num 21:18). In Isa 33:22, for example, מְחֹקֵק is used alongside מֶלֶךְ and שֹׁפֵט to describe YHWH's kingly rule over Jerusalem. The generic term "leaders," then, has been chosen here. The construction לְבִּי לְ (lit., "my heart is for") seems to connote concentration or mental perception. Though the syntax of verse 9a is unique, correlate constructions in the Hebrew Bible include שִׂים + לֵב + לְ ("pay attention"; cf. Ezek 40:4, in a list of verbs of perception) and שִׁית + לֵב + לְ ("consider, take note"; cf. Jer 31:21). A more similar collocation appears in 2 Samuel 14:1 (כִּי־לֵב הַמֶּלֶךְ עַל־אַבְשָׁלוֹם), but the phrase is similarly ambiguous.[54]

---

[49] E.g., Delbert R. Hillers, "A Note on Judges 5,8a," *CBQ* 27 (1965): 124–26, who recommends the translation "indeed, they desired demons." For a list of alternative translations, see Lindars, *Judges 1–5*, 240.

[50] Craigie ("Some Further Notes," 350) is a notable exception. While Craigie does not alter the consonantal text here, his semantic construal requires a logical arrangement for the stanza that deviates from what is implied by the accentuation of the MT.

[51] Following *GKC* §149e. Contra Burney, *Book of Judges*, 163; ESV. For similar examples of syntax, see Isa 22:14 and Job 6:28.

[52] *HALOT*, 346–47.

[53] Smelik, *Targum of Judges*, 443 and Marcos, *Judges*, 57. Rashi (Fishelis and Fishelis, *Judges*, 38) translates "lawgiver" and understands the referent to be those who teach the Torah in Israel.

[54] In 2 Sam 14:1, Tanakh translates "the king's mind was on Absalom," while the NIV suggests "the king's heart longed for Absalom." NLT and NET show their interpretive leanings when they translate "the king longed to see Absalom."

Verse 10

Those who sit on blankets. While the unique designation צְחֹרוֹת has caused some discussion,[55] the phrase יֹשְׁבֵי עַל־מִדִּין is more important for interpretation. The MT is basically unchallenged, though the versions include a range of interpretations.[56] One of only three occurrences of the form,[57] מִדִּין likely derives from מַד and refers to garments, blankets, or saddlebags that cover the beast of burden. Most assume this portrays the riders as rich.[58] Others interpret מִדִּין as a nominalization of the root דִין (to judge), a reading LXXB, Vulg., and (to some degree) TJon choose.[59] Schloen has endorsed a third reading, "Midian," attempting to avoid consonantal changes and reading the section in light of the "caravan hypothesis." That "the Midianites were caravaneers *par excellence*" suggests to him that they would be addressed expressly by the poet when caravan trade was in view.[60] While the third option is more plausible than the second, the generic language of the colon immediately preceding and following verse 10b commends the translation "blankets."

Tell of it! Difficulties of a more textual nature arise with the verb שִׂיחוּ. LXX and Syr. understand the verse to end before the verb; LXXB retains the מִן preposition from the beginning of the next verse (with ἀπὸ) and LXXA and Syr. remove it. By removing the intervening (and troublesome) preposition,

---

[55] The exact color and its potential implications are uncertain, because the adjective appears only here in the Hebrew Bible. Generally these "white" or "tawny" donkeys are assumed to be "precious" (Fishelis and Fishelis, *Judges*, 38) or "healthy" (Sasson, *Judges 1–12*, 293). LXXA lacks a designation altogether (simply translating ὑποζυγίων) while LXXB reads ὄνου θηλείας μεσημβρίας ("she-donkey at midday"). Based on the Greek evidence, Lindars (*Judges 1–5*, 243) has suggested that the term אֲתֹנוֹת was included as a later gloss. For a list of translation alternatives and bibliography, see *HALOT*, 1019.

[56] E.g., LXXA reads καθήμενοι ἐπὶ λαμπηνῶν, "those who ride on wagons."

[57] The exact form מִדִּין occurs also in Josh 15:61 and Isa 10:2. However, in the former, the text designates a placename ("Middin"); in the latter, the text represents the joining of the preposition מִן to the abstract noun דִין ("from justice").

[58] E.g., Marcos, *Judges*, 59*; Lindars, *Judges 1–5*, 244.

[59] TJon combines both interpretive options in its amplified translation: "[who] rode on she-asses saddled with variegated stitching and went through the whole territory of the land of Israel and were chosen to dispense judgment." Smelik, *Targum of Judges*, 445. So also Robert G. Boling, *Judges*, AB 6A (New York: Doubleday, 1975), 102, 110, who translates "O you who sit on the judgment seat."

[60] Schloen, "Caravans, Kenites, and *Casus belli*," 26–27. For the same conclusion based on Sisera's association with Midian in Ps 83:10[9], see Michael David Coogan, "A Structural and Literary Analysis of the Song of Deborah," *CBQ* 40 (1978): 148; followed by Susan Niditch, *Judges: A Commentary*, OTL (Louisville: Westminster John Knox, 2008), 72.

these versions link קוֹל with שִׂיחוּ.⁶¹ While some commentators do the same, neither the syntax nor the poetry requires it.⁶² In fact, keeping שִׂיחוּ (a pl. impv. associated with perception) in verse 10 with the list of addressees creates a parallel to verse 3, in which two other audiences are called with similar imperatives.

Verse 11

At the sound of those who distribute water. The meaning of MT's מְחַצְצִים is unclear. Attested only here, what appears to be a *piel* subst. ptc. likely derives from either (1) the noun חֵץ ("arrow"), meaning "those who shoot arrows" or (2) the root חצץ ("to divide").⁶³ An overlooked alternative relates מְחַצְצִים to חָצָץ, "gravel" or "pebbles," as proposed by Rashi.⁶⁴ LXX avoids the issue, making sense of קוֹל by reading מְחַצְּרִים (cf. 1 Chr 15:24; 2 Chr 5:12) and translating with ἀνακρουομένων ("music makers").⁶⁵

The problem of 11a is compounded by what follows; in 11b, a second prepositional phrase locates the action בֵּין מַשְׁאַבִּים, often translated as "between the places for drawing water." Assuming that the *hapax legomenon* מַשְׁאַבִּים derives from the root שאב, one imagines water holes at which those responsible for distributing water ("dividers"; חצץ) proclaim Israel's recent military conquests.⁶⁶ Others associate such a locale with public

---

⁶¹ Nowhere in the Hebrew Bible is שיח collocated with מִן. While attested frequently with direct objects, שיח generally appears with בְּ (e.g., Ps 105:2) or לְ (e.g., Job 12:8). See *DCH*, 8:125–6.

⁶² E.g., Boling, *Judges*, 110. The editors of *BHS* and *BHQ* also recommend this redivision.

⁶³ So the Tanakh: "Louder than the sound of archers," though the alternative translation, "thunder peals," is included as a footnote. Note the use of the comparative מִן. Cf. *GKC* §133e.

⁶⁴ While Rashi relates the sound to that of a river over pebbles, the sound of feet walking over pebbles (perhaps the feet of travelers?) is also possible. See Fishelis and Fishelis, *Judges*, 39.

⁶⁵ English translations follow suit (e.g., ESV, NRSV, "musicians"; NIV, "singers"; NLT "village musicians"). Presumably Boling's "cymbals" is indebted to this reading (*Judges*, 110).

⁶⁶ So the majority of commentators. See also *DCH* 6:296. Scholars have proposed a variety of historical situations to explain this difficult text. If one accepts Schloen's historical reconstruction ("Caravans, Kenites, and *Casus belli*," 25), then the "watering places" would have offered a natural place for caravanning travelers to pause, water their donkeys, and share recent news. Similarly, Block (*Judges, Ruth*, 229) proposes that "the watering holes served as community gathering places, where gossip was exchanged and significant events celebrated."

distribution of the spoils of war.⁶⁷ While the poem's thematic emphasis on "spoils" commends the latter interpretation, the lack of "spoils" as an explicit object makes the reading less likely given its prominence elsewhere in the song. Consequently, the translation above opts for the former interpretation, "those who distribute water."

The righteous acts of YHWH. Translations of צִדְקוֹת vary among commentators and English versions. While "righteous acts" is the standard translation, commentators such as Lindars and Chisholm render the phrase in 11b "victories" or "victorious deeds" of YHWH, given the form's martial context.⁶⁸ The feminine plural צִדְקוֹת is collocated with יהוה in only two other references—namely, 1 Samuel 12:7 and Micah 6:5. Both contexts highlight God's salvation of Israel in the Exodus and subsequent military endeavors, as many commentators have noted; however, more important in each case is the larger context—an indictment of Israel's unfaithfulness in contrast to the appropriate actions (צִדְקוֹת) of YHWH.⁶⁹ Thus, even though the referent of the lexeme is a military victory in each passage, the term's connotation accords with standard צדק terminology: "right behavior or status in relation to some standard of behavior accepted in the community."⁷⁰ Given the evaluative bent of the passage, "righteous acts" is an apt translation.

The righteous acts of his villagers. The semantic content of צִדְקֹת in 11b–c raises a second interpretive difficulty—how to render the genitive in 11c. Most agree that in 11b the genitive denotes possession; interpretations of 11c

---

⁶⁷ Assuming the root חצץ. E.g., Barry G. Webb, *The Book of Judges*, NICOT (Grand Rapids: Eerdmans, 2012), 196.

⁶⁸ Lindars, *Judges 1–5*, 247; Chisholm, *Judges and Ruth*, 237. Echols (*"Tell Me, O Muse,"* 31) follows Lindars over against Block (*Judges, Ruth*, 229) and others who opt for the vocabulary of "righteous acts." Cf. Sasson (*Judges 1–12*, 277, 294), who opts for "vindication" (a plural of abstraction) and therefore deems the subsequent collocation צִדְקֹת פִּרְזֹנוֹ an objective genitive (i.e., "vindication for his hamlets in Israel"). David J. Reimer, "צדק," *NIDOTTE*, 752, calls the standard translation "colorless" and suggests that rendering the lexeme as "triumphs" is "more attractive" given its context.

⁶⁹ In both texts the covenant relationship of the people and their Sovereign is in the background. Reimer ("צדק," p. 750) is right to caution that the Hebrew Bible never explicitly identifies the covenant as the standard that dictates the right behavior to which צדק terminology refers. Certain contexts, however, reflect clearly that covenantal background. The judicial vocabulary of the Samuel and Micah passages (e.g., שׁפט, עֵד in 1 Sam 12:5; רִיב in Mic 6:1, 2), in tandem with the assertion that Israel is YHWH's people, elucidate the covenantal nature of the proceedings. Given the covenantal concerns of the book of Judges, and the interest of the present song to gauge the faithfulness of Israel to YHWH's muster, the same is plausible in this context.

⁷⁰ Reimer, "צדק," p. 750.

vary more widely. TJon, for example, interprets the genitive as possessive in both lines, whereas LXX, Syr., and Vulg. do not.[71] Similar disagreement persists among contemporary commentators. Given the absence of a textual cue to attribute a different sense to an identical construction in parallel lines, I translate the construct phrase in 11c as a subjective genitive, following the pattern of the previous colon.

Verse 12

Awake, awake, Deborah. Departing from the tradition preserved in the MT, Vulg., Syr., and TJon, LXXA includes the phrase ἐξέγειρον μυριάδας μετὰ λαοῦ ("awaken myriads with the people") between the MT's 12a and 12b. Similarly, LXXA includes an extra verb in the summons to Barak and concludes the verse by once again addressing Deborah.[72] The shorter reading in the rest of the versions suggests that the phrases are amplifications.

Take captive your captives. Minor disagreement over the interpretation of the consonants שביך persists. The MT's שֶׁבְיְךָ, "your captives," has the support of the Vulg., TJon, and LXXA–B, while Syr. (followed by *BHK*) reads the ptc. שֹׁבֶיךָ, "your captors." The collocation in the first reading appears five times in the Hebrew Bible; the latter is attested in Isaiah 14:2, with an indirect object marked by לְ rather than the direct object found here. Considering the version evidence and the fact that Barak does not seem to be Sisera's captive,[73] the MT's reading is preferred.

Verse 13

Then the remnant triumphed. The complexity of verse 13 invites creative corrections and interpretations. The chief difficulty involves determining the degree to which one should harmonize the statement in 11d with its parallel components in 13a–b. Both segments are introduced with the consonants אז ירד. While the MT points the first verb as a *qal* pf. 3cp from the root ירד, a different vocalization (יְרַד) appears in 13a–b. If the MT is preserved in verse 13, the form is probably

---

[71] Smelik, *Targum of Judges*, 447, provides the translation "for the righteous deeds of the Lord, for the righteous deeds of the one who lives in the unwalled cities in the land of Israel." LXX and Syr. translate with a prepositional phrase ("in Israel"), and the Vulg. opts for an objective genitive. Following Lindars (*Judges 1–5*, 247), Marcos (*Judges*, 58*) argues that these variants are exegetically motivated in accordance with a late holy war tradition.

[72] ἐνισχύων and καὶ ἐνίσχυσον, Δεββωρα, τὸν Βαρακ, respectively.

[73] Lindars (*Judges 1–5*, 249) reconciles Barak's apparent freedom with the reading "captors" by raising the possibility that the ptc. is "conative, i.e., 'those who would capture you.'"

(1) an irregular *qal* impv. from the root ירד or (2) an apocopated *piel* impf. from רדה or רדד.⁷⁴ An impv. following אז is unlikely (without an intervening quotative), just as the *piel* rendering of either רדה or רדד is surprising.⁷⁵ Dissatisfied with either option, most simply assume the vocalization should mimic that of 11d, following the precedent of LXXB, Syr., and TJon. While these translations present a plausible reading, the *piel* pointing of the MT also makes good sense in the line. In the Hebrew Bible, the root רדה appears in poetic texts describing wartime conquest and is semantically related to the noun שָׂרִיד and the root שׁבה—both of which occur in the immediate context.⁷⁶ This attestation of the lexeme suggests that the line emphasizes the triumph (רדה) of the weak remnant over their mighty foes by using a playful phonemic twist on the earlier statement in verse 11.⁷⁷ Reinforcing this textual appraisal, another example of *near*—but not exact—repetition appears again in verse 15d.⁷⁸

Against the mightiest people. If שָׂרִיד is the subject of the verb, the remainder of the line is problematic. *BHQ* recommends transposing the *ʾatnaḥ* before עַם and, consequently, repointing עַם to be read in const. with יהוה.⁷⁹ In so doing, "remnant" (שָׂרִיד) is balanced by the fitting parallel term "people of YHWH"—the subject of the root ירד in verse 11d. While LXXB and several recensions follow this tradition, LXXA, Vulg., and TJon retain the accentuation of the MT and leave יהוה as the subject of 13b.⁸⁰ The transposition reflected in one Greek tradition and favored by modern commentators is doubtful for two reasons: (1) The language of YHWH (not his people) acting "against the warriors" (בַּגִּבּוֹרִים) is invoked again in verse 23, where the מַלְאַךְ יְהוָה curses Meroz for neglecting to fight with YHWH. It seems

⁷⁴ רֵד is the expected form of the *pe-yod qal* impv. See *GKC*, 522.

⁷⁵ Provided a *piel* form is the correct reading, this verse contains the only two *piel* forms of either of the possible roots. Aside from what appears to be a *hiphil* form in Isa 41:2, all other occurrences of רדה are *qal*. As for רדד, the *hiphil* is attested twice and the *qal* three times. *GKC* §69g classifies the form in the MT as a *piel* but rejects the preserved vocalization and recommends restoring *qal* perfects.

⁷⁶ Consider Num 24:19: "And one from Jacob shall exercise dominion (רדה) and destroy the survivors (שָׂרִיד) of cities." The parallel of Isa 14:2 is even more persuasive: "They will take captive (שבה) those who were their captors, and rule over (רדה) those who oppressed them." So too Smith and Bloch-Smith, *Judges 1*, 330.

⁷⁷ Rashi (Fishelis and Fishelis, *Judges*, 40) translates, "He gave me dominion (ירדה לי) over the mighty of the gentiles." I follow Sasson (*Judges 1–12*, 278) who translates, "Then a survivor triumphs / Over the mightiest people."

⁷⁸ On which, see below.

⁷⁹ Marcos, *Judges*, 59*.

⁸⁰ 13b (MT) is one of the "remote doublets" identified by Tov in "The Textual History of the Song of Deborah in the A Text of the LXX," 225–27. YHWH is the subject of the verb both times the line appears in LXXA.

likely that this retrospective reference to the battle would evoke the same language as that of the battle's description. (2) Juxtaposing the action of the people with YHWH's direct involvement is a poetic device employed frequently by the composer. The poet accomplishes this effect in 11b–c through formal parallelism, and elsewhere (e.g., v. 2, 9) by inviting listeners to "bless YHWH" following lines honoring the faithful leaders of Israel.

If we retain the accentuation of the MT in 13a, we must also address the syntactical function of עָם. According to the recommended rendering, the noun עָם is governed by the substantival adjective אַדִּירִים. Whether the MT has been corrupted or the form is morphologically anomalous,[81] TJon treats the adjective אַדִּירִים as in construct by supplying the translation גברי עממיא, "champions of the nations." Assuming TJon accurately preserves the Hebrew syntax, the construction is likely superlative.[82]

Verse 14

Their root in Amalek. Though only explicit in 14c, the verb ירד is implied in verses 14a–b, d. But what shall we make of the phrase שָׁרְשָׁם בַּעֲמָלֵק in 14a? While ancient and modern interpreters have replaced עמלק with עמק (cf. v. 15c),[83] Vulg., Syr., and TJon agree with the MT. Since Judges 12:15 associates the Amalekites geographically with the territory of Ephraim, the association of Amalek with the tribe is comprehensible.[84] Because lines a–b and d begin with a similar prepositional phrase (מִן), to assume continuity in the remainder of the lines' syntax is reasonable. The phrase שָׁרְשָׁם בַּעֲמָלֵק should then be read in parallel to "your people" (14b; עֲמָמֶיךָ), "leaders" (14c; מְחֹקְקִים), and "musterers" (14d; מֹשְׁכִים), respectively.[85] By

---

[81] According to *UT*, 430, an enclitic ם- (akin to that attested in Ugaritic) is attached to the construct plural substantive אַדִּירֵי, resulting in the translation "the mighty ones of the people." Alternatively, Sasson (*Judges 1–12*, 295) labels the construction לְאַדִּירִים עָם "superlative" and frets little over the apparently anomalous morphology.

[82] Smelik (*Targum of Judges*, 453) rightly suggests that the amplified translation of TJon "offers the most viable explanation of the MT's odd syntax." On similar superlative constructions, see *GKC* §132c; 133g–h.

[83] E.g., LXXA (ἐν κοιλάδι), which may have been determined by theological considerations. The association of the two entities may have seemed problematic, since the hostility of the Amalekites to Israel had a long history. The expansion of TJon highlights this conflict: "Out of the House of Ephraim arose Joshua, son of Nun. He was the first to wage war with those of the House of Amalek" (Smelik, *Targum of Judges*, 453). In defense of the reading "valley" (עמק), see also Lindars, *Judges 1–5*, 252–53.

[84] Asserted by Barthélemy, in *BTAT*, 85. See n. 89 below.

[85] The verb משׁך normally denotes "mustering" in the context of war (cf. Judg 4:6). While some have suggested that the collocation משׁך + ב in reference to a concrete

reading the consonants שרשם as a substantive, based on loan-words several scholars have argued that the word means something like "officers."[86] However, מִ already implies the idea of *"men from"* (cf. LXXA, λαὸς); thus, "those whose root(s) are in Amalek" is functional—though admittedly unsatisfying.

What "root" connotes in the context is another question. Following TJon, many Jewish interpreters assume that the association of Ephraim and Amalek was contentious.[87] Barthélemy suggests that "root" implies an "impregnable installation,"[88] which presumably describes Ephraim's settlement among the Amalekites. Because the narrator had already emphasized Ephraim's failure to drive out the land's inhabitants (cf. Judg 1:29), the "hill country of the Amalekites" in 12:15 might refer to an area controlled by this group of Israelite oppressors.[89] Quinn Daniels, however, argues that when the root *šrš* is used to describe "a relationship between social bodies," in biblical, but especially extrabiblical, literature, it means "relative" or "descendent" (within a dynastic succession; e.g., Isa 11:10).[90] Most persuasively, he points to Hosea 9:16, which also describes the "root" of Ephraim; in this context, that root is "dried up" in an instance of infertility (or the mortality of children). This "reproductive interest" suggests the reference in the song is to "Ephraim's prominent 'patrilineages'" who "came to represent the vitality of all Ephraim's social and political future."[91]

---

instrument—that is, the staff of the scribe—makes "wield" or "hold" a better translation (e.g., Lindars, *Judges 1–5*, 255), 2 Kgs 25:19 seems to associate scribes ("secretary of the commander of the army") with the task of gathering the troops (using צבע rather than משך). Perhaps something similar is described here.

[86] Most notably, Craigie, "Some Further Notes," 351–52, whose argument is conjectural. For a concise summary of relevant positions, see Lindars, *Judges 1–5*, 253.

[87] Smelik, *Targum of Judges*, 453; BTAT, 85.

[88] "Il s'agit d'une relative utilisant le mot 'racine' au sens d'installation inexpugnable" (*BTAT*, 86).

[89] Given the presence of Amalekite activity in the Jezreel Valley during the time of Gideon, their ongoing influence in Ephraim is plausible. See H. Cazelles, "Déborah (Jud. V 14), Amaleq et Mâkîr," *VT* 24 (1974): 237, who points to Judg 6:33, Exod 17:8–16, and Num 24:20 to corroborate the implication of Judg 12:15 that the Amalekites pushed to the North long before the reign of Saul. For a similar observation, see Block, *Judges, Ruth*, 232. Contra Ernst Axel Knauf, "Zum Text von Ri 5:14," *Bib* 64 (1983): 429, who dismisses the possibility of Ephraim's settlement in Amalek at the time of the song's composition and suggests instead that the phrase is a gloss intended originally for 5:24 (made plausible, he argues, by 1 Sam 15:6) and inserted in a shared margin between the two verses.

[90] Quinn Daniels, "The Root of Ephraim among Amalek in the Song of Deborah," *JBL* 142 (2023): 251.

[91] Daniels, "Root of Ephraim," 253.

Verse 15

The officials of Issachar. In the MT שָׂרַי represents a plural noun with a first-person suffix ("my officials"). To whom the suffix applies is difficult to discern, considering that the immediate context refers to Deborah and Barak in the third person. Presumably for this reason, most ancient versions (e.g., TJon [const.], Vulg., LXXB [abs.]) treat the noun as pl. but omit the suffix, though LXXA omits the word entirely.[92] The Masoretic vocalization appears confused, but the *consonantal* text is not problematic. Since a const. subst. followed by a prepositional phrase is not foreign to the Hebrew Bible,[93] the best reading is שָׂרֵי בְּיִשָּׂשכָר, "officials who are in Issachar," or more simply, the "officials of Issachar."

And Issachar likewise with Barak. Many scholars have problematized the repetition of Issachar in verse 15 and have needlessly omitted or replaced it in verse 15b (cf. LXX).[94] Considering that the song uses repetition liberally and to various ends, the translation above makes good sense.[95] Moreover, both Syr. and TJon retain the repetition.

In the ranks of Reuben were great leaders of heart. With Syr., many interpreters challenge the MT in 15d in conjunction with 16c; two *nearly* identical phrases envelope an address to Reuben. Their degree of similarity leads many to harmonize them (i.e., to emend חִקְקֵי in 15d to חִקְרֵי).[96] To do so, however, neutralizes the play on words that the MT and both versions of the LXX

---

[92] See also *GKC* §87g and Fishelis and Fishelis, *Judges*, 41.

[93] Cf. 2 Sam 1:21; Ps 2:12; 84:7; Isa 28:9; Ezek 13:2; and Neh 7:43. See *IBHS*, 155.

[94] While the LXX omits Ισσαχαρ in 15b, LXXB supports the repetition by simply stating, "chiefs in Issachar [were] with Deborah and Barak" (καὶ ἀρχηγοὶ ἐν Ισσαχαρ μετὰ Δεββωρας καὶ Βαρακ). Though the translators omitted the second occurrence of the word, their rendering is consistent with the MT (on which, see *BTAT*, 87).

[95] The tricola comprising 5:15a–c includes a bicolon featuring semantic synonymous parallelism and a third colon related to the initial pair through synthetic or constructive parallelism; the final line provides clause constituents missing from the first two parallel lines:

	Adverbial	Adverbial	Verb	Subject	Adverbial
v. 15a		עִם־דְּבֹרָה		וְשָׂרַי בְּיִשָּׂשכָר	
v. 15b		כֵּן בָּרָק		וְיִשָּׂשכָר	
v. 15c	בְּרַגְלָיו		שֻׁלַּח		בָּעֵמֶק

[96] See, e.g., *HALOT*, 346–47; Lindars, *Judges 1–5*, 259. So also Syr.

retain.⁹⁷ Just as verse 11d is similar, but not identical, to verse 13a–b, the near repetition of verses 15d and 16c represents an effective focusing strategy.

Verse 16

Between the sheepfolds. The MT places Reuben between הַמִּשְׁפְּתַיִם, a word that has become an exegetical crux. *DCH* summarizes scholarly disagreement with five options based on different proposed etymologies: fireplaces, saddlebags, divided sheepfolds, double wall, or grazing places.⁹⁸ The ancient versions reflect the same interpretive difficulties: LXXA simply transliterates its Hebrew *Vorlage* (τῶν μοσφαθαιμ), while LXXB reads the term as "burdens" (τῆς διγομίας; i.e., load for the beast of burden; saddlebags). TJon translates the term twice with "war camps" and "borders," which may be the meaning of the doublet in verse 15 of LXXA: ἐν μέσῳ χειλέων.⁹⁹ Vulg. also translates *inter duos terminos*, "between two borders."

Other texts provide little assistance. As in Genesis 49:14, here the grammatical subject is stationary (sitting [יָשַׁב] Judg 5:16; cf. crouching [רֹבֵץ] in Gen 49:14).¹⁰⁰ A form lacking the initial מ occurs in the similar literary setting of Psalm 68:14 (שְׁפַתָּיִם). This alternate spelling occurs elsewhere only in Ezekiel and where it tends to be translated "hooks" or "edges."¹⁰¹ However, the context of the lexeme in Psalm 68 leads most to associate שְׁפַתָּיִם with הַמִּשְׁפְּתַיִם from Judges. Lindars may be right to assume that the phrase is "a proverbial expression for people who stay at home."¹⁰²

Verse 17

And in his bays he remains. The context suggests that the hapax legomenon מִפְרָץ relates to Asher's seaside land allotment. Ancient translators offer a number of sea-related glosses—channels (LXXA, τὰς διακοπὰς), outlets (LXXB,

---

⁹⁷ LXXA–B use two different Greek words to translate the lexemes in 15d and 16c (and thus resist harmonization), but the pair of words is *different* in each version (LXXA: ἀκριβασμοί/ἐξιχνούμενοι; LXXB: ἐξιχνούμενοι/ἐξετασμοί). For a discussion of the connotation of such a play on words in the MT, see Sasson, *Judges 1–12*, 278, 299–300.

⁹⁸ *DCH* 5:564–65.

⁹⁹ "TJon translates the term twice": On which, see Smelik, *Targum of Judges*, 458–60. While both words probably interpret the term preserved in the MT as הַמִּשְׁפְּתַיִם, only the Aramaic תחומיא ("borders") is governed by the locative preposition בֵּין ("between"). "Which may be the meaning": Thus Marcos, *Judges*, 61*, though NETS prefers "in the midst of shores."

¹⁰⁰ Note that Issachar is in a "resting place" (מְנוּחָה).

¹⁰¹ See *HALOT*, 1683.

¹⁰² Lindars, *Judges 1–5*, 260.

διεξόδοις), ports (Vulg., *portibus*)—which commend such an interpretation. John Gray asserts plausibly that the noun should be associated with פרץ, thus denoting "breakings" or "gaps" into the main land mass.[103]

Verses 18–20

On the heights of the field. The ancient reading of verse 18 is surprisingly uniform, thereby rendering unlikely the suggested emendations (e.g., שָׂדֶה to שְׂדֵהוּ) of the *BHS* editors. Even TJon's amplification is in line with the MT, albeit in a recontextualized theological framework.[104] The translation "on the heights of the field" may relate to mixed terrain in the Jezreel Valley.[105] Verses 19–20 are also clear enough in the MT to produce near agreement among ancient and contemporary interpreters.

Verse 21

The ancient wadi, Wadi Kishon. The form קְדוּמִים occurs only here and is most likely an abstract subst. related to קֶדֶם, meaning "before" (positionally or temporally; e.g., Job 23:8), "east" (e.g., Gen 3:24, 10:30), or "primeval/ancient" (e.g., Deut 33:15, 27; Prov 8:22–23).[106] While certain Greek recensions offer alternative readings,[107] LXXB supports the MT, reading "wadi of ancients" (χειμάρρους ἀρχαίων), as does TJon, which associates the wadi with miracles performed "of old." Others support the spelling of the MT but treat the designation as a proper name: Vulg., *Cadumim*, and LXXA, χειμάρρους καδημιμ.

March on, my soul, with might! While the *BHS* editors recommend the removal of the phrase, the major textual witnesses all render some version of the phrase. Given the presence of this self-reference through the Psalter, נפש should not be translated "neck," as scholars such as Boling have suggested.[108] In the Psalms, when נפשי is the subject of a *yiqtol*, the jussive sense seems to be absent. To the degree that this signals a standard in Hebrew poetry or

---

[103] Gray, "Israel in the Song of Deborah," 439, n. 59, contra TJon, which assumes the same etymology in its paraphrase but prefers the connotation of destruction: "The cities of the nations which had destroyed [them], they rebuilt them and lived in them." See Smelik, *Targum of Judges*, 464.

[104] A convincing argument is made by Smelik, *Targum of Judges*, 464–65, esp. n. 770.

[105] Thus Block, *Judges, Ruth*, 234, in accord with Boling, *Judges*, 113, who insists on a similar construction in 2 Sam 1:21 (contra *BHS* and most ancient versions). For a brief assessment of modern translations of this verse, see Anthony Abela, "Two Short Studies on Judges 5," *Bible Translator* 53 (2002): 134–35.

[106] "(Positionally or temporally; e.g., Job 23:8)": Contra *HALOT*, 1069–70. "East" (e.g., Gen 3:24, 10:30), or "primeval/ancient": Following *BTAT*, 88. Cf. זְקֵנִים in Gen 21:2, 7.

[107] For a list of other possibilities, see Marcos, *Judges*, 62*.

[108] Boling, *Judges*, 103, 113, translates, "You shall trample the throat of the mighty."

grammar more widely, at least one other translation is possible, namely, a simple declaration: "I/my soul march[es] mightily."

Verse 22

Then the hooves of the horses hammered. Despite the tendency by commentators, Vulg., and certain LXX MSS to pluralize סוס by reclaiming the initial מ of מִדַּהֲרוֹת, the MT requires no revision. As elsewhere in the Hebrew Bible, סוס functions as a collective singular (e.g., Deut 17:16; Josh 11:4; 1 Kgs 20:1).[109]

Verse 23

Said the envoy of YHWH. That TJon introduces the מלאך יהוה as a prophet (נביא) is an interpretive choice whose exegetical significance has already been explored.[110] The unanimous witness of the ancient translations to the MT's מלאך יהוה suggests that no revision is necessary. The structure of the poem and all extant witnesses counsel against the suggestion of *BHS* to transpose verse 23 after verse 17.[111]

Verse 26

Her hand to the tent peg she stretched out. The MT describes Jael's action using the verb תִּשְׁלַחְנָה, a 3fs verbal form with a 3fs pronominal suffix featuring an energic nun (more frequently pointed נָּה).[112]

To the workers' mallet. While the first half of the verse seems clear, the MT's לְהַלְמוּת עֲמֵלִים is comprised of two challenging hapax legomena. Syr. and Vulg. agree with the MT in their rendering of both words. TJon also speaks of a "hammer" but uses the verbal root הלם again to speak of "shattering" the wicked and makes no reference to workmen.[113] LXXA reads εἰς ἀποτομὰς κατακόπων ("to the cutting off of weary ones," NETS), thereby associating the עֲמֵלִים with those who are miserable (as in Job 3:20; 20:22)

---

[109] On "collective singulars" with plural predicates, see *BHRG*, 249 (§35.3).

[110] See p. 30, n. 54 above. For his own analysis of this interpretation, see Smelik, *Targum of Judges*, 470.

[111] Ending this stanza with a curse (ארר) and beginning the next with a blessing (ברך) seems intentional.

[112] Contra Lindars, *Judges 1–5*, 278, who claims the "pointing of the MT as a pl. form is clearly wrong." For other examples of the 3fs suffix pointed as it is here, see Job 17:16 (תֵּרַדְנָה) and Obad 13 (תִּשְׁלַחְנָה; though Serge Frolov, "How Old Is the Song of Deborah?" *JSOT* 36 [2011]: 168, suggests the verb in Obad 13 is actually a 3fs form with no suffix and thereby claims the same spelling in Judg 5 is evidence of its late composition). For further explanation and additional examples, see Joüon, §61f; *IBHS*, 517, n. 63.

[113] According to Smelik (*Targum of Judges*, 474–75), the idea of "workmen" is restored in the Western tradition.

rather than those who toil or work hard (as in Prov 16:26, Qoh 2:18; 3:9). The latter nuance makes better sense of the mallet (הַלְמוּת) with which the pl. subst. is associated.

Verse 28

The mother of Sisera lamented through the veil. The song's single *wayyiqtol* occurs here, though its presence is not universally acknowledged. The MT, Vulg., and Syr. read a *piel* 3ms from יבב (most likely "to lament," or "to yell," though the root occurs only here in the Hebrew Bible). LXXA–B omit the verb entirely while other recensions (Alexandrinus; Origen) supply καὶ κατεμάνθανεν ("gaze," "observe," "inspect"). Because TJon supplies a verb meaning "to peer," following Kittel scholars have conjectured the reading וַתַּבֵּט (from the root נבט, "to behold, look at, watch").[114] While Rashi opts for the latter reading, he notes that earlier rabbinic tradition associated יבב with "an expression of wailing," as in Numbers 29:1.[115] Since early translations provide no consensus and either rendering makes good sense poetically,[116] I adopt the translation that seems most sensible contextually; to translate "lament" best introduces the quotation that follows.

Why do his chariots tarry to come? In verse 28c, LXXB interprets the Hebrew בשש according to the root בוש I ("to be ashamed"; ᾐσχύνθη) rather than בוש II ("to hesitate/tarry").[117] As in the other apparent instance of the root, Exodus 32:1, בוש II suits the context better by providing a semantic parallel to אחר, "to delay," in verse 28d. This reading is supported by LXXA, which supplies ἠσχάτισεν, "[they] come late, lag behind."

Verse 29

The wisest of her women answered. The form חַכְמוֹת in the MT is a pl. adjective agreeing in number and gender with the noun שָׂרוֹתֶיהָ and (arguably) the verb תַּעֲנֶינָּה, though the verbal form might also be read as a singular verb with a 3fs suffix.[118] Except for Syr., all ancient versions recognize a 3fs suffix on

---

[114] *BTAT*, 88–89, traces the reading back to Kittel. On the root יבב, see *HALOT*, 382; on the conjectured root נבט, see *HALOT*, 661.

[115] Fishelis and Fishelis, *Judges*, 46.

[116] Reading "peer" invokes a word pair that occurs in Ps 102:20, thereby emphasizing the parallelism of 28a–b through semantic overlap. Reading "lament" emphasizes the parallel nature of Sisera's mother's speech with that of her attendant(s): both quotations would be introduced by a verb of speech (יבב and ענה, respectively).

[117] *HALOT*, 117.

[118] For an example of this rendering, see Lindars, *Judges 1–5*, 283, who recommends emending חַכְמוֹת to חַכְמַת.

the verb, though several construe the verbal form itself as plural.[119] While the *dagesh* does not normally appear in the plural form—with the notable exception of Micah 7:10, in which the verb תִּרְאֶינָּה is pointed similarly—the vocalization of the form would be even more anomalous if the verb were morphologically singular.[120] Based on these considerations, there is no need to emend the text to חַכְמַת as in Vulg. and Syr. and recommended by the *BHS* editors; the consistently plural morphology supported by LXX and TJon should be retained.

Verse 30

On the basis of supposed dittography in 30d (שְׁלַל צְבָעִים) and assumed unnecessary verbiage in 30e (צֶבַע), *BHS* has proposed several deletions from verse 30. Given the distinct poetic features of climactic parallelism, these adaptations seem arbitrary and unnecessary.[121] Barthélemy rightly directs attention to LXXA–B, whose verbal sequences and reconstructed pointing match those of the MT.[122] These proposals aside, the interpretation of the MT's לְצַוְּארֵי שָׁלָל remains a problem. In LXXA–B, the phrase τράχηλον αὐτοῦ attests to the form לְצַוָּארוֹ, a sg. noun with a 3ms pronominal suffix. The phrase על צוריה in TJon (though out of sequence) also supports this rendering. The editors of *BHS* propose the Akkadian loanword שֵׁגָל ("queen") as an alternative to the final instance of שׁלל, while Boling favors the ptc. שֹׁלֵל ("plunderer").[123] These emendations are certainly plausible, but so is the reading of the MT. Indeed, Barthélemy's proposal that the subst. refers to the necks of the *women* is certainly

---

[119] Namely LXXA (ἀνταπεκρίναντο πρὸς αὐτήν), LXXB (ἀπεκρίθησαν πρὸς αὐτήν), and TJon (ענין לה). See also Marcos, *Judges*, 64*, and Smelik, *Targum of Judges*, 479, n. 851.

[120] See, e.g., Gen 16:6, in which the 3fs form of ענה II with a sg. suffix is spelled וַתְּעַנֶּהָ. Note, however, the following dissimilarities: the form is a *qal* rather than a *piel*, a *wayyiqtol* rather than a *yiqtol*, and does not bear the *atnaḥ*. After observing the oddity of the *dagesh* and drawing attention to the parallel in Micah, Sasson (*Judges 1–12*, 309) opines confidently that "despite a doubling of the last nun . . . [the 3fp of the verb ענה] is a decent enough verbal form." Groß and Gaß, *Richter*, 301, draw on GKC §20i to demonstrate how the pausal form might require the *dagesh* forte. Contra Joüon, 243 (§88Mk), and *IBHS*, 101, n. 29 (6.3.2.b), who designate the verb (and its subject) as morphologically singular.

[121] Contra Lindars, *Judges 1–5*, 284.

[122] *BTAT*, 89, followed by Marcos, *Judges*, 64*. While the LXX opts for more amicable vocabulary by reading the consonants רחם as the root meaning "show compassion/friendliness," rather than רֶחֶם, "womb," the *semantic* discontinuity does not negate the apparent *syntactical* continuity of the MT and the *Vorlage* of LXXA–B.

[123] "The editors of *BHS* propose": *HALOT*, 1415; so also *BHK*. "While Boling favors": Boling, *Judges*, 115. TJon may also lend credence to such an interpretation, as the end of v. 30 records the distribution of "goods of the wealthy and the objects of desire to his champions, who plundered [them]." See Smelik, *Targum of Judges*, 479.

reasonable. In 30d–e, the poet subtly returns to the "one-two pattern" introduced in 30b; the women described as "a womb or two" (רַחַם רַחֲמָתַיִם) earlier are now adorned not with a single piece of embroidered cloth (רִקְמָה), but two (רִקְמָתַיִם).[124]

Verse 31

May those who love him. The pronominal suffixes in verse 31 are difficult. While verse 31b supplies a 3ms suffix to the subst., the preceding cola addresses YHWH directly and affixes a 2ms pronominal suffix to the subst. אֹיֵב. Presumably in view of this earlier colon, Vulg., Syr., and two Greek MSS read a 2ms suffix in 31b. Some modern scholars follow suit so as to harmonize the pronominal objects,[125] but LXXA–B (οἱ ἀγαπῶντες αὐτόν) and TJon (ורחמוהי) agree with the MT. Considering that this sort of pronominal shift is common in Hebrew poetry, I retain the 3ms object in 31b.

---

[124] *BTAT*, 90. Followed by Marcos, *Judges*, 65*. Though he prefers to emend the const. ending to a 3ms suffix following the LXX, Lindars (*Judges 1–5*, 286) acknowledges that this interpretation is plausible.

[125] See, e.g., Burney, *Book of Judges*, 165; Lindars, *Judges 1–5*, 286; and the editors of *BHS*.

Bibliography

Abela, Anthony. "Two Short Studies on Judges 5." *Bible Translator* 53 (2002): 133–37.
Ackerman, Susan. *Warrior, Dancer, Seductress, Queen: Women in Judges and Biblical Israel*. Anchor Bible Reference Library. New York: Doubleday, 1998.
Ackermann, James. "Prophecy and Warfare in Early Israel: A Study of the Debora-Barak Story." *Bulletin of the American Schools of Oriental Research* 220 (1975): 5–13.
Aitken, James K. "Fat Eglon." In *Studies on the Text and Versions of the Hebrew Bible in Honour of Robert Gordon*, edited by Geoffrey Khan and Diana Lipton, 141–54. Vetus Testamentum, Supplements 149. Leiden: Brill, 2012.
Albright, William F. "The Song of Deborah in the Light of Archeology." *Bulletin of the American Schools of Oriental Research* 62 (1936): 26–31.
———. *Yahweh and the Gods of Canaan: A Historical Analysis of Two Contrasting Faiths*. Jordan Lectures in Comparative Religion Series 7. London: Athlone, 1968.
Alonso-Schökel, Luis. "Erzählkunst im Buche der Richter." *Biblica* 42 (1961): 143–72.
Alter, Robert. *The Art of Biblical Narrative*. New York: Basic Books, 1981.
Amit, Yairah. *The Book of Judges: The Art of Editing*. Translated by Jonathan Chipman. Biblical Interpretation Series 38. Boston: Brill, 1999.
———. "The Story of Ehud (Judges 3:12–30): The Form and the Message." In *Signs and Wonders: Biblical Texts in Literary Focus*, edited by J. Cheryl Exum, 97–123. Society of Biblical Literature Semeia Studies. Atlanta: SBL, 1989.
Andersson, Greger. *The Book and Its Narratives: A Critical Examination of Some Synchronic Studies of the Book of Judges*. Örebro Studies in Literary History and Criticism 1. Örebro: Örebro University, 2001.
Assis, Elie. "Chiasmus in Biblical Narrative: Rhetoric of Characterization." *Prooftexts: A Journal of Jewish Literary History* 22 (2002): 273–304.
———. "The Choice to Serve God and Assist His People: Rahab and Yael." *Biblica* 85 (2004): 82–90.
———. "The Function of Repetition and Contradiction in the Paradigm of the Judges (2:11–19)." *Scriptura* 119 (2020): 1–10.

———. "The Hand of a Woman: Deborah and Yael (Judges 4)." *Journal of Hebrew Scriptures* 5 (2005): 1–12.

———. "Man, Woman and God in Judg 4." *Scandinavian Journal of the Old Testament* 20 (2006): 110–24.

———. *Self-Interest or Communal Interest: An Ideology of Leadership in the Gideon, Abimelech and Jephthah Narratives (Judg 6–12)*. Translated by Stephanie Nakache. Vetus Testamentum, Supplements 106. Leiden: Brill, 2005.

———. "The Structure and Meaning of the Samson Narratives (Jud. 13–16)." In *Samson: Hero or Fool? The Many Faces of Samson*, edited by Erik Eynikel and Tobias Nicklas, 1–12. Themes in Biblical Narrative 17. Leiden: Brill, 2014.

Auffret, Pierre. "En ce jour-la Debora et Baraq chanterent: Étude structurelle de Jg 5, 2–31." *Scandinavian Journal of the Old Testament* 16 (2002): 113–50.

Backfish, Elizabeth H. P. "The Function of Alliteration in the Prosaic and Poetic Accounts of the Deborah Cycle." *Journal for the Study of the Old Testament* 44 (2020): 551–62.

Bar-Efrat, Shimon. *Narrative Art in the Bible*. New York: T&T Clark International, 2004.

———. "Some Observations on the Analysis of Structure in Biblical Narrative." *Vetus Testamentum* 30 (1980): 154–73.

Barré, Michael L. "The Meaning of *pršdn* in Judges 3:22." *Vetus Testamentum* 41 (1991): 1–11.

Bartelmus, Rudiger. "Forschung am Richterbuch seit Martin Noth." *Theologische Rundschau* 56 (1991): 221–59.

Becking, Bob. "Deborah's Topical Song: Remarks on the Gattung of Judges 5." In *Biblical Narratives, Archaeology, and Historicity: Essays in Honour of Thomas L. Thompson*, edited by Łukasz Niesiolowski-Spanò and Emanuel Pfoh, 190–97. Library of Hebrew Bible/Old Testament Studies 680. London: T&T Clark, 2019.

Beldman, David J. H. *The Completion of Judges: Strategies of Ending in Judges 17–21*. Siphrut: Literature and Theology of the Hebrew Scriptures 21. Winona Lake, Ind: Einsenbrauns, 2017.

———. *Judges*. Two Horizons Old Testament Commentary. Grand Rapids: Eerdmans, 2020.

Berlin, Adele. *Dynamics of Biblical Parallelism*. Biblical Resource Series. Rev. and exp. ed. Grand Rapids: Eerdmans, 2008.

———. *Poetics and Interpretation of Biblical Narrative*. Bible and Literature Series 9. Winona Lake, Ind.: Eisenbrauns, 1994.

Berman, Joshua A. *Narrative Analogy in the Hebrew Bible: Battle Stories and Their Equivalent Non-Battle Narratives*. Vetus Testamentum, Supplements 103. Leiden: Brill, 2004.

Blenkinsopp, J. "Ballad Style and Psalm Style in the Song of Deborah: A Discussion." *Biblica* 42 (1961): 61–76.

Block, Daniel I. "Deborah among the Judges: The Perspective of the Hebrew Historian." In *Faith, Tradition, and History: Old Testament Historiography in Its Near Eastern Context*, edited by A. R. Millard, James K. Hoffmeier, and David W. Baker, 229–53. Winona Lake, Ind.: Eisenbrauns, 1994.

———. *Deuteronomy*. NIV Application Commentary. Grand Rapids: Zondervan, 2012.

———. *Judges, Ruth*. New American Commentary 6. Nashville: Broadman & Holman, 2001.

———. "A Prophet like Moses: Another Look at Deut 18:9–22." In *The Triumph of Grace: Literary and Theological Studies in Deuteronomy and Deuteronomic Themes*, 349–61. Eugene, Ore.: Cascade, 2017.

———. "Will the Real Gideon Please Stand Up? Narrative Style and Intention in Judges 6–9." *Journal of the Evangelical Theological Society* 40 (1997): 353–66.

Bluedorn, Wolfgang. *Yahweh versus Baalism: A Theological Reading of the Gideon–Abimelech Narrative*. Edited by David J. A. Clines and Philip R. Davies. Journal for the Study of the Old Testament, Supplement Series 329. Sheffield: Sheffield Academic Press, 2009.

Boda, Mark J. "Judges." In *Numbers–Ruth*, vol. 5 of *The Expositor's Bible Commentary*, edited by Tremper Longman III and David E. Garland, 1043–288. Rev. ed. Grand Rapids: Zondervan, 2017.

———. "Recycling Heaven's Words: Receiving and Retrieving Divine Revelation in the Historiography of Judges." In *Prophets and Prophecy and Ancient Israelite Historiography*, edited by Mark J. Boda and Lissa Wray Beal, 43–67. Winona Lake, Ind.: Eisenbrauns, 2013.

Boda, Mark J., and Mary L. Conway. *Judges*. Zondervan Exegetical Commentary on the Old Testament. Grand Rapids: Zondervan Academic, 2022.

Boling, Robert G. *Judges*. Anchor Bible (Commentary) 6A. New York: Doubleday, 1975.

Bonfiglio, Ryan P. "Choosing Sides in Judges 4–5: Rethinking Representations of Jael." In *Joshua and Judges*, edited by Athalya Brenner and Gale A. Yee, 161–73. Texts at Contexts. Minneapolis: Fortress, 2013.

Bowman, Richard G. "Narrative Criticism: Human Purpose in Conflict with Divine Presence." In *Judges and Method: New Approaches in Biblical Studies*, edited by Gale A. Yee, 19–45. Minneapolis: Fortress, 2007.

Brenner, Athalya. "A Triangle and a Rhombus in Narrative Structure: A Proposed Integrative Reading of Judges IV and V." *Vetus Testamentum* 40 (1990): 129–38.

Brotzman, Ellis R., and Eric J. Tully. *Old Testament Textual Criticism: A Practical Introduction*. 2nd ed. Grand Rapids: Baker, 2016.

Burney, C. F. *The Book of Judges: With Introduction and Notes*. 2nd ed. London: Rivingtons, 1920.

Butler, Trent C. *Judges*. Word Biblical Commentary 8. Nashville: Thomas Nelson, 2009.

Calderone, P. "ḤDL-II in Poetic Texts." *Catholic Biblical Quarterly* 23 (1961): 451–60.

Cazelles, H. "Déborah (Jud. V 14), Amaleq et Mâkîr." *Vetus Testamentum* 24 (1974): 235–38.

Chaney, Marvin Lee. "ḤDL-II and the Song of Deborah: Textual, Philological, and Sociological Studies in Judges 5, with Special Reference to the Verbal Occurrences of ḤDL in Biblical Hebrew." PhD diss., Harvard University, 1976.

Chisholm, Robert B., Jr. *A Commentary on Judges and Ruth.* Kregel Exegetical Library. Grand Rapids: Kregel Academic, 2013.

———. "Ehud: Assessing an Assassin." *Bibliotheca Sacra* 168 (2011): 274–82.

———. "Identity Crisis: Assessing Samson's Birth and Career." *Bibliotheca Sacra* 166 (2009): 147–62.

———. "What's Wrong with This Picture? Stylistic Variation as a Rhetorical Technique in Judges." *Journal for the Study of the Old Testament* 34 (2009): 171–82.

Claassens, L. Juliana M. "The Character of God in Judges 6–8: The Gideon Narrative as Theological and Moral Resource." *Horizons in Biblical Theology* 23 (2001): 51–71.

Clines, David J. A. *The Theme of the Pentateuch.* Journal for the Study of the Old Testament, Supplement Series 10. 2nd ed. Sheffield: Sheffield Academic, 1997.

Conway, Mary L. *Judging the Judges: A Narrative Appraisal Analysis.* Linguistic Studies in Ancient West Semitic 15. University Park, Pa.: Eisenbrauns, 2020.

Coogan, Michael David. "A Structural and Literary Analysis of the Song of Deborah." *Catholic Biblical Quarterly* 40 (1978): 143–65.

Cooke, George A. *The History and Song of Deborah: Judges IV and V.* Oxford: Horace Hart, 1892.

Coppens, Joseph. "La Théophanie de Jud 5:4–5." *Ephemerides Theologicae Lovanienses* 43 (1967): 528–31.

Cottrill, Amy C. "Moral Injury and Humanizing the Enemy in Judges 5." In *Moral Injury: A Guidebook for Understanding and Engagement,* edited by Brad E. Kelle, 149–60. Lanham, Md.: Rowman & Littlefield, 2020.

Craigie, Peter C. "A Note on Judges V 2." *Vetus Testamentum* 18 (1968): 397–99.

———. "Some Further Notes on the Song of Deborah." *Vetus Testamentum* 22 (1972): 349–53.

Daniels, Quinn. "The Root of Ephraim among Amalek in the Song of Deborah." *Journal of Biblical Literature* 142 (2023): 243–65.

Dijk-Hemmes, Fokkelien van. "Mothers and a Mediator in the Song of Deborah." In *A Feminist Companion to Judges,* edited by Athalya Brenner, 110–14. Feminist Companion to the Bible 4. Sheffield: Sheffield Academic, 1993.

Echols, Charles L. *"Tell Me, O Muse": The Song of Deborah (Judges 5) in the Light of Heroic Poetry.* Library of Hebrew Bible/Old Testament Studies 487. London: T&T Clark, 2008.

Edenburg, Cynthia. *Dismembering the Whole: Composition and Purpose of Judges 19–21.* Society of Biblical Literature Ancient Israel and Its Literature 24. Atlanta: SBL, 2016.

Exum, J. Cheryl. "The Centre Cannot Hold: Thematic and Textual Instabilities in Judges." *Catholic Biblical Quarterly* 52 (1990): 410–31.

———. "The Theological Dimension of the Samson Saga." *Vetus Testamentum* 33 (1983): 30–45.

Fensham, F. C. "The Numeral Seventy in the Old Testament and the Family of Jerubbaal, Ahab, Panammuwa and Athirat." *Palestine Exploration Quarterly* 109 (1977): 113–15.

Fishbane, Michael. *Biblical Interpretation in Ancient Israel.* New York: Oxford, 1985.

Fishelis, Schmuel, and Avraham Shelomoh Fishelis. *Judges: A New English Translation of the Text, Rashi and a Commentary Digest*. Edited by A. J. Rosenberg. Judaica Books of the Prophets. New York: Judaica, 1983.

Fokkelman, Jan P. *Reading Biblical Narrative: An Introductory Guide*. Translated by Ineke Smit. Louisville: Westminster John Knox, 1999.

———. *Reading Biblical Poetry: An Introductory Guide*. Translated by Ineke Smit. Louisville: Westminster John Knox, 2001.

———. "The Song of Deborah and Barak: Its Prosodic Levels and Structure." In *Pomegranates and Golden Bells: Studies in Biblical, Jewish, and Near Eastern Ritual, Law, and Literature in Honor of Jacob Milgrom*, edited by David P. Wright, David Noel Freedman, and Avi Hurvitz, 595–628. Winona Lake, Ind.: Eisenbrauns, 1995.

Freeman, James A. "Samson's Dry Bones: A Structural Reading of Judges 13–16." In *Literary Interpretations of Biblical Narratives*, vol. 2, edited by Kenneth R. R. Gros Louis, 145–60. Nashville: Abingdon, 1982.

Fritz, Volkmar. "Das Debora-Lied Ri 5 als Geschichtsquelle." In *Studien zur Literatur und Geschichte des alten Israel*, 165–85. Stuttgarter Biblische Aufsatzbände 22. Stuttgart: Katholisches Bibelwerk, 1997.

Frolov, Serge. "How Old Is the Song of Deborah?" *Journal for the Study of the Old Testament* 36 (2011): 163–84.

———. *Judges*. The Forms of the Old Testament Literature 6b. Grand Rapids: Eerdmans, 2013.

Giles, Terry, and William J. Doan. *Twice Used Songs: Performance Criticism of the Songs of Ancient Israel*. Peabody, Mass.: Hendrickson, 2009.

Globe, Alexander. "Judges V 27." *Vetus Testamentum* 25 (1975): 362–67.

———. "The Literary Structure and Unity of the Song of Deborah." *Journal of Biblical Literature* 93 (1974): 493–512.

———. "The Muster of the Tribes in Judges 5, 11e–18." *Zeitschrift für die alttestamentliche Wissenschaft* 87 (1975): 167–84.

———. "The Text and Literary Structure of Judges 5,4–5." *Biblica* 55 (1974): 168–78.

Gooding, David W. "The Composition of the Book of Judges." *Eretz-Israel* 16 (1982): 70–79.

Gottwald, Norman K. *The Tribes of Yahweh: The Sociology of the Religion of Liberated Israel, 1250–1050 B.C.E.* Maryknoll, N.Y.: Orbis, 1979.

Gray, John. "Israel in the Song of Deborah." In *Ascribe to the Lord: Biblical and Other Studies in Memory of Peter C. Craigie*, edited by Lyle Eslinger and J. Glen Taylor, 421–55. Journal for the Study of the Old Testament, Supplement Series. Sheffield: JSOT, 1988.

Greenspahn, Frederick E. "The Theology of the Framework of Judges." *Vetus Testamentum* 36 (1986): 385–96.

Groom, Sue. *Linguistic Analysis of Biblical Hebrew*. Waynesboro, Ga.: Paternoster, 2003.

Groß, Walter, and Erasmus Gaß. *Richter: Übersetzt und ausgelegt*. Herders Theologischer Kommentar zum Alten Testament. Freiburg: Herder, 2009.

Gunn, David M. *Judges*. Blackwell Bible Commentaries. Malden: Wiley-Blackwell, 2005.

Hackett, Jo Ann. "Violence and Women's Lives in the Book of Judges." *Interpretation* 58 (2004): 356–64.

Halpern, Baruch. *The First Historians: The Hebrew Bible and History*. San Francisco: Harper & Row, 1988.

Hamley, Isabelle. *God of Justice and Mercy: A Theological Commentary on Judges*. London: SCM Press, 2021.

Hauser, Alan J. "Two Songs of Victory: A Comparison of Exodus 15 and Judges 5." In *Directions in Biblical Hebrew Poetry*, edited by Elaine R. Follis, 265–84. Journal for the Study of the Old Testament, Supplement Series 40. Sheffield: JSOT, 1987.

Heller, Roy L. "What Is Abimelek Doing in Judges?" In *Raising Up a Faithful Exegete: Essays in Honor of Richard D. Nelson*, edited by K. L. Noll and Brooks Schramm, 225–35. Winona Lake, Ind.: Eisenbrauns, 2010.

Hess, Richard S. *Israelite Religions: An Archaeological and Biblical Survey*. Grand Rapids: Baker Academic, 2007.

———. "Judges 1–5 and Its Translation." In *Translating the Bible: Problems and Prospects*, edited by Stanley E. Porter and Richard S. Hess, 142–60. Journal for the Study of the New Testament, Supplement Series 173. Sheffield: Sheffield Academic, 1999.

Hillers, Delbert R. "A Note on Judges 5,8a." *Catholic Biblical Quarterly* 27 (1965): 124–26.

Holmstedt, Robert D. "Analyzing זֶה Grammar and Reading זֶה Texts of Ps 68:9 and Judg 5:5." *Journal of Hebrew Scriptures* 14 (2014): 1–26.

Hoop, Raymond de. "Judges 5 Reconsidered: Which Tribes? What Land? Whose Song?" In *Land of Israel in Bible, History, and Theology*, edited by Jacques van Ruiten and J. Cornelis de Vos, 151–66. Vetus Testamentum, Supplements 124. Boston: Brill, 2009.

Huehnergard, John. *An Introduction to Ugaritic*. Peabody, Mass.: Hendrickson, 2012.

Janzen, David. "Why the Deuteronomist Told about the Sacrifice of Jephthah's Daughter." *Journal for the Study of the Old Testament* 29 (2005): 339–57.

Klein, Lillian R. *The Triumph of Irony in the Book of Judges*. Journal for the Study of the Old Testament, Supplement Series 68. Sheffield: Almond, 1988.

Knauf, Ernst Axel. "Zum Text von Ri 5:14." *Biblica* 64 (1983): 428–29.

Knierim, Rolf. "Old Testament Form Criticism Reconsidered." *Interpretation* (1973): 435–68.

Knight, Michelle. "Geometry and Psalmody: Characterization and the Role of Deborah's Song (Judges 5)." In *"Now These Records Are Ancient": Studies in Ancient Near Eastern and Biblical History, Language and Culture in Honor of K. Lawson Younger, Jr*, edited by James K. Hoffmeier et al., 287–98. Ägypten und Altes Testament 114. Münster: Zaphon, 2022.

———. "The Prophet's Song of Victory: Judges 5 within a Trajectory of Theological Training in the Book of Judges." *Bulletin for Biblical Research* 33 (2023): 287–303.
Knohl, Israel. "The Original Version of Deborah's Song, and Its Numerical Structure." *Vetus Testamentum* 66 (2016): 45–65.
Kooij, Arie van der. "On Male and Female Views in Judges 4 and 5." In *On Reading Prophetic Texts: Gender-Specific and Related Studies in Memory of Fokkelien van Dijk-Hemmes*, edited by Bob Becking and Meindert Dijkstra, 135–52. Biblical Interpretation Series 18. New York: Brill, 1996.
Kronholm, T. "פֶּרֶא." In vol. 2 of *Theological Dictionary of the Old Testament*, edited by G. Johannes Botterweck, Helmer Ringgren, and Heiz-Josef Fabry, translated by David E. Gene, 98–101. New York: Doubleday, 1992.
Kugel, James L. *The Idea of Biblical Poetry: Parallelism and Its History*. Baltimore: Johns Hopkins University Press, 1998.
Kupitz, Yaakov S., and Katell Berthelot. "Deborah and the Delphic Pythia: A New Interpretation of Judges 4:4–5." In *Images and Prophecy in the Ancient Eastern Mediterranean*, edited by Martti Nissinen and Charles E. Carter, 95–124. Forschungen zur Religion und Literatur des Alten und Neuen Testaments 233. Göttingen: Vanderhoeck & Ruprecht, 2009.
Landers, Solomon. "Did Jephthah Kill His Daughter?" *Bible Review* 7 (1991): 28–31, 42.
Lewis, Theodore J. "The Songs of Hannah and Deborah: *HDL*-II ('Growing Plump')." *Journal of Biblical Literature* 104 (1985): 105–8.
Lilley, J. P. U. "A Literary Appreciation of the Book of Judges." *Tyndale Bulletin* 18 (1967): 94–102.
Lindars, Barnabas. *Judges 1–5: A New Translation and Commentary*. International Critical Commentary. New York: T&T Clark, 1995.
Liss, Hanna. "Die Fabel des Yotam in Ri 9,8–15: Versuch einer strukturellen Deutung." *Biblische Notizen* 89 (1997): 12–18.
Magness, Jodi. "Toilets and Toilet Humor in the Story of Eglon's Murder by Ehud (Judges 3:15–26)." *Journal of Biblical Literature* 142 (2023): 65–89.
Malamat, Abraham. "Cushan Rishathaim and the Decline of the Near East around 1200 B.C." *Journal of Near Eastern Studies* 13 (1954): 231–42.
———. *Mari and the Early Israelite Experience*. Schweich Lectures 1984. Oxford: Oxford University Press, 1989.
Marcos, Natalio Fernandez. *Judges*. Vol. 7 of *Biblia Hebraica Quinta*. Stuttgart: Deutsche Bibelgesellschaft, 2011.
Martens, Elmer A. "Accessing Theological Readings of a Biblical Book." *Andrews University Seminary Studies* 34 (1996): 223–37.
Martin, Lee Roy. "From Gilgal to Bochim: The Narrative Significance of the Angel of Yahweh in Judges 2:1." *Journal for Semitics* 18 (2009): 331–43.
———. *The Unheard Voice of God: A Pentecostal Hearing of the Book of Judges*. Journal of Pentecostal Theology Supplemental Series 32. Blandford Forum: Deo Publishing, 2008.

———. "Yahweh Conflicted: Unresolved Theological Tension in the Cycle of Judges." *Old Testament Essays* 22 (2009): 356–72.

Mathys, Hans-Peter. *Dichter und Beter: Theologen aus spätalttestamentlicher Zeit.* Orbis biblicus et orientalis 132. Freiburg: Universitätsverlag Freiburg Schweiz Vandenhoeck, 1994.

Mattingly, Gerald L. "Amalek (Person)." In vol. 1 of *Anchor Bible Dictionary*, edited by David Noel Freedman et al., 169–71. New York: Doubleday, 1992.

Mayfield, Tyler. "The Accounts of Deborah (Judges 4–5) in Recent Research." *Current in Biblical Research* 7 (2009): 306–35.

McCann, J. Clinton, Jr. *Judges*. Interpretation: A Bible Commentary for Teaching and Preaching. Louisville: John Knox, 2002.

Miller, Robert D. "When Pharaohs Ruled: On the Translation of Judges 5:2." *Journal of Theological Studies* 59 (2008): 650–54.

Moran, William L. "Ancient Near Eastern Background of the Love of God in Deuteronomy." *Catholic Biblical Quarterly* 25 (1965): 77–87.

Murray, D. F. "Narrative Structure and Technique in the Deborah-Barak Story, Judges 4:4–22." In *Studies in the Historical Books of the Old Testament*, edited by J. A. Emerton, 155–89. Vetus Testamentum, Supplements 30. Leiden: Brill, 1979.

Na'aman, Nadav. "Literary and Topographical Notes on the Battle of Kishon (Judges IV–V)." *Vetus Testamentum* 40 (1990): 423–36.

Neef, Heinz-Dieter. "Deboraerzählung und Deboralied: Beobachtungen zum Verhältnis von Jdc. IV und V." *Vetus Testamentum* 44 (1994): 47–59.

———. "Eglon als 'Kälbermann'? Exegetische Beobachtungen zu Jdc 3:12–30." *Vetus Testamentum* 59 (2009): 284–94.

———. "Meroz: Jdc 5,23a." *Zeitschrift für die alttestamentliche Wissenschaft* 107 (1995): 118–22.

Nel, P. J. "Character in the Book of Judges." *Old Testament Essays* 8 (1995): 191–204.

Nelson, Richard D. *Judges: A Critical and Rhetorical Commentary*. New York: T&T Clark, 2017.

Niditch, Susan. *Judges: A Commentary*. Old Testament Library. Louisville: Westminster John Knox, 2008.

Niehr, H. "He-of-the-Sinai." In *Dictionary of Deities and Demons in the Bible*, edited by Karel van der Toorn, Bob Becking, and Pieter W. van der Horst, 387–88. 2nd extensively rev. ed. Leiden: Brill, 1999.

O'Connell, Robert H. *The Rhetoric of the Book of Judges*. Vetus Testamentum, Supplements 63. Leiden: Brill, 1996.

Oeste, Gordon K. "Butchered Brothers and Betrayed Families: Degenerating Kinship Structures in the Book of Judges." *Journal for the Study of the Old Testament* 35 (2010): 295–316.

———. *Legitimacy, Illegitimacy, and the Right to Rule: Windows on Abimelech's Rise and Demise in Judges 9*. Library of Hebrew Bible/Old Testament Studies 546. New York: T&T Clark, 2011.

Ottoson, Magnus. *Gilead: Tradition and History*. Translated by Jean Gray. Coniectanea biblica, Old Testament 3. Lund: CWK Gleerup, 1969.

Park, Song-Mi Suzie. "Left-Handed Benjaminites and the Shadow of Saul." *Journal of Biblical Literature* 134 (2015): 701–20.

Rabin, Chaim. "Judges 5:2 and the 'Ideology' of Deborah's War." *Journal of Jewish Studies* 6 (1955): 125–34.

Rad, Gerhard von. *The Theology of Israel's Historical Traditions*. Vol. 1 of *Old Testament Theology*. Translated by D. M. G. Stalker. Old Testament Library. Louisville: Westminster John Knox, 2001.

Rainey, Anson F., and R. Steven Notley. *The Sacred Bridge: Carta's Atlas of the Biblical World*. Jerusalem: Carta, 2006.

Reimer, David J. "צדק." In vol. 3 of *New International Dictionary of Old Testament Theology and Exegesis*, edited by Willem A. VanGemeren, 744–69. Grand Rapids: Zondervan, 1997.

Ross, Jillian. *A People Heeds Not Scripture: Allusion in Judges*. Eugene, Ore.: Pickwick, 2023.

Sakenfeld, Katharine Doob. "Whose Text Is It?" *Journal of Biblical Literature* 127 (2008): 5–18.

Sasson, Jack M. "'A Breeder or Two for Each Leader': On Mothers in Judges 4 and 5." In *A Critical Engagement: Essays on the Hebrew Bible in Honour of J. Cheryl Exum*, edited by David J. A. Clines and Ellen van Wolde, 333–54. Hebrew Bible Monographs 38. Sheffield: Sheffield Phoenix, 2011.

———. "Ethically Cultured Interpretations: The Case of Eglon's Murder (Judges 3)." In *Homeland and Exile: Biblical and Ancient Near Eastern Studies in Honour of Bustenay Oded*, edited by Gershon Galil, Mark Geller, and Alan Millard, 571–95. Vetus Testamentum, Supplements 130. Leiden: Brill, 2009.

———. *Judges 1–12: A New Translation with Introduction and Commentary*. Anchor Bible (Commentary) 6D. New Haven: Yale University, 2014.

Schloen, J. David. "Caravans, Kenites, and *Casus belli*: Enmity and Alliance in the Song of Deborah." *Catholic Biblical Quarterly* 55 (1993): 18–38.

Schneider, Tammi J. *Judges*. Berit Olam. Collegeville, Minn.: Liturgical Press, 2000.

Smelik, Willem F. *The Targum of Judges*. Oudtestamentische Studiën 26. New York: Brill, 1995.

Smith, Mark S. *Poetic Heroes: Literary Commemorations of Warriors and Warrior Culture in the Early Biblical World*. Grand Rapids: Eerdmans, 2014.

———. "What Is Prologue Is Past: Composing Israelite Identity in Judges 5." In *Thus Says the Lord: Essays on the Former and Latter Prophets in Honor of Robert R. Wilson*, edited by Stephen L. Cook and John J. Ahn, 43–58. Library of Hebrew Bible/Old Testament Studies. London: T&T Clark, 2009.

Smith, Mark S., and Elizabeth Bloch-Smith. *Judges 1: A Commentary on Judges 1:1–10:5*. Hermeneia. Minneapolis: Fortress, 2021.

Smith, Mark S., and Wayne T. Pitard. *Introduction with Text, Translation and Commentary of KTU/CAT 1.3–1.4*. Vol. 2 of *The Ugaritic Baal Cycle*. Vetus Testamentum, Supplements 114. Leiden: Brill, 2009.

Soggin, Jan Alberto. "'Ehud und 'Eglon: Bemerkungen zu Richter 3:11b–31." *Vetus Testamentum* 39 (1989): 95–100.

———. *Judges: A Commentary*. Translated by John Bowden. Old Testament Library. Philadelphia: Westminster, 1981.

Spronk, Klaas. "Deborah, a Prophetess: The Meaning and Background of Judges 4:4–5." In *The Elusive Prophet: The Prophet as a Historical Person, Literary Character and Anonymous Artist*, edited by Johannes de Moor, 232–42. Oudtestamentische Studiën 45. Leiden: Brill, 2001.

Stager, Lawrence E. "Archaeology, Ecology, and Social History: Background Themes to the Song of Deborah." In *Congress Volume: Jerusalem, 1986*, 221–34. Leiden: Brill, 1988.

———. "The Song of Deborah: Why Some Tribes Answered the Call and Others Did Not." *Biblical Archaeology Review* 15 (1989): 50–64.

Stek, John H. "The Bee and the Mountain Goat: A Literary Reading of Judges 4." In *A Tribute to Gleason Archer: Essays on the Old Testament*, edited by Walter C. Kaiser and Ronald F. Youngblood, 53–86. Chicago: Moody, 1986.

Stemmer, Nathan. "The Introduction to Judges, 2.1–3.4." *Jewish Quarterly Review* 57 (1967): 239–41.

Sternberg, Meir. *Expositional Modes and Temporal Ordering in Fiction*. Baltimore: Johns Hopkins University Press, 1978.

———. *The Poetics of Biblical Narrative*. Edited by Robert M. Polzin. Indiana Studies in Biblical Literature. Bloomington: Indiana University Press, 1985.

Stone, Lawson G. "Eglon's Belly and Ehud's Blade: A Reconsideration." *Journal of Biblical Literature* 128 (2009): 649–63.

———. "From Tribal Confederation to Monarchic State: The Editorial Perspective of the Book of Judges." PhD diss., Yale University, 1988.

———. "Judges." In *Joshua, Judges, Ruth*, edited by Philip W. Comfort, 185–494. Cornerstone Biblical Commentary. Carol Stream, Ill.: Tyndale House, 2012.

———. "Judges, Book of." In *Dictionary of the Old Testament: Historical Books*, edited by Bill T. Arnold and H. G. M. Williamson, 592–606. Downers Grove, Ill.: InterVarsity Press, 2005.

Sweeney, Marvin A. "Davidic Polemics in the Book of Judges." *Vetus Testamentum* 47 (1997): 517–29.

Tanner, J. Paul. "The Gideon Narrative as the Focal Point of Judges." *Bibliotheca Sacra* 149 (1992): 146–61.

Thelle, Rannfrid Irene. "Matrices of Motherhood in Judges 5." *Journal for the Study of the Old Testament* 43 (2019): 436–52.

Thomas, D. W. "Some Observations on the Hebrew Root *ḥdl*." In *Volume du Congrès: Strasbourg, 1956*, 8–16. Vetus Testamentum, Supplements 4. Leiden: Brill, 1957.

Tidiman, Brian. *Le Livre des Juges*. Vaux-sur-Seine: Édifac, 2004.

Tobolowsky, Andrew. "The Problem of Reubenite Primacy: New Paradigms, New Answers." *Journal of Biblical Literature* 139 (2020): 27–45.

Tov, Emmanuel. *Textual Criticism of the Hebrew Bible*. 4th rev. and exp. ed. Minneapolis: Fortress, 2022.

———. "The Textual History of the Song of Deborah in the A Text of the LXX." *Vetus Testamentum* 28 (1978): 224–32.
Waard, Jan de. "Jotham's Fable: An Exercise in Clearing Away the Unclear." In *Wissenschaft und Kirche: Festschrift für Eduard Lohse*, edited by Kurt Aland and Siegfried Meurer, 362–70. Texte und Arbeiten zur Bibel 4. Bielefeld: Luther-Verlag, 1989.
Watson, Wilfred G. E. *Classical Hebrew Poetry: A Guide to Its Techniques*. Journal for the Study of the Old Testament, Supplement Series 26. Sheffield: JSOT, 1984.
Watts, James W. "Biblical Psalms outside the Psalter." In *The Book of Psalms: Composition and Reception*, edited by Peter W. Flint and Patrick D. Miller, 288–309. Vetus Testamentum, Supplements 99. Leiden: Brill, 2005.
———. *Psalm and Story: Inset Hymns in Hebrew Narrative*. Journal for the Study of the Old Testament, Supplement Series 139. Sheffield: JSOT, 1992.
Way, Kenneth C. "The Literary Structure of Judges Revisited: Judges as a Ring Composition." In *Windows to the Ancient World of the Hebrew Bible: Essays in Honor of Samuel Greengus*, edited by B. T. Arnold, N. L. Erickson, and J. H. Walton, 247–60. Winona Lake, Ind.: Eisenbrauns, 2014.
Webb, Barry G. *The Book of Judges*. New International Commentary on the Old Testament. Grand Rapids: Eerdmans, 2012.
———. *The Book of Judges: An Integrated Reading*. Journal for the Study of the Old Testament, Supplement Series 46. Sheffield: JSOT, 1987.
Weinfeld, Moshe. "Divine Intervention in War in Ancient Israel and in the Ancient Near East." In *History, Historiography and Interpretation: Studies in Biblical and Cuneiform Literatures*, edited by H. Tadmor and Moshe Weinfeld, 121–47. Jerusalem: Magnes Press, 1984.
———. "The Period of the Conquest and of the Judges as Seen by the Earlier and the Later Sources." *Vetus Testamentum* 17 (1967): 93–113.
Weiser, Artur. "Das Deboralied: Eine gattungs- und traditionsgeschichtliche Studie." *Zeitschrift für die alttestamentliche Wissenschaft* 71 (1959): 67–97.
Weitzman, Steven Phillip. *Song and Story in Biblical Narrative: The History of a Literary Convention in Ancient Israel*. Bloomington: Indiana University, 1997.
Wiseman, D. J. "'Is It Peace?': Covenant and Diplomacy." *Vetus Testamentum* 32 (1982): 311–26.
Wolde, Ellen van. "Deborah and Yaʻel in Judges 4." In *On Reading Prophetic Texts: Gender-Specific and Related Studies in Memory of Fokkelien van Dijk-Hemmes*, edited by Bob Becking and Meindert Dijkstra, 283–95. Biblical Interpretation Series 18. New York: Brill, 1996.
Wong, Gregory T. K. *The Compositional Strategy of the Book of Judges: An Inductive, Rhetorical Study*. Vetus Testamentum, Supplements 111. New York: Brill, 2006.
———. "Ehud and Joab: Separated at Birth?" *Vetus Testamentum* 56 (2006): 399–412.
———. "Song of Deborah as Polemic." *Biblica* 88 (2007): 1–22.

Wright, Jacob L. "Deborah's War Memorial: The Composition of Judges 4–5 and the Politics of War Commemoration." *Zeitschrift für die alttestamentliche Wissenschaft* 123 (2011): 516–34.

———. "War Commemoration and the Interpretation of Judges 5:15b–17." *Vetus Testamentum* 61 (2011): 505–21.

Wyatt, N. "Astarte." In *Dictionary of Deities and Demons in the Bible*, edited by Karel Van der Toorn, Bob Becking and Pieter W. van der Horst, 109–14. 2nd extensively rev. ed. Leiden: Brill, 1999.

Yee, Gale A. "By the Hand of a Woman: The Metaphor of the Woman Warrior in Judges 4." In *Women, War, and Metaphor: Language and Society in the Study of the Hebrew Bible*, edited by Claudia V. Camp and Carole R. Fontaine, 99–132. Semeia 61. Atlanta: Scholars Press, 1993.

Younger, K. Lawson. "Heads! Tails! Or the Whole Coin?! Contextual Method & Intertextual Analysis: Judges 4 and 5." In *The Biblical Canon in Comparative Perspective*, vol. 4 of *Scripture in Context*, edited by K. Lawson Younger, William W. Hallo, and Bernard F. Batto, 109–46. Ancient Near Eastern Texts Relating to the Old Testament 11. Lewiston: Edwin Mellen, 1991.

———. "Judges 1 in Its Near Eastern Literary Context." In *Faith, Tradition, and History: Old Testament Historiography in Its Near Eastern Context*, edited by A. R. Millard, James K. Hoffmeier, and David W. Baker, 207–27. Winona Lake, Ind.: Eisenbrauns, 1994.

———. *Judges, Ruth*. NIV Application Commentary. Rev. ed. Grand Rapids: Zondervan, 2020.

Zucker, David J., and Moshe Reiss. "Subverting Sexuality: Manly Women; Womanly Men in Judges 4–5." *Biblical Theology Bulletin* 45 (2015): 32–37.

Author Index

Abela, Anthony, 166n105
Ackerman, Susan, 55n63
Ackermann, James, 51n48, 53n53
Aitken, James K., 102n55
Albright, William F., 150, 150n19, 153, 153n32
Alonso-Schökel, Luis, 33–34n2, 35n5, 42n21, 53n57
Alter, Robert, 101, 101n52
Amit, Yairah, 8n33, 9, 9n34, 9n36, 62n76, 82n9, 83n10, 110n66, 122n3, 122n6, 123n7
Andersson, Greger, 4–5n17
Assis, Elie, 9n35, 36n8, 48n38, 50, 50n44, 53n55, 54n60, 60n73, 62, 62n76, 64n83, 90n27, 94n34, 95n36, 98, 98n45, 98n48, 112, 112n67, 112n68, 127
Auffret, Pierre, 19, 20n15, 29n50

Backfish, Elizabeth H. P., 17n3
Bar-Efrat, Shimon, 33n2, 67, 67n85, 67n86
Barré, Michael L., 102n57
Bartelmus, Rudiger, 1n2
Becking, Bob, 25, 25n36
Beldman, David J. H., 11–12, 11n41, 12n42, 24, 24n31, 24n32
Berman, Joshua A., 34n4
Berthelot, Katell, 52n51
Blenkinsopp, Joseph, 18, 18n8
Bloch-Smith, Elizabeth, 18n8, 46n3, 52n52, 60n72, 155n40, 161n69
Block, Daniel I., 10n39, 21n21, 30n53, 44n28, 46n34, 47n37, 52n50, 53n53, 55n61, 86n17, 93n31, 97n42, 100n49, 110n66, 113n73, 116n80, 122n3, 133, 133n27, 134n29, 148n12, 158n66, 159n68, 163n89, 166n105
Bluedorn, Wolfgang, 81n6, 114, 114n75, 123n9
Boda, Mark J., 51n49, 52n52, 122n3, 137n37, 151n23
Boling, Robert G., 24n30, 53n53, 157n59, 158n62, 158n65, 166, 166n105, 166n108, 169, 169n123
Bonfiglio, Ryan P., 62, 62n77
Bowman, Richard G., 30n55
Brenner, Athalya, 46n35, 64n83, 72, 72n95, 73n97
Brotzman, Ellis R., 4n17
Burney, C. F., 147n8, 148–49n14, 154n41, 156n51, 170n125
Butler, Trent C., 28n44, 30n53, 50, 50n45, 81n6, 101n54, 133n26

Calderone, P., 151n24
Cazelles, H., 163n89
Chaney, Marvin Lee, 41n19, 151n24
Chisholm, Robert B., Jr., 46n32, 60n72, 82n8, 86n17, 88n19, 89n23, 90n27, 98n46, 132n24, 133n26, 139, 139n61
Claassens, L. Juliana M., 113, 113n72
Clines, David J. A., 67n85
Conway, Mary L., 52n52, 89n23
Coogan, Michael David, 17, 17n7, 18n11, 19n13, 157n60
Cooke, George A., 154n44
Coppens, Joseph, 150n17
Cottrill, Amy C., 49n41

Craigie, Peter C., 148, 148n12, 153, 153n32, 155n47, 156n50, 163n86

Daniels, Quinn, 163, 163n90, 163n91
Dijk-Hemmes, Fokkelien van, 59, 70n90
Doan, William J., 4, 4n15, 4n16

Echols, Charles L., 17, 17n4, 17n5, 17n6, 18, 22, 22n22, 147n10, 148n11, 154, 154n40, 154n44, 155n47, 159n68
Edenburg, Cynthia, 8n31
Exum, J. Cheryl, 98n47, 98n48, 113, 113n69, 117, 117n81, 123n8, 129n18

Fensham, F. C., 107n64
Fishbane, Michael, 150n20
Fishelis, Avraham Shelomoh, 149n15, 156n53, 157n55, 158n64, 161n77, 164n92, 168n115
Fishelis, Schmuel, 149n15, 156n53, 157n55, 158n64, 161n77, 164n92, 168n115
Fokkelman, Jan P., 6n23, 10n37, 17, 17n7, 18n10, 18n11, 20n15, 20n18, 20n19, 21n20, 24, 24n33, 43n23, 43n26
Freeman, James A., 97n43
Fritz, Volkmar, 142n1
Frolov, Serge, 22n23, 23n26, 24, 24n34, 25, 25n35, 167n112

Gaß, Erasmus, 145n1, 147n10, 169n120
Giles, Terry, 4, 4n15, 4n16
Globe, Alexander, 17, 17n7, 20n16, 23n28, 26n37, 31n56, 149n15, 149n16, 150n21
Gooding, David W., 113n71, 128n17
Gottwald, Norman K., 151n24
Gray, John, 166, 166n103
Greenspahn, Frederick E., 122n3
Groom, Sue, 74n99
Groß, Walter, 145n1, 147n10, 169n120
Gunn, David M., 124n10

Hackett, Jo Ann, 49n41, 53n53
Halpern, Baruch, 89n21
Hamley, Isabelle, 36n80
Hauser, Alan J., 29n52
Heller, Roy L., 122, 122n6, 123n7, 129n18

Hess, Richard S., 44n28, 151n24, 155n47
Hillers, Delbert R., 156n49
Holmstedt, Robert D., 151, 151n22, 151n23
Hoop, Raymond de, 28n45
Huehnergard, John, 150n19

Janzen, David, 86n15, 86n16, 115n78

Klein, Lillian R., 62n75, 89n22, 96n40, 98n44
Knauf, Ernst Axel, 163n89
Knierim, Rolf, 22n24, 22n25, 23, 23n27
Knight, Michelle, 52n51, 73n97
Knohl, Israel, 152n30
Kooij, Arie van der, 59, 59n69
Kronholm, T., 147n10
Kugel, James L., 5, 5n20, 6n21
Kupitz, Yaakov S., 52n51

Landers, Solomon, 96n39
Lewis, Theodore J., 151n24
Lilley, J. P. U., 123n8, 123n9
Lindars, Barnabas, 146–47n7, 147n8, 148n11, 150n20, 156n49, 157n55, 157n58, 159, 159n68, 160n71, 160n73, 162n83, 162–63n85, 163n86, 164n96, 165, 165n102, 167n112, 168n118, 169n121, 170n124, 170n125
Liss, Hanna, 84n12

Magness, Jodi, 102n56
Malamat, Abraham, 45n31, 100n51
Marcos, Natalio Fernandez, 145–46n3, 153n37, 155n48, 156n53, 157n58, 160n71, 161n79, 165n99, 166n107, 169n119, 169n122, 170n124
Martens, Elmer A., 8n29
Martin, Lee Roy, 30n54, 116n79, 117n82
Mathys, Hans-Peter, 3, 3n8, 3n9, 3n10, 38, 38n13, 43n24
Mattingly, Gerald L., 104–5n59
Mayfield, Tyler, 1n2
McCann, J. Clinton, Jr., 100n49
Miller, Robert D., 147n8
Moran, William L., 44n28
Murray, D. F., 33n2, 48n38, 71, 71n92

Na'aman, Nadav, 19n12
Neef, Heinz-Dieter, 30, 30n54, 88n20, 102n56, 155n46
Nel, P. J., 39n14, 121, 121n1
Nelson, Richard D., 60n73, 67n87, 90n28, 155n47
Niditch, Susan, 23n28, 30n55, 50n43, 157n60
Niehr, H., 150n19
Notley, R. Steven, 59n71

O'Connell, Robert H., 43n22, 88n18, 89n25, 135n32
Oeste, Gordon K., 83n10, 136n36
Ottoson, Magnus, 40n17

Park, Song-Mi Suzie, 89n21
Pitard, Wayne T., 147n10

Rabin, Chaim, 147n9, 148n13
Rad, Gerhard von, 97n41, 98n44
Rainey, Anson F., 59n71
Reimer, David J., 159n68, 159n69, 158n70
Reiss, Moshe, 58n68
Ross, Jillian, 11n40

Sakenfeld, Katharine Doob, 62n75, 62n77
Sasson, Jack M., 20, 20n17, 28n48, 31n57, 45, 45n30, 50n43, 51n48, 58n67, 81, 82n7, 89, 89n24, 102n56, 115n76, 149n16, 150n19, 152, 152n26, 154n44, 155n47, 157n55, 159n68, 161n77, 162n81, 165n97, 169n120
Schloen, J. David, 27n42, 151n24, 157, 157n60, 158n66
Schneider, Tammi J., 81, 81n5, 88n20, 94n35
Smelik, Willem F., 147n9, 150n20, 152n27, 153n37, 153n38, 154n42, 156n53, 157n59, 160n71, 162n82, 162n83, 163n87, 165n99, 166n103, 166n104, 167n110, 167n113, 169n119, 169n123
Smith, Mark S., 1n1, 18n8, 46n33, 52n52, 57n66, 60n72, 147n10, 155n47, 161n76
Smith, W. Robertson, 147n8

Soggin, Jan Alberto, 88n20, 152n25
Spronk, Klaas, 52n50, 53n53
Stager, Lawrence E., 29n49, 49n42, 153, 153n33, 153n34, 153n35
Stek, John H., 35n7, 39n15, 48n38
Stemmer, Nathan, 133n27
Sternberg, Meir, 9n34, 35n6, 58, 58n68
Stone, Lawson G., 101n52, 102, 102n56, 102n58, 115n77, 115n78, 123, 123n9, 127n16, 128, 133n27, 134n29, 134n31
Sweeney, Marvin A., 125n13

Tanner, J. Paul, 113n71, 128n17
Thelle, Rannfrid Irene, 55, 56n64
Thomas, D. W., 151n24
Tidiman, Brian, 27n43, 154n41
Tobolowsky, Andrew, 142n1
Tov, Emmanuel, 145n3, 146n4, 161n80
Tully, Eric J., 4n17

Waard, Jan de, 83n11
Watson, Wilfred G. E., 148–49n14
Watts, James W., 2, 2n4, 2n5, 3, 3n6, 3n7, 4, 5n18, 5n19, 7, 7n25, 7n26, 7n27, 7n28, 37
Way, Kenneth C., 124n11, 126n15
Webb, Barry G., 53n54, 65n84, 95, 95n37, 95n38, 106n62, 107n64, 122n5, 132n24, 133, 133n25, 133n27, 159n67
Weinfeld, Moshe, 44n27, 132n24
Weiser, Artur, 17, 17n7
Weitzman, Steven Phillip, 3, 3n11, 3n12, 3n13, 4, 4n14, 61n74
Wiseman, D. J., 63n78
Wolde, Ellen van, 28n48, 37n10, 46, 46n36, 52n52, 64n81
Wong, Gregory T. K., 1n1, 8n31, 8n32, 12n42, 23n29, 24, 24n31, 25, 44, 44n29, 53, 53n56, 89, 89n23, 107n64, 132n23, 136n35,
Wright, Jacob L., 29n51, 73n96
Wyatt, N., 77n1

Yee, Gale A., 63n79, 71, 71n93, 72, 72n94,
Younger, K. Lawson, 2n3, 10n39, 20n19, 41n18, 81n6, 100, 100n50

Zucker, David J., 58n68

Scripture Index

Genesis
3:24 166, 166n106
10:30 166, 166n106
16:6 169n120
18:11 152n25
21:2 166n106
21:7 166n106
24:10 100
34 82
36:16 104n59
49:1–27 28
49:10 156
49:14 165
49:14–15 28n47
49:15 28n47

Exodus
2:7 51
2:14 51n47
3:8 105n60
5:4 147
14:25 29
15 3, 24
15:1 146
17:8–16 163n89
17:8–18 104n59
17:14–16 104–5n59
18:9 105n60
18:10 105n60
20:6 57
21:6 155n45
22:8[9] 155n45
30:15 79–80n2
32:1 168
32:25 147

Leviticus
10:6 147
13:45 147
21:10 147

Numbers
1:2–3 63
1:4 51n47
5:10 57
5:18 147
6 147
6:5 147, 148n12
7:9 57
13:3 57
13:31–33 73n98
14:39–45 104n59
21:4 115n77
21:17 6
21:18 156
24:19 161n76
24:21 163n89
29:1 168
32 29
32:1–5 29n51

Deuteronomy
1:30–31 53
1:36 88
3:5 152
3:18 53
3:20 10
3:22 53
4:9 131n20
4:9–14 130
4:23 131n20
4:31 131n20

4:38	73n98	33:15	166
6–7	112n68	33:18–19	143n3
6:6–15	130	33:27	166
6:10	49n42	34:10	55n61
6:12	131n20	**Joshua**	73
7:1	134n31	7:1–9	37n11
7:1–2	142n2	8:30–34	81n6
7:7	73n98	10:20	49n42
7:21–24	53	10:34–35	101n53
8:11	131n20	10:40	37n11
8:11–20	131	11	45
8:14	131n20	11:4	167
8:17	131	11:20–23	37n11
8:19	131, 131n20	11:23	69n89
9:1	49n42	12:12	101n53
9:4–6	73n98	13	134n31
9:7	131n20	13:1–7	134
10:14–19	73n98	13:6	134, 142
11:29	81n6	14:8	88
12:8	11n40	15:63	37n11, 69n89
12:10	10	16:10	37n11, 69n89
17:8	52	17:12	69n89
17:8–9	51	18:1	69n89
17:16	167	20:7	81n6
18	55n61	21:21	81n6
18:17–19	60	23:1	10
20:3–4	57	23:6–13	134
20:10	63n78	24	81n6
20:16–18	63n78, 142n2	**Judges**	1n1, 2, 4, 4–5n17, 8,
23:4	100		18, 26n41, 88, 121, 141, 165
25:17–19	104n59	1	2, 143n3
25:19	10, 131n20	1:1	8
26:7	115n78	1:1–2:5	8
26:13	131n20	1:1–3:6	8, 8n30, 9, 9n34, 11
27:4	81n6	1:5–7	10
31:19	87	1:7	107
31:19–21	131n20	1:19	73, 143
31:19–22	37	1:21	69n89
31:21	131n20	1:22–26	142
32	24n34, 147	1:27–36	37n11, 69n89
32:1–43	131	1:29	163
32:9	131	1:30	143n3
32:9–14	73n98	1:33	58
32:17	154	2	126, 131
32:18	131n20	2:1	55n61
32:42	147	2:1–2	142
32:47	131	2:1–5	9, 125, 126
33:1–4	131	2:2	126
33:1–29	28		

2:3	9, 92, 125, 128, 142	3:10	88, 95, 107, 110n65
2:4–5	141	3:12	45, 77, 78, 100, 101, 106, 106n63, 123, 131
2:6–3:6	9, 34, 37		
2:7	8, 141	3:12–30	78, 112
2:10	10, 10n38, 130, 143	3:12a	78
2:10–19	77	3:12c	78
2:10ff	125	3:13	78, 107
2:11	128	3:14	78, 103, 123n7
2:11–13	77	3:15	78, 88, 91, 110
2:11–19	88	3:17	101
2:11–23	9	3:19	90
2:13	77n1, 81	3:19–20	90
2:14	29, 99, 103, 123, 143	3:21	90
2:15	85, 130n19	3:25	90, 91, 117
2:17	81, 124	3:27	78
2:17–19	130	3:28	90, 102, 110
2:18	105n60, 123–24n9	3:28–29	78
2:19	10, 81, 121, 123, 124, 130, 136, 137	3:29	78, 102, 107
		3:30	40n16, 78, 110, 110n65
2:20–22	126, 142	3:31	65, 66, 94, 122n3, 137n37
2:20–10:5	125	4	1–2, 4, 33, 36n8, 37, 39, 40, 41, 43, 44, 46, 48, 49, 53, 54, 55, 59, 60, 62, 66, 67, 70, 72, 73, 74, 75, 76, 90, 94, 94n33, 111, 112
2:21	9, 10, 132		
2:21–22	110, 125, 132		
2:22	10, 130, 132, 133, 136, 138		
2:22–3:4	45, 136		
2:23	10	4–5	2, 2n3, 17n3, 33, 38, 39, 45, 49, 61, 69, 70, 73, 112, 123
3:1	10, 110, 133, 133n28, 134		
3:1–2	130	4–9	136
3:1–5	142	4:1	39–40n15, 45, 77, 78, 102, 123, 131
3:1–6	9, 125, 125n13, 134		
3:2	133, 134, 136	4:1–2	34, 106n63
3:2a	133n28	4:1–5	34, 35, 39, 46n35
3:2c	133n28	4:1–5:31	33n1
3:3	134	4:2	34, 36, 39–40n15, 46, 47, 74n99, 78, 107
3:4	37, 58, 60, 110, 130, 133, 134, 136, 138		
		4:2b	47
3:5	108, 125, 134n31	4:3	26n41, 34, 39–40n15, 52n52, 73, 78, 103, 123n7
3:5–6	82		
3:6	98	4:3c	38
3:7	77, 77n1, 84, 109, 123, 125n13, 128, 131	4:4	24, 34, 47, 55n61, 71, 79–80n2
		4:4a	51, 71
3:7–8	106n63	4:4b	52, 52n50
3:7–11	78, 88	4:4–5	52
3:7–4:23	118	4:4–5a	50
3:7–16:31	8n30, 10, 77, 99, 117, 122	4:5	34, 47, 78
		4:5a	47
3:8	45, 107, 109, 123n7	4:5b	52
3:9	88, 109	4:5d	56
3:9–10	91, 109		

4:6	34, 41, 42, 48, 58, 67, 74n99, 135, 162n85
4:6–7	47, 56, 80
4:6–8	68
4:6–9	68
4:6–10	34, 35
4:6–16	34
4:7	46, 46n36, 48, 74n99
4:7b	54
4:8	60, 67
4:9	2, 43, 53, 53n58, 54, 59, 62, 68, 71, 75, 90, 95
4:9b	68
4:9b–c	63
4:9e	70
4:9e–10	54
4:9f	54, 68
4:9f–10	34
4:9g	68
4:10	41, 44, 48, 56, 74, 74n99
4:10–11	75
4:10c	54, 75
4:11	62
4:11–13	34, 35
4:12	74n99
4:13	26n41, 30, 48, 59, 74, 74n99
4:14	28, 35, 42, 44, 48, 54, 60, 90, 95, 135
4:14c	54
4:14e	56
4:14–16	34
4:15	35, 48, 74, 76, 103, 111, 113
4:15a	35
4:15–16	44
4:15b–16	35
4:17	30, 35, 45, 46, 46n36, 48, 62, 68
4:17b	62
4:17–21	34, 35
4:17–22	34, 48, 64
4:18	48, 64, 90
4:19	64
4:20	71n91
4:20–21	64
4:21	35, 54, 60, 64, 90
4:22	34, 35, 36, 37, 48, 68, 90
4:23	37, 39–40n15, 43, 110n65, 111
4:23–24	34, 35, 36, 37, 39, 40, 46, 46n35, 49, 55, 61, 64, 74
4:24	24, 37, 39–40n15, 40, 68, 68n88, 69, 78, 107
5	1–4, 7, 13, 17, 22, 23, 23n28, 24, 24n34, 25, 28, 28n48, 32, 33, 38, 40, 40n17, 41, 41n18, 48, 69, 73, 74, 75, 79, 91, 112, 119, 121, 127, 131, 142, 142n1, 143, 145, 145n1, 145n2, 146, 146n4, 147, 167n112
5:1	13, 22, 24, 25, 33, 37, 61, 146
5:1–23	49
5:1–31	118, 126
5:2	13, 18, 19, 21, 25, 30, 41, 43, 56, 57, 65, 70, 135, 146–48, 156, 162
5:2a	156
5:2b	148, 156
5:2–3	18, 55, 57, 79
5:2–8	18, 19, 25
5:2–31	126
5:2–31b	7, 23, 26n41, 80, 93, 99, 119, 129, 141, 153, 153n36, 155
5:3	13, 18, 19, 41, 103, 117, 148–49, 150n21, 153n31, 155, 158
5:3d	26, 43
5:4	13–14, 19
5:4–5	18, 19, 26, 29, 29n52, 57, 131, 149, 150, 150n17
5:4c	149
5:4e	149n16
5:5	4–5n17, 14, 18, 41, 149–51, 155
5:5a	149n16
5:5a–b	150
5:5b	26, 43, 150
5:5b–c	149n16
5:5c–d	149n16
5:6	14, 19, 27n42, 65, 66, 137n37, 151–52
5:6–7	27, 69, 74, 75, 79
5:6c–d	152n26
5:6d	152
5:7	14, 25, 41, 55, 57, 151n24, 152–54
5:7b–c	26

5:7c	19	5:15a–c	164n95
5:8	14, 19, 23, 26, 41, 43, 114, 154–56	5:15b	164, 164n95
		5:15c	162, 164n95
5:8a	26, 43n25, 154	5:15d	29n50, 161, 164, 165
5:8b	27	5:15d–16	20
5:8c	156	5:15d–16c	28n47
5:8d	19	5:16	15, 165
5:9	14, 19, 20, 21, 27, 30, 43, 56, 57, 65, 70, 135, 148, 156, 162	5:16a	29
		5:16c	164
5:9–10	57, 79	5:17	15, 165–66, 167
5:9–11c	19	5:17–18	20
5:9–23	18, 19, 27, 30	5:17b	29
5:9a	19, 156	5:18	15, 44, 166
5:9b	156	5:18–20	166
5:10	14, 19, 27, 27n42, 85, 103, 157–58	5:19	15, 20, 23, 109, 143
		5:19d	31, 103
5:10–11	27	5:19–20	29n52, 46, 166
5:10b	157	5:19–22	42, 76
5:10c	152	5:20	15
5:11	14, 19n12, 20, 23, 27, 27n43, 41, 43, 55, 69, 70, 85, 135, 152, 158–60, 161	5:20–21	17, 57
		5:20–21b	20
		5:20–22	26
5:11a	158	5:21	15, 56, 57, 131, 166–67
5:11b	27, 158	5:21c–22	20
5:11b–c	43, 159, 162	5:22	16, 23, 30, 44, 167
5:11c	159	5:23	16, 20, 24, 30, 65, 69, 74, 103, 126n14, 161, 167
5:11d	19, 29, 43, 44, 160, 161, 165		
5:11d–13	19, 27	5:23–24	57, 66
5:12	14–15, 19, 27, 56, 57, 61, 91, 160	5:24	16, 65, 163n89
		5:24–27	21
5:12a	160	5:24–30	65
5:12b	160	5:24–31	18, 30
5:12c–d	44	5:24–36	75
5:13	15, 19n12, 20, 20n19, 23, 43, 56, 74, 160–62	5:24a	65
		5:24b	65
5:13a	103	5:24c	65
5:13a–b	19, 160, 165	5:25	16, 21
5:13b	19, 103, 161, 161n80	5:26	16, 21, 167–68
5:14	15, 156, 162–63	5:26–30	44
5:14–15c	20, 29, 44	5:26c–e	21
5:14–18	40, 69	5:27	16, 21
5:14a	162	5:28	16, 21, 31, 70, 75, 168
5:14a–b	162	5:28–30	21
5:14b	162	5:28–31	49
5:14c	29n50, 162	5:28a–b	168n116
5:14d	162	5:28c	31, 168
5:15	15, 56, 61, 91, 156, 164–65	5:28d	168
5:15–17	24	5:29	16, 168–69
5:15a	164n95	5:29–30	21

5:30	16–17, 21, 31, 91, 143, 169–70, 169n123
5:30b	170
5:30d	169
5:30d–e	170
5:30e	169
5:31	17, 21, 24, 33, 37, 38, 39–40n15, 44, 49, 57, 79, 104, 135, 170
5:31–6:1	127, 132n22
5:31a	38
5:31a–b	69
5:31b	137, 170
5:31c	22, 38
6–7	92, 112
6–9	87, 99, 136
6:1	77, 105, 123, 123n7, 128, 129, 136, 137
6:1–5	106n63
6:1–7:25	118
6:2–3	79
6:2–4	26n39
6:2–6	105
6:6–7	80
6:7–10	112
6:8	79–80n2, 127, 128
6:8–10	87
6:9	105, 105n60
6:10	105, 126
6:10–12	126
6:11	92
6:11–26	126n14
6:11–7:25	113
6:12	92n30
6:13	92
6:14	92n30, 113n70, 135
6:16	92n30, 113n70
6:20–21	92n30
6:22	92
6:23	92n30, 113n70
6:25	113n70
6:25–27	92
6:27	92
6:33	163n89
6:34	113, 113n70
6:40	113n70, 114
7:2	113n70
7:4	113n70
7:5	113n70
7:7	113n70
7:8	80
7:9	95, 113n70
7:10	92
7:12	106
7:15	80, 92, 95, 113, 136
7:22	113, 113n70
7:23	80
7:25	106
8	106, 113n70
8:1–3	86
8:1–9:57	118
8:5	45
8:22	80, 84, 113, 114
8:27	80, 92, 93, 128
8:27–35	84
8:28	110n65, 123n7, 124, 128
8:29–31	106n63
8:30	106
8:33	81, 82, 123n7, 124, 128, 137
8:33–35	106n63
8:34	80, 87, 114
8:34–35	136
9	84, 94, 94n33, 122, 122n6
9–12	88
9:1–6	106n63
9:2	84, 106
9:3	81n6, 82
9:4	81n4, 82, 94, 128
9:5	106
9:6	82
9:7	84, 114
9:9	114n74
9:14	95
9:15	83
9:16	83
9:16–19	136
9:16–20	82, 83
9:18	106
9:22	82, 123n7
9:23	114
9:24	106
9:53–54	59n69
9:53–57	108
9:54	93
9:55	82
9:56	106, 107, 108, 110n65, 114

9:57	107, 114	15:3–5	97
10	94, 126	15:7–8	97
10:1–16	118	15:11	86n17, 97, 108
10:6	77n1, 85, 115, 124, 128	15:11–12	87
10:6–10	125	15:14	98
10:6–21:25	125	15:18	97
10:7	116	15:18–19	98
10:8	85, 123n7	15:20	86, 97
10:9	85	16	109
10:10	85	16:3	97
10:11–14	96, 126	16:16	97, 115n77
10:13	98, 115, 117, 144	16:17–20	98
10:13–14	85, 86	16:23–24	117
10:16	85, 85n13, 115	16:24	109
10:17–18	85	16:28	97
10:17–12:15	118	16:28–30	98
10:18	94	16:31	86
11:1	94	17	10n39, 122
11:3	94	17–18	10
11:6	95	17–21	11, 125
11:7–11	95	17:1–21:25	8
11:10	95	17:11–13	144
11:11	95	18:27–30	144
11:12	45	18:31	81n4
11:12–27	95	19–21	10
11:13	108	19:23–26	144
11:15–27	96	20:14–18	144
11:28	95, 108	20:16	89
11:29	116	**1 Samuel**	
11:32	95, 116	2:1–10	7, 7n26
11:33	85, 110n65, 116	6:18	152
11:34	23	8:5	81n4
11:40	85	12:5	159n69
12	86	12:7	159
12:7	124	12:9	46n34
12:15	162, 163, 163n89	12:11	52n50
13	86	13:19–23	26n41
13:1	96, 124	13:22	26n41
13:1–16:31	118	14:19	68n88
13:3–20	126n14	15:1–11	37n11
13:5	86, 96, 98	15:2–3	104–5n59
13:25	98	15:6	163n89
14:3	87, 97	**2 Samuel**	
14:4	86, 97, 98, 117	1:21	89, 89n23
14:5	109	1:22	164n93, 166n105
14:6	98	3:1	102n58
14:7	97	7:10	79–80n2
14:18–19	97	14:1	81n4
14:19	98		156

18:25	68n88	59:5	28n46
22:29	31n56	68	149n16, 150, 150n17, 165
22:35	134n30	68:8–9	150
23:5	81n4	68:14	165
		80:3	28n46

1 Kings

11:26	51	83:9	46n34
17:9–10	51	83:10[9]	157n60
20:1	167	84:7	164n93
		102:20	168n116

2 Kings

2:12	55n62	105:2	158n61
13:14	55n62	123:2	153n36
19:2	50n43		

Proverbs

22:14	50n43, 51	1:9	152n25
25:19	162–63n85	1:25	147
		4:15	147

1 Chronicles

5:18	134n30	8:22–23	166
12:2	89	13:18	147
15:24	158	15:31	147
		16:26	168
		29:18	147

2 Chronicles

5:12	158	
28:19	147	

Ecclesiastes/Qoheleth

		2:18	168
		3:9	168

Nehemiah

7:43	164n93

Song of Songs

		2:7	153n36

Esther

9:19	152	2:17	153n36
		3:4	153n36

Job

3:10	115n78	3:5	153n36
3:20	167	3:8	134n30
5:7	115n78	8:4	153n36
6:28	156n51		

Isaiah

11:16	115n78	2:3	152n25
12:8	158n61	5:25	149
17:16	167n112	10:1	115n78
20:22	167	11:10	163
21:4	115n77	14:2	160, 161n76
22:15	152n25	22:14	156n51
23:8	166, 166n106	22:16	156
		28:9	164n93

Psalms

2:12	166	33:22	156
7:17[16]	164n93	40:26	44n27
18:35	115n78	41:2	161
18:38	134n30	51:17	28n46
19:6	31n56	53:3	79–80n2
35:23	152n25	63	150n18
58:10[9]	28n46	63:19–64:2 [64:1–3]	150
	107		

Jeremiah
- 28:1 — 50n43
- 31:21 — 156
- 39:10 — 79–80n2

Ezekiel
- 13:2 — 165
- 24:14 — 164n93
- 38:11 — 147
- 40:4 — 152
- 44 — 156
- 44:20 — 147

Daniel
- 8:10 — 44n27

Hosea
- 9:16 — 163

Joel
- 4:9 — 28n46

Amos
- 2:7 — 79–80n2
- 4:1 — 79–80n2
- 5:11 — 79–80n2

Obadiah
- 13 — 167n112

Micah
- 1:4 — 149
- 2:7 — 115n77
- 6:1 — 159n69
- 6:2 — 159n69
- 6:5 — 159
- 7:10 — 169

Habakkuk
- 1:3 — 115n78
- 2:19 — 28n46
- 3:14 — 153

Zechariah
- 1:1 — 50n43
- 1:7 — 50n43
- 2:8 — 152
- 11:8 — 115n77
- 13:7 — 28n46

Hebrews
- 11:32 — 141
- 11:32–34 — 52n50
- — 141

www.ingramcontent.com/pod-product-compliance
Lightning Source LLC
Chambersburg PA
CBHW021355300426
44114CB00012B/1236